Virtual Reality Systems for Business

ROBERT J. THIERAUF

Q

QUORUM BOOKS
Westport, Connecticut • London

Library of Congress Cataloging-in-Publication Data

Thierauf, Robert J.
    Virtual reality systems for business / Robert J. Thierauf.
       p. cm.
    Includes bibliographical references and index.
    ISBN 0–89930–946–1
    1. Virtual reality in management. I. Title.
HD30.2122.T48 1995
650'.0285'6—dc20   95–3779

British Library Cataloguing in Publication Data is available.

Library of Congress Catalog Card Number: 95–3779
ISBN: 0–89930–946–1

First published in 1995

Quorum Books, 88 Post Road West, Westport, CT 06881
An imprint of Greenwood Publishing Group, Inc.

Printed in the United States of America

The paper used in this book complies with the
Permanent Paper Standard issued by the National
Information Standards Organization (Z39.48–1984).

10 9 8 7 6 5 4 3 2 1

The most effective way to bring business information to life is to allow the person to *experience* it in a virtual world as opposed to reading about and viewing it. Such an approach saves a person's time and is less costly.

Contents

Figures

Abbreviations

ABC	activity-based costing
AI	artificial intelligence
API	Application Programmer's Interface
AT	Advanced Texture
ATM	asynchronous transfer mode
ATR	Advanced Telecommunications Research
BISDN	broadband integrated-services digital network
BOOM	Binocular Omni-Orientation Monitor
BPR	business-process reengineering
BT	British Telecommunications
CAD	computer-aided design
CAM	computer-aided manufacturing
CASE	computer-aided software engineering
CBT	computer-based training
CCITT	Consultative Committee of International Telegraph and Telephone
CDK	Cyberspace-Developer Kit
CD-ROM	compact disk–read-only memory
CIG	computer image generating
CIM	computer-integrated manufacturing
COF	customer-order flow
CPU	central processing unit

CRT	cathode ray tube
CSF	critical success factor
CSS	Continuous-System Simulator
DARPA	Defense Advanced Research Projects Agency
DASD	direct-access storage device
DBC	Data Broadcasting Corporation
DBMS	database management system
D-DBMS	distributed database management system
DEMOS	Distributed Earth Model and Orbiter Simulation
DIVE	Dismounted Infantry Virtual Environment
DOD	Department of Defense
DOF	degrees of freedom
DOS	disk operating system
DSS	decision support system
DXF	Drawing Interchange Format
EDI	electronic-data interchange
E-mail	electronic mail
ERP	enterprise-resources planning
ERT	extended range transmitter
FAA	Federal Aeronautics Association
GIS	geographic information system
GPSS	General-Purpose Systems Simulator
HCI	human computer interface
HDTV	high-definition TV
HIT	Human Interface Technology
HMD	head-mounted display
HMSI	Head-Mounted Sensory Interface
HRMS	human-resource-management system
IFIPS	International Federation of Information Processing Societies
IMS	Interactive Market Systems
I/O	input/output
ISDN	integrated-services digital network
IST	Institute for Simulation and Training
IVR	Immersive Virtual Reality
JIT	just-in-time
KPI	key performance indicator
LAN	local area network

LCD	liquid-crystal display
MAN	metropolitan area network
MB	megabytes
Mbps	megabits per second
MCC	Mission Control Center
MIS	management information system
MMU	manned maneuvering unit
NASA	National Aeronautics and Space Administration
ODR&E	Office of Director for Research and Engineering
ONA	Open-Network Architecture
OOAD	object-oriented analysis and design
OODBMS	object-oriented database management system
OOP	object-oriented programming
OSI	Open-Systems Interconnection
PC	personal computer or microcomputer
PID	Personal Immersive Display
PIMS	Profit Impact of Marketing Strategies
PMS	Picturephone Meeting Service
QA	quality assurance
R&D	research and development
RB2	Reality Built for Two
RDBMS	relational database management system
ROI	return on investment
SE	Synthetic Environments
SEALS	SE-Air-Land Units
SGI	Silicon Graphics Inc.
SIMNET	Simulation Network
SMDS	Switched Multimegabit Digital Service
SONET	Synchronous Optical Network
SQI	Structured Query Language
TACOM	Tank Automatic Command
TFT	thin-film transistor
2-D	two-dimensional
3-D	three-dimensional
3-DS	three-dimensional storage
TQM	total quality management
UPC	universal product code
VEGAS	Virtual EGress Analysis System

VEOS	Virtual Environment Operating System
VET	Virtual Environment Theater
VIEW	Virtual Interface Environment Workstation
VIRART	Virtual Reality Research Team
VLAN	virtual local-area network
VMS	Virtual Meeting System
VR	virtual reality
VRT	Virtual Reality Toolkit
VSS	Virtual Scene System
WAN	wide area network
WTK	WorldToolKit

Preface

In the early days of virtual reality (VR), its cause was embraced by fringe people bent on exploiting it as a new kind of electronic LSD. To the distress of serious pioneers, this new computer technology was trivialized. Now, however, the dust has settled, and sincere interest is rising in ways to use VR for business. Essentially, virtual world technology has grown up and is moving out by being applied to numerous and diverse business areas: product sales, industrial product design, manufacturing simulation, and financial modeling, to name a few. Real-world VR business applications are using current-generation hardware platforms and VR-software tools.

Although it may take a while for VR technology to realize its full potential, experts seem to agree that by the middle to late 1990s there will be photorealistic 3-D visualization capabilities along with the appropriate hardware and software to create realistic simulations within most virtual business worlds. The typical company, however, will be able to get its feet wet by employing current VR technology as set forth in this text. Hence, this text sets the stage for the future in which the typical company will be able to buy a VR application just as easily as it can purchase a spreadsheet or word-processing package today. From this perspective, VR will have the capability *of enriching*, rather than replacing, the real world of the typical business user.

Virtual reality gets its power from the fact that people can comprehend images more quickly than they can understand columns of numbers or lines of text. It has been reported that a person can absorb the equivalent of about a billion bits of information per second while his or her ability to read is limited to only about 100 bits, or characters, per second. In addition, because about half the brain is dedicated to visual processing, VR is the most natural way for a person to understand and manipulate computerized data in three dimensions. Thus, VR has the capability of changing the way in which people use computers. This viewpoint will be evident in this text, especially in the last four chapters on business-oriented VR applications.

The structure of this text on VR systems for business follows a logical flow for a comprehensive treatment of this emerging new computer technology. The topical areas that are enhanced by emerging real-world applications are as follows:

Part 1: An Overview of Virtual-Reality Systems for Business. In Chapter 1, I discuss the need to rethink how a typical business organization is operated along with the essential components of virtual worlds. I also treat the historical and current VR developments, complemented by an introduction to the subject matter of this text. In Chapter 2, I take a closer look at the elements that comprise a VR system and VR applications that are nonbusiness related.

Part 2: Computer Hardware and Software in Virtual-Reality Systems for Business. In Chapter 3, I explore hardware components found in a typical VR environment, complemented by an exposition of leading VR products along with criteria for evaluation of VR vendors. In Chapter 4, I focus on VR software currently available from a number of vendors. Not only do I describe well-known VR software, but I also state the criteria for the evaluation of this software. In Chapter 5, I set forth the essentials of databases and data communications and networking as they relate to VR systems for business.

Part 3: Building Virtual-Reality Systems for Business. In Chapter 6, I initially set forth considerations that are helpful in getting started on a VR-systems project. This is followed by VR-system-development methodologies for end users as well as computer professionals.

Part 4: Applications of Virtual-Reality Systems for Business. In Chapter 7, I explore the fundamentals of retailing and marketing along with the need to rethink these areas. In turn, I describe typical VR applications for these two areas. The remaining chapters follow the same format. In Chapter 8, I look at design and manufacturing; in Chapter 9, I focus on accounting and finance; and in Chapter 10, I examine training and human resources. These chapters demonstrate that virtual worlds can have a dramatic impact on the typical business organization.

Because of the magnitude of this undertaking, I wish to thank the following who have gone beyond the call of duty. More specifically, I would like to thank the many hardware and software vendors who have supplied materials that have been included throughout the text, in particular in Chapters 3 and 4. My graduate students at Xavier University are to be commended for their comments and helpful suggestions. Most of these students are employed full-time by a number of organizations in the Midwest where they are computer professionals. Finally, a special note of thanks goes to Eric Valentine for his encouragement throughout this unusual project.

PART I

An Overview of Virtual-Reality Systems for Business

1

Introduction to Virtual-Reality
Systems for Business

ISSUES EXPLORED

- To demonstrate that VR technology must give consideration first to the human element to be successful in business or otherwise
- To explore how VR is different from prior information processing
- To explore the essential components of VR as a means of defining it
- To set forth important considerations that form the basis for developing typical VR applications in business
- To explore the past and future developments of VR as they affect the typical organization

OUTLINE

Introduction to VR in a Business Environment

   How VR Is Different from Prior Information Processing

VR and Its Tie-In with Artificial Intelligence

   Relationship of VR and Artificial Intelligence to Object Worlds

VR and Its Tie-In with Creativity

Basic Types of VR Systems

   Desktop VR Systems versus Immersion VR Systems

Essential Components of a VR System

   Sensory Feedback System

   VR Defined

Virtual Corporation

INTRODUCTION TO VR IN A BUSINESS ENVIRONMENT

Today and into the twenty-first century and beyond, creative agility is essential for businesses to meet the ever-increasing pressure of competition. Not only are national events reshaping businesses at a very rapid rate, but also global happenings are causing even more changes in corporate United States. Since many businesses are at a crossroads point, they can either go forward or backward. To assist businesses in moving in a positive direction, virtual reality (VR) is a great, untapped resource. Some computer experts think that VR will eventually have an impact as great as the invention of writing. Although this viewpoint may be overambitious, it will not be for any want of ambition or confidence among pioneers in the field. Essentially, the only thing that can stop the widespread use of VR is the speed of light and the ability to write complex software programs.

To assist businesses in this important new direction, this text will provide an adequate background for the development and implementation of VR systems in business. Initially, this chapter serves not only as an introduction to the reader, but also to the subject matter of the entire text. From this latter perspective, an overview is given for the topical areas to be covered that can assist a typical manager or management information system (MIS) professional in getting started on the development and implementation of VR systems in their business areas.

Going beyond the technical aspects of VR systems for business, there is a most important point that must be made regarding the human element. The VR systems that are installed must serve the needs of those who use them. Because users are not always able to express their needs, VR developers need to get out and learn the business of the organizations they serve so that they have the necessary knowledge to get involved in VR systems. Although I recommend that developers encourage users to consider new VR technology, both users and developers must understand that the users are to be served effectively or they will choose not to be served at all. Hence, users must be considered by VR developers at all stages of the development and implementation processes. Human needs must precede those of VR technology.

How VR Is Different from Prior Information Processing

At this point, it is helpful to state how VR is different from information processing, in particular, decision support systems (DSSs) that are and have been popular within an individualized or group processing mode. Traditionally, decision makers have relied on the display of data in spreadsheets or in some type of two-dimensional (2-D) mode. The human brain, however, can process real-time, multidimensional data much more efficiently and faster than 2-D data. Virtual-reality technology provides the capability that allows information to appear as graphical objects that respond to changing data and give instantaneous information updates. These objects have attributes such as position, size, orientation, color, shape, and behaviors that extend the dimensions of the data space from more than two dimensions.

Since VR systems are designed to make participants think that they are in another world, the computer creates a sensory-based environment that interactively and dynamically responds to and is controlled by the user. In VR-based systems, visuals, sounds, and sensations mimic actual experiences, leaving the user free to explore the environment, gather information, and solve problems. The ways in which the user interacts with the system is of vital importance. This certainly is not the case with current information processing. However, with the merger of VR with DSSs, there can be a focus on the powerful functionalities of multidimensional presentation of data, dynamic interaction with data, and multiuser networking in a shared virtual space, thereby allowing the technology to emerge as an alternative to the standard ways in which decision makers understand and visualize complex and changing data.

Essentially, a combined VR-DSS approach can surround its decision makers with an artificial environment mimicking real life wherein the decision makers interact with objects and settings as they would in the real world. There is no passive viewing of computer graphics, the way it is done on most of today's screens. While some advanced information processing lets decision makers manipulate objects on a screen, VR turns them into full participants in a 3-D (three-dimensional) setting that envelops them completely with real-time interaction.

VR AND ITS TIE-IN WITH ARTIFICIAL INTELLIGENCE

Virtual reality and artificial intelligence (AI) are tied in together by the fact that both model some aspect of the real world. For example, an airplane manufacturer, like Boeing, models a new aircraft, like the model 777, through its design process. In a similar manner, Boeing's pilots have a model of how the new plane will operate that is quite different from a model of how a Stealth bomber operates. In addition, air-traffic controllers have a different model of the airplane's performance from that of aircraft designers and pilots. In effect, people have need of different models to get a handle on their view of the world around them.

So the question can be raised, how is VR tied in with AI? In the example cited, Boeing designs a new aircraft and develops a prototype that operates in a virtual world. The airplane's three-dimensional (3-D) design can be thoroughly simulated in a real-time and interactive mode whereby improvements can be made before the first airplane is built. Then the plane is built by using factory workers and expert systems (i.e., AI) on the production floor, whereby production errors are eliminated. In turn, the plane is flown by pilots who are assisted by expert systems that help in determining where problems are and how they can be corrected by the pilots while in the air. As can be seen from this example, both VR and AI are complementary and helpful to companies in a wide range of industries. Each technology has its own particular strengths that can be used in a product or service that will meet a company's total-quality-management (TQM) requirements. In effect, VR is a natural cousin of AI. As humans become comfortable with operating in virtual worlds, they will expect to react in intelligent ways. For example, playing a 3-D chess game in VR will be hollow if the system cannot play an intelligent game. Artificial intelligence will help put the intelligence into the VR equation of today and tomorrow.

Relationship of VR and Artificial Intelligence to Object Worlds

The relationship of VR to AI can be carried a step further by relating to object-oriented technology. In an object-oriented sense, each of these models as set forth above descends from a base class, a real-world model. Each inherits something from other models, encapsulates public and private knowledge, and has actions and attributes in common with other models. As an example of the melding of AI with VR, Autodesk is marketing its VR software product called the Cyberspace Developer Kit (CDK). It is a library of the C++ class that gives developers a method of creating virtual worlds and interacting with them. The tie-in to AI is object-oriented programming.

Primarily, Autodesk is known for computer-aided design (CAD), modeling, and animation—all of the essentials of the CDK. However, to be usable for VR Autodesk has added support for a variety of input and output devices. Since the toolkit is C++ based, the user can also work from the base classes and derive his or her own controls. In addition to the facilities for modeling and interaction, the CDK has the ability to place constraints on the objects in the universe. This includes properties such as gravity, mass, and density. This extends the use of the tool to educational purposes and enhances the ability to add reality to virtual worlds.

In summary, object-oriented technology is a way to build models for experiments in artificial life. Since this is a programming system, the user combines the CDK's modeling capabilities with those of an AI (i.e., a neural network or any of several other techniques) to create entities that learn. For example, instead of building physical robots that learn avoidance and navigation, users can study these phenomena very cost effectively. Autodesk's CDK is effective in this scenario. If users want to build virtual spaces, this VR software package will provide the tools needed. The addition of some AI allows the user to extend the capabilities of virtual worlds.

VR AND ITS TIE-IN WITH CREATIVITY

Although present VR software does not include the built-in capability of enhancing an individual's creativity skills per se, it does, however, allow the user to go beyond traditional boundaries of design and to view designs in new and unusual ways. From this view, present VR software would qualify as a creative computer technique to assist a typical designer. To demonstrate this point, Eastman Kodak quickly gained new insights after it used a supercomputer to process in 3-D the intricate interactions of such variables as heat, temperature, and pressure in the injection process that the company uses to make plastic items from film spools to camera cases. To see six or seven variables actually is an unusual experience since polymers do an unexpected dance to untangle themselves. Hence, Kodak engineers started to see things that could not be seen through equations.

By making those polymer pirouettes visible, Kodak engineers can design lighter, thinner parts that require less material and meet environmental standards. Larry Smarr, who has almost single-handedly pushed the United States into a dominant position in the use of supercomputers for visualization, says that he wants researchers to become "infonauts" such that they can swim among those polymer molecules to enter the interior of galactic black holes.[1]

BASIC TYPES OF VR SYSTEMS

To better understand virtual systems that are useful in a business environment or otherwise, it is helpful to look at VR's four basic types. The *first* is a desktop VR system that allows the user to navigate through 3-D on a personal computer (PC), workstation, or a monitor. As such, the user does not use specialized headgears, wired gloves, and bodysuits in a VR environment. Such an approach can be utilized for typical business applications. The *second* type is partial immersion whereby the user navigates through 3-D space on a PC, workstation, or a monitor with enhancements, such as gloves and 3-D goggles. For more realistic approaches to selected business areas, this can be quite beneficial to the user for better grasping the area under study. The *third* type is the use of full immersion whereby the user employs headgear, gloves, and bodysuits. As will be discussed in the text, total immersion allows the user, for example, to walk through and interact with a computer-generated architectural model of a building. The *fourth* and last type consists of 3-D environmental systems that are externally generated but with little or no body paraphernalia. To help distinguish between the first type and other types of immersion systems, they are discussed below.

Desktop VR Systems versus Immersion VR Systems

Desktop VR systems, noted above as the first basic type, are an important vehicle for business applications. Utilizing in many cases the same VR software as immersion VR systems, desktop VR retains the benefits of real-time visualization and interaction within a virtual world, but without some of the inherent problems still associated with immersion systems. As the name implies, desktop VR systems are based on standard desktop computers. A 486 IBM-compatible PC with a powerful graphics card, as an example, can deliver the required illusion of VR. The user can interact with virtual worlds by using a mouse, a keyboard, or a 3-D controller. The desktop version can also be utilized by several people who can wear stereoscopic glasses and view the same screen as well as view the program simultaneously.

At this time, it is expected that desktop VR systems may well have the greatest impact on the business community in the next several years. Using the broadest VR definition, it includes early products like Microsoft's Flight Simulator, but typically it refers to navigating through a truly 3-D–rendered landscape. Architectural walk-through packages, a leading application for this type of VR program, allow designers a sense of their creations by walking through simulated models. As such, users are drawn into the simulated reality as if it were the real thing.

Additionally, VR business applications are expected to make use of partial immersion whereby the user navigates through 3-D space on a monitor with possible enhancements, such as gloves and 3-D glasses. In some cases, users can control an input device to reach into a VR world and manipulate virtual objects. By using a DataGlove from VPL Research, or even a Logitech 2D/6D mouse with such software as the VREAM System from VREAM or Sense8's WorldToolKit (WTK), users can manipulate objects in real time. Some of the heads-up displays currently used in fighter aircrafts and proposed for automobiles are a type of this VR. In addition, partial immersion could be used to display computer-generated template information on top of a machine that is being assembled or repaired.

Currently, immersion VR systems have several drawbacks. Chief among them is the fact that the user can suffer from what is commonly called "simulator sickness" within approximately thirty minutes of using a headset. Sensor lag, wherein the detection of head movements by magnetic sensors can cause noticeable delay in the view being updated, can cause disorientation. Frequent recalibration of the equipment may also be necessary. In contrast, desktop VR systems are not affected by any of these problems. The fact that interaction with the virtual worlds is controlled from the desktop immediately makes desktop VR suitable for one or many people at presentations. The absence of a headset for one or many people overcomes the problem of the clarity of the screen, giving a great level of resolution and detail. Moreover, by introducing familiar techniques for visualization and virtual-world creation, users will find themselves in a more traditional operating environment. In many cases, desktop VR systems are replacing traditional techniques of communicating or presenting images, such as artist's impressions, 3-D models, textbooks, or interactive video. In essence, desktop VR has the capability of providing an interactive, real-time, and 3-D visualization of almost any scenario or environment.[2]

As will be seen throughout this text, there will be a great accent on the use of desktop VR systems. Users are not interested in headsets since the quality is somewhat poor. They are interested in quality of image and the speed of the virtual world. While the resolution and accuracy of headsets are bound to improve for immersion VR systems, they do not reflect the needs of the business users. The advantages of desktop VR systems make it the most suitable solution for the business community.

ESSENTIAL COMPONENTS OF A VR SYSTEM

A key aspect of VR work is that the brain can process information better when it is presented through sight, sound, and touch instead of through text or numbers. Scientists also have found that responses to certain visual cues, including hand-eye coordination and the ability to detect the edges of objects and to recognize movement across a meadow of grass, are encoded in genes. From the beginning of the human race, people have developed these responses to the world around them.

Today, a user can enter visually a virtual environment and respond by interacting with the environment. Sensors feed data from the user back into the VR application, which uses that data to modify the behavior of the virtual environment. The diagram of such a sensory feedback system is found in Figure 1.1.

Sensory Feedback System

To better understand the process in Figure 1.1, there is a continuous interplay between the user through sensors, on the one hand, with the reality engine or the other. The VR cycle starts with the user's responding to what is being seen

Figure 1.1
Diagram of Sensory Feedback within a Virtual Environment—A Closed-Loop System

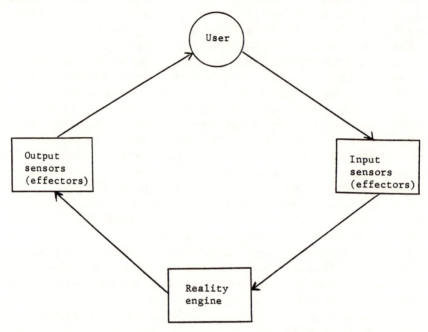

and heard by turning his or her head or moving some type of device, like a joystick. These *input sensors* are processed by the *reality engine* that operates in real time—sensing, recalculating, redrawing, and displaying the world at least ten times per second. The sound in a VR system has to be even more precise because gaps or broken sound can severely distract the user. In turn, the reality engine creates another set of sights and sounds in the form of *output sensors* to which the user responds. The modified virtual environment now presents new stimuli to the user. This process is repeated such that there is a sensory feedback system operating in a virtual environment.

The heart of a VR system is the reality engine, or software that lets a user interact with the generated world. The reality engine takes a stored set of objects and landscapes and merges the "virtualized" user into that environment. Every time the user moves or acts, the engine updates the world and re-creates it for the user within the closed loop system. A further discussion of these components of a sensory feedback system within a VR environment is given in the next chapter.

VR Defined

Typically today, VR is interchanged with the term "cyberspace." Virtual Reality involves the computer-based creation of a totally artificial world or the reproduction of a remote but real location and the immersion of the senses of a participant in that 3-D environment. Utilizing such aids as a head-mounted display (HMD) to visually enter and move around in the VR environment, a glove that senses the position and flexing of a hand and fingers, and other feedback tools, a participant can move around and manipulate objects in the VR as if it were a real world. Virtual reality enables users to enter simulated computer-generated environments in real time that includes three-dimensionality through sound, sight, and touch. However, from a business-application perspective, all of the above hardware that the individual must put on may not be necessary. From this view, VR technology enables users to view data in numerous ways by utilizing the technology found in database and network environments. No matter the viewpoint, there are certain elements that are found in VR worlds when defining it.

Because there is no generally accepted definition of VR, it would be helpful to look at its essential elements. *First*, VR is a computer system that permits the user to interact with the VR system. *Second*, a 3-D environment is simulated, so that it appears real to the user of the VR system. *Third*, the user is involved in the manipulation of the virtual world through the utilization of the user's body and mind in a real-time operating mode. These three basic elements result in a computer-generated simulation in real time of some 3-D environment in which the user views and manipulates it in an interactive manner. To put it more simply, VR can be defined as a computer-generated, simulated, and real-time 3-D environment in which the user views and manipulates the environment interactively. It should be noted that this definition ties in with Figure 1.1, which is focused on a sensory-feedback system.

VIRTUAL CORPORATION

Going beyond the concept of VR is one known today as the *virtual corporation* or *virtual company*. Such an organization is a temporary network of independent suppliers, customers, and even rivals that are linked by information technology to share skills, costs, and access to one another's markets. The idea of a virtual corporation is based on the development of alliances with others to exploit business opportunities. While some alliances will last for a long time, others will be opportunistic and short-lived. Fundamentally, the bottom line is that a virtual corporation forces the rethinking of what a corporation can be. It allows a corporation the capability of reshaping itself continuously over time to fit its customers' shifting needs.

Another way of viewing the virtual corporation is from the standpoint of outsourcing just about everything in the pursuit of flexibility, low overhead, and leading-edge technology to meet customer needs. In reality, virtual corporations have been around since time immemorial in spirit, if not in name, because they define, in part, the bootstrapping endeavors behind many corporations. Still, virtual corporations are now more relevant than ever.

Today, large companies increasingly realize that smaller companies have been doing this all along and getting higher productivity from its usage. For example, Compaq is an aggressive outsourcer from the world of high technology that has prospered at the expense of larger, more integrated rivals. Compaq's success is based on keeping tight control over its area of expertise and then doing a lot of subcontracting. The focus is on keeping overhead low, owning as few resources as possible, and keeping productivity high through a number of alliances. The key is for Compaq to give up something of value in order to create something of more enduring worth for its customers.

Virtual Data Center

The concept of the virtual corporation can also be applied to its data center. In a *virtual data center*, the data center can no longer be thought of or defined as a physical or geographical entity but rather as an information utility. With the continual decline in the per-unit cost of computing driving the proliferation of computing power into almost every aspect of business, thinking of a data center as something only behind the glass wall grossly undervalues the concept of the whole computing area and its everyday operations.

In the age of distributed data processing, client/server computing, and open systems, the computing area must be defined in much broader terms, that is, the data center must be thought of as being everywhere. It is the whole corporation wherever its computing operations are, whether it is in corporate finances or in a memorandum being written by an executive on his or her laptop during a flight somewhere in the world. Moreover, it is the business-crucial computing functions and practices on a twenty-four-hour-a-day, seven-day-a-week operation, security, backup, and so forth, that must be applied and practiced by every person using a computer, whether that person is a chief executive officer (CEO) or an end user at some remote location.

Implementing this idea of a virtual-data center will have important ramifications for the whole computing world. Needless to say, managing a broadly defined information utility will be much more difficult than managing the physical data center ever was. Additionally, there will be many policy questions that will have to be resolved. For example, how does the typical computer manager handle this virtual world? What are the boundaries in the world of the virtual data center where external relationships, linked by technologies like electronic data interchange, determine where one company begins and another ends? How will computer manager balance the need of governance with the demand for service? How will the company develop its computer applications? And how does the computer manager instill the necessary disciplines and practices in end users that are so necessary to the secure and proper functioning of their organization? The relationship of the virtual data center to selected areas of a typical corporation will be treated in the final part of the text. Thus, some of these questions will be addressed and resolved based on the present level of information technology and its tie-in with changing virtual environments.

HOW TO GET VR SYSTEMS FOR BUSINESS UP AND RUNNING IN A TYPICAL COMPANY

To get VR systems up and running in a typical company requires a coordinated effort by the computer department. Not only must there be an effective working relationship with the functional departments that will implement VR technology, but also the computer department must have a thorough working knowledge of VR technology. More specifically, this includes the areas of VR hardware and software along with databases and data communications and networking required for specific applications. Depending on the VR application, there may be need to provide stereoscopic video and full 3-D audio, thereby giving users the impression of being in a separate, self-contained world. While the user sees and hears sights and sounds that exist only in the computer's memory, computerized clothing can be used to register the user's body position and utilize that data in such a way that enables parts of the body to interact with objects in a virtual world. In other VR applications, the use of this specialized clothing may not be required. Because of the importance of hardware, software, databases, and data communications in a VR environment, they are set forth within the context of the material presented later in this text.

VR Hardware

Important advances have been made in VR technology that include the HMD and the wired glove. These two computer peripherals were developed by VPL Research, Inc. (Palo Alto, California). The names given to these products are EyePhones and DataGlove. The EyePhones are a stereoscopic, head-mounted computer display that look like a pair of goggles. Worn over the eyes, the EyePhones are held on the head by straps so that all external light is blocked out. Inside the EyePhones are two color-display screens, one for each eye. The images that appear on the two screens are slightly different, giving the illusion of depth when seen together. On the other hand, the DataGlove is a black glove made of Lycra, with flex sensors running along the back of each finger. The sensors use fiber-optic technology to determine the bend of each joint, and are very light and flexible so as not to interfere with finger movement.

Wearers of the EyePhones and the DataGlove are transported into a VR environment. The 3-D view that the EyePhones present exists as a database of polygons in a computer. By sensing the position of the user's head, the EyePhones can realistically adjust the 3-D view in real time as the user looks right and left. In contrast, the DataGlove senses the position and digitation of the user's hands, enabling the user to manipulate objects in VR and to send commands to the computer by using hand gestures. Both VR devices are used in concert with the Convolvotron, a digital-audio system developed by Crystal River Engineering (Groveland, California). The Convolvotron uses digital audio-filtering technology to position sounds in 3-D space through the use of normal

597221

stereo headphones. The system allows sounds to accompany objects in VR. As objects move, the sound they make follows them realistically.

Suppliers of VR headsets and data gloves, like VPL Research, sell the headsets for about $10,000 to $50,000 each and the gloves for about $5,000 to $10,000 each. Since the VR system can use two powerful graphics computers, one for each eye, the total system can cost up to $250,000. To reach the mass market, a race is on to cut the costs of those key items drastically. Mattel markets a $50 version of the data glove. Run by a separate $99 Nintendo game cartridge, Mattel's Power Glove allows its user to play virtual handball on a virtual court against a virtual opponent. Mattel has sold a million of the gloves since it introduced them in 1989.

Currently, VPL Research is working on a $200 DataGlove for PC users. It would allow the user to manipulate items on the PC screen. To this must be added a pair of stereo glasses (about $1,000) and a VR chip board (another $1,000 to $2,000) for a PC. Cheaper still may be TV eyeglasses under development at leading U.S. and Japanese companies. Although intended as TV receivers, they could be used to project VR scenes. As a person uses a laptop PC to write a report, he or she could put on the TV glasses and see the text suspended in the air. Some VR experts envision a portable window into the virtual world several years from now, an attachment that would fit over a PC or laptop screen and serve the same purpose as more cumbersome headsets or stereo glasses. Silicon Graphics (Mountain View, California) makes the powerful graphics workstations that run most VR applications.[3] A further exposition of VR hardware will be given in Chapter 3.

VR Software

Today, as with VR hardware, there is a wide range of software available that is suited to meet the needs of computer professionals and noncomputer personnel. One VR package, for example, is Virtus WalkThrough (product of Virtus Corporation, Cary, North Carolina). Basically, it is a modeling and visualization package that takes the concept of VR from esoteric experiment to a practical tool. It lets architects and interior designers create conceptual designs of buildings and interiors and then move through and around them on-screen. WalkThrough lets the user move about freely, viewing the design from many different perspectives, in real time. The program renders scenes in such a way that the user can move through a suite of rooms in seconds. It does all this with files no bigger than word-processing documents.

Creating and editing models in Virtus WalkThrough is almost as quick and easy as moving around in them. Top View, the default 2-D Design View, is where the user does most of the drawing. The user can open windows for the Front, Back, Left, Right, and Bottom Views. An object drawn in Design View immediately appears in Walk View as a rendered 3-D object. Virtus WalkThrough, which costs around $200, lets the user experience on a PC what not even the most expensive graphics workstation can reproduce. Virtus Walk-Through provides ease of model navigation and creation, speed, and minute file size. It is an important conceptualization tool for those who need to look at a design from all angles.[4] This software is but one example of the type of software that will be presented in Chapter 4.

VR Databases and Data Communications and Networking

Complementary to VR hardware and software are those relating to databases and data communications and networking. Perhaps one of the most formidable impediments to widespread use of VR technology in business applications has nothing to do with hardware or software but rather with databases. If the vast majority of business applications utilize databases, it becomes obvious that relational or object-orientated databases represent a large financial investment. Certainly, VR technology will not be widely implemented if it is seen as incompatible with current investments in database technology. In other words, VR has its best chance for acceptance by business if it can be seen as something that exploits, extends, and otherwise complements database applications.

From this perspective, VR technology is best viewed as a high-level interface to an organization's databases. It can provide user access to, user understanding of, and user interaction with relational or object-oriented information in a way that has not formerly been possible. As an example, Maxus Systems International (using Sense8 Corporation's WTK) has developed a VR program for stock-market analysts. By rendering large amounts of financial information into a virtual world, analysts fly over stocks (or even market segments); and by noticing shape, size, motion, color, and the like of a particular stock, analysts can instanteously understand the performance of that stock in relation to others. In addition, stock-market analysts can even fly into the stock symbol and obtain formatted data on the particular stock. Today, the Maxus program has been subsequently enhanced by Avatar Partners whereby they added a number of additional features that include texture mapping, 3-D sound, and voice recognition of certain user commands.

In this example or many other business VR applications, there is a need to get at information not at the same location but at some location nearby or around the world. This is where data communications and networking come into play. Information may be available on a local area network (LAN), a metropolitan area network (MAN), or a wide area network (WAN). No matter where the data is located, it must be accessible to meet the requirements of the VR application. If access to needed databases is not available to users, the application of VR to a typical company will be limited.

From a different perspective, data-communication networks also allow users to meet with other users from whom they are physically distant. With high-speed data networks, it is possible to offer the user a tele-VR service. Virtual video teleconferencing allows businesspeople to hold meetings around conference tables in virtual space.

Lastly, it should be noted that an integral part of the emerging area of VR data communications and networking is telepresence. *Telepresence* makes it possible to perform long-distance activities. For example, an automobile engineer in Detroit might make a change in a simulated dashboard prototype while colleagues in an East Coast city and a West Coast city watch and see how it would look. In a similar manner, telepresence allows for the remote manipulation of equipment. A construction company, for example, could build a system that lets an operator in one city direct a robot operating anywhere in the world. The operator would work the controls that signal the robot to do the task. With VR, the image is so exact that the human operator makes no mistakes in directing the operation. The important aspects of databases and data communications and networking will be treated in Chapter 5.

VR Development

To build and implement virtual worlds successfully for companies, there must be an effective collaborative effort of people from the appropriate departments since virtual worlds are rarely created in a day. For a virtual world to be convincing, it must offer richness and variety to one or more of the human senses. While systems designers have often done this for years in noninteractive business environments, to do so in a truly interactive mode is far more difficult. No longer are the computing paths fixed for business applications; they tend to be different for each user as well as for each time a user enters a virtual world. Hence, the reactive nature of each world must also be designed into the VR processes. As such, virtual worlds must respond to the stimuli provided by their users, and must do so in a fashion that is both convincing and complex. Virtual-reality tools that support this design process must offer much of this responsiveness so that the systems designer is not burdened with trivial behavior common to large classes of virtual environments. In Chapter 6, the steps to follow in VR development will be explored.

In addition, barriers to the successful development of VR technology will be covered in this chapter as well as in subsequent chapters. Some of these barriers can be attributed to hardware, primarily the poor quality of displays and physical interfaces. These will improve rapidly over the next several years. Another barrier is software that relates to the virtual-world-design process. To achieve widespread acceptance, VR must be easy to use and easy to create. Also, other barriers include high cost, the need for more central-processing-unit (CPU) power, and the lack of standards and uniform concepts for data display. Low resolution of visual quality, lack of tactile feedback, uncomfortable data goggles, and the need for fiber-optic cable to transmit sounds and images are still other barriers to successful VR.

TYPICAL CURRENT VR BUSINESS APPLICATIONS

Today, there are a number of business applications that are a natural fit for practical VR. Among these VR business applications are those found later in the text: (1) retailing and marketing (Chapter 7), (2) design and manufacturing (Chapter 8), (3) accounting and finance (Chapter 9), and (4) training and human resources (Chapter 10). In the material to follow, representative VR business applications are set forth. The reader should have no difficulty in recognizing other areas that are logical candidates for VR.

Retailing and Marketing

For retailing organizations and marketing departments, the compilation and retrieval of field intelligence is useful for an effective marketing program. Coordination between all sales and marketing activities is enhanced with the systemization of this information. Retailing and marketing personnel can all benefit from being able to view interactive presentations as opposed to relying on prerecorded audiovisual material or brochures. As a starting point, retailing and marketing personnel can view sales forecasts in multicolor 3-D bar charts that allow the personnel to interact with suggested changes in the forecasts that are updated in real time. Marketing and design departments for retail stores can also use 3-D modeling, visualization, and computer-aided design (CAD) tools to build an entire prototype store. The addition of VR makes CAD designs more real since users can interact within the models by manipulating those models' orientations.

Currently, Matsushita Electric Works (Tokyo, Japan) has a showroom in place that has a "virtual kitchen" equipped with U.S.-developed headsets and data gloves. Prospective buyers of the company's custom-built kitchens can experience what the kitchens will look and feel like when completed. A customer gives the kitchen dimensions to a salesperson and states what appliances and cabinets he or she wants. The salesperson then enters this information into a VR computer program. The customer puts on the headgear and the data glove. The new kitchen appears and allows the customer to move around the room, getting a feel for what working in it would be like. The customer can open doors of the virtual appliances and cabinets to make sure that they are unobstructed. Not only can customers lay out their dream kitchens, but they also can turn on faucets, pick up dishes, and the like. Typically, the customer spends about thirty minutes to one hour before the kitchen is finalized. At the end of the sales process, the order is placed with the factory, and the customer has his or her custom-built kitchen within two weeks. Other retailing and marketing applications of this type will be given later in the text.

Design and Manufacturing

In the most profitable industries, there is intense competition among organizations that produce similar products or provide similar services. A company can become a leader by having a competitive edge. Conversely, failure to remain competitive can spell disaster. The basic purpose of using VR systems from this perspective is to ensure that products or services meet the criteria required by consumers and competitors. For example, Boeing Aircraft is using VR systems for designing a new aircraft when it is still a gleam on a designer's workstation and before the company commits to build it. As such, the interior of a virtual aircraft can be designed with customers' participation. They may decide that they need a higher or a lower ceiling. At this time, it is still fairly easy to make design changes before actually building the aircraft, and it is much more economical to do so at this stage. In a similar manner, very specific design changes can be made at the beginning rather than at the end. That is, when one designer peered into the maintenance hatch of that virtual airplane at Boeing, the individual saw that the pressure gauge dial remained obscured to view no matter how the person tried to get at the gauge.

Today, architects are among the biggest VR users. Architectural walk-through programs that run on PCs and workstations are readily available. The programs offer a highly realistic view of both the inside and outside of a building from different perspectives and allow changes to be made in the plans. Something else that has increased the use of VR for designers is the utilization of CAD for 3-D computing to build prototypes. These prototypes can be picked up and put to use in order to test the effectiveness of their design.

Referring again to Boeing, production workers are using "augmented" or "see-through" reality. That is, workers wear clear goggles with 3-D images reflected onto the lenses. The goggles superimpose a virtual image of the desired result on a real object, so that workers will know what to do with the object without consulting manuals or blueprints. An assembler, for example, inside a fuselage would see the real openings for hydraulic ducts or communications cables with a virtual image of the installed ducts or cables superimposed on them. The goggles could also reflect schematic and wiring diagrams, location of drill holes, and other information. The net result is better quality in less time.

Virtual reality is being put to work in a variety of ways, including telerobotic systems for removing hazardous wastes, toxic chemicals, and bombs. The National Aeronautics and Space Administration (NASA) is undertaking work in telerobotics, particularly in hazardous environments where it is too risky to send humans, and is also looking at virtual planetary exploration. In addition, designers can use VR to design sales and marketing displays. Virtual reality CAD lets the user walk into a store on the screen and rearrange the goods for maximum sales impact. More illustrations will be given later in the text.

Accounting and Finance

Senior managers from a company's functional departments who have specific fiscal responsibilities are particularly concerned with the financial status of all of the organization's components. An effective financial-information system must provide their management with all information needed to make crucial financial decisions. From this broad perspective, senior managers and their staffs can utilize a VR system to wander through virtual hills and valleys of financial information to get a spatial sense of relationships among inventories, expenses, sales, and income. Hence, they can take into account hundreds and even thousands of different variables. In this way, senior managers and their staffs can steer through financial information as if it were presented in a visual way, instead of in rows and columns of figures that accountants have favored in the past.

As far as VR on Wall Street is concerned, new kinds of computer VR systems allow stock exchange traders to render complex processes in a visually intuitive manner. These systems allow users to participate in an alternative, computer-generated reality. In effect, VR helps simplify the complex processes involved in financial markets. It assists in revealing new relationships that had been hidden under a blizzard of numbers. Additional applications of VR systems for finance and accounting will be given later in the text.

Training and Human Resources

The training and education of people before they are employed by a company is an important concern of our society today. It is a truism that participation is crucial to learning, yet students are often essentially passive in the classroom. However, by applying VR techniques to learning, such techniques make a big difference in the final results of education. For example, educators have devised a VR program for algebra in which students act as part of the equations. An equal sign could be represented by a balance beam; in the equation $6x=4y + 50$, students would become blocks of different sizes representing $6x$ or $4y$ and would try to bring the pieces into equilibrium. In a similar manner, difficult concepts like events in the field of quantum mechanics (where electrons can act as both waves and particles) may become easier for students to understand if they are submerged in a virtual quantum world. Thus, simpler visual presentations of such complex material increase comprehension so much that even mediocre students have the potential to be good students.

This increase is comprehension is not confined to students. For example, Eastman Kodak engineers quickly gained new insights after they used a supercomputer to process in 3-D the intricate interactions of such variables as heat, temperature, and pressure in the injection process that the company uses to make plastic items from film spools to camera cases. To see six or seven variables is a new experience for Kodak engineers. They saw new relationships that were not possible through equations. By making those polymer pirouettes visible, Kodak now designs lighter, thinner parts that require less material and meet environmental standards.

In the area of human resources, the dedicated efforts of competent people is one of the most crucial success factors in any company. A key task is creating conditions that will both attract and retain personnel with the necessary combination of skill and experience to carry out all necessary activities in the organization. While adequate monetary compensation is a basic condition that must be satisfied, other requirements, such as a challenging job, a professional environment, and sufficient material and managerial support, must be met to realize the greatest potential in all personnel. Moreover, an organization's personnel must be satisfied without losing sight of the organization's goals. Thus, a continuous evaluation of personnel compensation is needed. This can be assisted by utilizing a human-resource–management system (HRMS). This evaluation must take into account employee performance and the current market value of employee contributions.

In light of these comments about the importance of an HRMS, VR can help senior management in reassigning workers' activities so that there is an improvement in productivity. A VR human-resource system can assist in getting a better handle on a number of fringe-benefit programs that best meet the needs of a company's employees. In addition, the tie-in for a HRMS to VR can help ensure that relationships that were not known or were obscure before are better defined and understood. In the final chapter of the text, training and human resource applications are set forth.

PIONEERS IN THE VR FIELD

Today, it is recognized that research into VR environments began with Ivan Sutherland. In 1965, Sutherland presented a paper at the International Federation of Information Processing Societies (IFIPS), titled "The Ultimate Display." Basically, Sutherland's original challenge was to make the virtual worlds look, act, sound, and feel real. In comparing Sutherland's vision of the Ultimate Display and the research currently being undertaken as well as proposed, the problem is much broader than the development of a display device. It becomes obvious that all components of a VR system must be considered, including the human element.[5]

A most interesting and colorful VR pioneer is Jaron Lanier who coined the term "virtual reality" in the early 1980s. He was the founder and chairman of VPL Research Inc., which he started in 1984. The company sold many virtual-space hardware products, such as the DataSuit and DataGloves. The company seemed poised to cash in on consumer VR. Instead, VPL could not make good on its loans. The patents owned by VPL have gone to French venture capitalists

Thompson INITS. Lanier has left to start another company although VPL is still in operation.

Lanier hopes that VR will be a creative force that will liberate people from the current dreary forms of vicarious entertainment. He has had a hand in several breakthroughs in the technology, but sometimes his visions go over people's heads. For example, Lanier thinks VR will be, like music, a creative medium that can express pure emotions. This kind of talk is easily misinterpreted. As a result, his ideas have been distorted by the press.

Another pioneer is Myron W. Krueger, who coined the term ''artificial reality'' in a book by the same name in the early 1970s. The idea was expanded upon by William Gibson a decade later in a series of science-fiction novels that described ''cyberspace'' systems, that is, VR systems. Krueger has been working over twenty years developing interactive works that challenge the divisions between artwork and viewer; the viewer is part of the art. When he began working with interactive art in 1969, Krueger held the opinion that the most important aspect of the work was the viewer's influence on the piece. Krueger has developed the MANDALA system that provides a silhouette of the human form via ''blue-screen'' image-processing techniques. The resulting image, with the user's image remixed, is projected on a wall opposite the blue screen, and the participants can see their own image. A MANDALA user wears no special VR equipment.

For the past quarter century, Dr. Thomas A. Furness has been pioneering the development of virtual interfaces. Now, as director of the Human Interface Technology (HIT) Laboratory and professor of industrial engineering at the University of Washington (Seattle, Washington), he is trying to make interface technologies both practical and affordable. As costs fall, he expects virtual worlds to become commonplace in such fields as industry, medicine, and education. Another noted VR pioneer is John Walker, founder of Autodesk. Walker sees VR as a replacement for the Mac interface.

Currently, a number of VR researchers and some of the original pioneers can be found in business organizations, military establishments, and educational institutions. The Digital Equipment Corporation, for example, is a most recent vendor to take a major interest in developing VR technology. The company has outlined its own internal research programs and bestowed a $1.4 million grant to supply equipment for scientists at the HIT Laboratory. In addition, such companies as Boeing, Sun Microsystems, Southwestern Bell, US West, Fujitsu, and Microsoft have invested funds and personnel in VR research at the HIT Laboratory.

In the military, NASA uses VR to analyze large, visualized, fluid-flow data sets and to show a fly through of the proposed Spacestation Freedom. At the Fake Space Lab, users walk inside a space shuttle via a simplified version of NASA's numerically simulated airflow. Other VR researchers have gravitated toward projects underway at the major universities in this country, like the University of North Carolina (Charlotte) and the University of Washington mentioned above. The premise of this extensive VR research is that it lets people step almost literally into a computer-generated environment and perform feats that would be impractical or even physically impossible in real life. Although only a few pioneers and institutions are noted above, many others could have been included. The history and lore of VR makes for quite a fascinating story. A summary of the important milestones in VR is set forth in Figure 1.2.

FUTURE RESEARCH DIRECTIONS OF VR

Future directions in VR research seem to be headed toward company and university involvement as well as government participation. As an example, a new VR interface, called CAVE (developed at the University of Illinois), is a cube with display screen faces surrounding a viewer, coupled with a head-tracking device. As the viewer moves within the bounds of the CAVE, the correct perspective and stereo projections of the environment appear on the display screens. As far as such immersion issues as field of view and intrusion are concerned, CAVE overcomes many of the problems encountered by other VR systems. Moreover, CAVE is effective in regard to such visualization issues as look around and collaboration. Real-time rendering of the virtual world is achieved through six Silicon Graphics VGX workstations, each attached to a rear projection display. Applications of CAVE include graphical planning for brain surgery, fractal exploratorium, and biomodeling.[6]

As far as the federal government is concerned, there are efforts underway to fund research in the VR industry. The VR Technology Task Group, part of the president's High Performance Computing, Communications and Information Technologies Committee, has determined that VR may be the nation's most important technology of the decade. The task force has released reports that recommend government funding for basic VR research at universities and major company laboratories.

Over the long term, Jaron Lanier suggests that VR be considered in three time frames: 10, 100, and 1000 years into the future. He states that three ethical issues will arise in the next 10 years: (1) The use of VR in scientific research, (2) VR's role in distancing the public from the horrors of war, and (3) VR's potential impact on children. He expects to play a vital role in developing VR for children, since it is inherently a nonpassive media and it encourages the physical and social activities that TV and Nintendo discourage. He addresses but disputes the potential for governmental misuse of VR as a means of control in 100 years. Cultural change is so slow that VR may only become common-place in 1000 years. Although the reader may agree or disagree with his assessment in the near and distant future, the fact is that virtual worlds in business and nonbusiness activities have the potential to affect the real world dramatically. In retrospect, I expect future generations will look back and call this era the "horse and buggy" days of VR environments.[7]

Figure 1.2
Summary of the Important Milestones in VR

Year	Important Milestones
1929	First mechanical flight simulator is demonstrated.
1952	Mechanical flight simulator is combined with video.
1966	First computer-controlled HMD is built by Ivan Sutherland.
1968	Electronic scene generators for flight simulators are created by David Evans and Ivan Sutherland.
1970	First fully functional HMD is demonstrated.
1971	GROPE-II, developed at the University of North Carolina, allows chemists to visualize molecules.
1972	First computer-based flight simulator is unveiled.
1975	Myron Kreuger developed his VIDEOPLACE—a projected environment.
1982	Flight simulator is merged with an HMD.
1984	NASAVIEW workstation is unveiled.
1985	University of North Carolina's Sitterson Hall is modeled in 3-D on a computer that allows virtual walk throughs. First practical stereo HMD is developed at NASA.
1986	VPL Research shipped its first DataGlove.
1989	VPL Research shipped its first commercial VR hardware system. Autodesk Inc. demonstrated its first PC-based VR system.
1991	Sense8 Corporation shipped its first WorldToolKit.
1992	A new VR interface, called the CAVE, is developed by the University of Illinois. First VR art show is held in the New York Gallery. Boston Computer Museum demonstrated Sense8/Intel applications as part of exhibit.

SUMMARY

For the most part, VR is a technology that has only recently come within reach for the typical company. Although the philosophical, cultural, and hallucinogenic implications remain, VR is becoming decidedly more serious as business, government, and education embrace the technology for a diverse range of applications. Demand for this new interactive, real-time, and 3-D technology should contribute to the development of better and less expensive hardware and software. In the past, the introductions of new computer technologies, such as microprocessors, has bolstered the growth of many new industries. Some believe that VR will be of comparable importance in influencing the growth of even more new industries in the years to come.

NOTES

1. Gene Bylinsky, "The Marvels of 'Virtual Reality,' " *Fortune*, June 3, 1991, p. 150.

2. Andy Tait, "Authoring Virtual Worlds on the Desktop," *Virtual Reality Special Report*, published by *AI Expert* (San Francisco: Miller Freeman, 1993), pp. 11–12.

3. Bylinsky, "Marvels of 'Virtual Reality,' " pp. 139, 142.

4. John Rizzo, "Virtus WalkThrough," *MacUser*, July 1991, pp. 73–76.

5. J. Michael Moshell and Richard Dunn-Roberts, "A Survey of Virtual Environments: Research in North America, Part One," *Virtual Reality World*, November–December 1993, pp. 4–5.

6. Carolina Cruz-Neira et al., "The Cave: Audio Visual Experience Automatic Virtual Environment," *Communications of the ACM*, June 1992, pp. 64–72.

7. Stephen Porter, "Interview: Jaron Lanier," *Computer Graphics World*, April 1992, pp. 61–66.

2

A Framework for Business-Oriented Virtual-Reality Systems

ISSUES EXPLORED

- To set forth the basic concepts of visualization as found in VR systems today
- To examine the basic components of immersion systems as found in a typical VR environment
- To take a look at the components of a reality engine
- To explore the basic elements of sensors (input and output) that are found in immersion VR systems
- To look at nonbusiness VR applications that complement the business applications set forth in the text

OUTLINE

Introduction to a Framework for VR Systems

Important Developments That Make VR Possible for Mass Appeal

Concept of Visualization

Virtual Worlds Fall into Four Areas

   Considerations for Standards

Essential Components of Immersion VR Systems

Output Sensors

   Visual

   Auditory

   Haptic

   Voice

INTRODUCTION TO A FRAMEWORK FOR VR SYSTEMS

In its fullest realization via a total immersion system, VR is essentially being there with all of one's senses intact and enhanced in an artificial 3-D environment. Fantasies of some future VR applications are evoked on the Enterprise's holodeck in the TV show *Star Trek: The Next Generation* and films like *Brainstorm* and *Lawnmower Man.* In these conceptualizations, a person may not be able to tell a computer-generated hallucination from flesh-and-blood reality. In order to get a better idea of what is required for total immersion in a VR environment at one end of the spectrum versus utilizing desktop VR systems at the other end, this chapter looks at a basic framework for VR systems, whether they are oriented toward business applications or not.

Even in a rudimentary desktop VR application that uses less than state-of-the-art technology, there is the illusion of entering a new kind of world. Virtual reality's artificial construct may be less than complete at this time, but it provides just enough visual, spatial, and auditory cues that confirm and consolidate a person's senses so that a person's own library of experiences begin to fill in the blanks. Gradually, especially in high-end systems driven by high-powered graphics workstations, VR comes to its fullest potential by extending the power of the person. Virtual reality is extremely successful on the assumption that the brain cell can process information better when it is presented through sight, sound, and touch than when it must grasp columns of numbers or lines of a text.

IMPORTANT DEVELOPMENTS THAT MAKE VR POSSIBLE FOR MASS APPEAL

Within the last few years, a number of technological developments have made it possible for VR to be an important part of the business organization. Hardware technology, in particular the PC, has advanced to the point where it is fast enough for the implementation of VR. This will be evident in Chapter 3. In a similar manner, the display technology is sufficiently advanced. From another viewpoint, useful VR software is now being marketed to assist the user in developing appropriate VR business applications. This item is related to the subject matter of Chapter 4. Important to both advances in hardware and software technologies are database management systems and data communications that have been developed sufficiently to accommodate the needs of VR, as will be demonstrated in Chapter 5. Overall, there is a critical mass of developers and users whose needs can be met by advancing information technology for VR business-oriented applications.

Although information technology has been sufficiently developed to make VR possible, it should be noted that there are a number of crucial challenges still facing the typical user. First and foremost, there is a need for business organizations to rethink their approaches on how their organizations are run. This important fact will be quite evident in Part IV—"Applications of Virtual-Reality Systems for Business." Second, the central-processing-unit (CPU) horsepower of PCs needs to be improved so that VR operations are in real time with no apparent timing lapses. Third, even faster graphics are necessary so that the viewer is linked directly with operations as they occur. Fourth, displays should be of greater quality, lower in price than presently, light in weight, and less bulky. Fifth, a most important challenge of VR is finding applications that can make the organization more productive. This item is tied in with making the organization more effective and efficient in its day-to-day operations. Essentially, this is a significant thrust of this text in that new business applications will be set forth for making the organization and its employees more productive.

CONCEPT OF VISUALIZATION

As noted in the previous chapter, the aim of AI is to build systems that can mimic human reasoning, a goal that has yet to be reached. On the other hand, VR is the antithesis of what AI has tried to do, that is, it aims to extend the power of the person. As such, the term *visualization* comes into play. Visualization is used to indicate graphic, 3-D representation of data to make its implications clearer to the user. Visualization also encompasses VR experiments, and scientists expect to discover whether it is useful for a more complete understanding of data. Currently, VR researchers hope that their work will progress from visualization to *realization*, or complete understanding.

As an example, interactive modeling and visualization of medical and biological data has the potential for improving patient care and reducing medical costs. Visualization environments for these domains must address all stages of data analysis, including registration, segmentation, 3-D reconstruction, rendering, analysis, and simulation. These components of the visualization environment are best implemented in a collaborative environment.

In another example, a visualization tool designed by Maxus Systems International is used by managers at TIAA-CREF—a New York pension fund with $105 billion in assets. Tracking the performance of a group of stocks against the larger market is a challenge for analysts, who must follow hundreds of ever-changing numbers. Using software from the Sense8 Corporation, the Maxus system converts the numbers to a 3-D schematic of colored squares that move and symbolize individual stocks within grids representing market and industry sectors. Portfolio managers use a mouse ''to fly'' into the lowest tier of stocks, which have plunged the fastest, and click on the security that has dropped the most. The process takes seconds, so portfolio managers can identify trends, recognize exceptions, and make decisions more quickly. The net result is that portfolio managers have a better understanding of the stock market than previously.

VIRTUAL WORLDS FALL INTO FOUR AREAS

Fundamentally, VR attempts to convey a sense of realism such that it is useful in modeling situations in the real world. Virtual reality is also useful in making abstract data seem more real. In both situations, realism can be enhanced by using motion and complex behavior on objects as well as improving image quality. When classified as movement and control, virtual worlds fall into four basic areas. *First*, there is no interaction. The static computer-generated worlds that are produced by architectural computer-aided–design (CAD) programs fall into this first category. There may be real-time walk throughs, but no interaction occurs. As such, these applications simply call for the user to move in real time through a 3-D database. For example, in an architectural walk through the user moves through a "virtual house." In reference to the definition given in the prior chapter, this is not considered to be true VR.

The *second* area contains worlds with movement and interaction. Most VR systems provide some form of motion control on objects, from simple dynamics to full simulation of the physical properties of the object in question. Essentially, each object reacts in a manner consistent with a set of rules, such as the laws of physics for that world. This is a crucial step toward true interactivity. If users, for example, collide with a ball in a virtual world, they would expect the ball to be affected in some way. As such, *collision detection* ensures that the user cannot walk through walls or that objects that are placed on a table do not drop through the table. This feature means that objects do not just exist in space but can sense, through touch, the existence of one another and that the user can interact with an object. Generally, collision detection becomes increasingly difficult to determine with a corresponding increase in the complexity of the objects contained in the virtual world.

The *third* area is behavioral modeling and control, which means that the objects in a virtual world "know" how to behave. In other words, when objects are manipulated such that the user interacts with this virtual environment through the use of some input device (a glove, wand, or joystick), they act as they would in life. Objects can detect circumstances arising in a virtual world and respond to them in a variety of preprogrammed ways, which can effectively override the laws of physics. As an example, if a car is pushed, it will roll in a straight line until stopped. A car with complex behavior can be made to accelerate, decelerate, or turn under its own initiative or make choices about its route depending on the state and position of other objects in the virtual world.

The importance of behavioral modeling and control goes beyond merely providing helpful approaches to users of largely static virtual worlds. The VR system can be used to visualize inherently complex dynamic processes, such as the movement of parts through a factory. With dynamic interaction between the user and the virtual world, useful work can be undertaken in a virtual environment. Visualization of real-world events can be accomplished and appropriate actions taken. Hence, the objects in the virtual world can be programmed to provide important visual and aural cues for situations requiring immediate attention as well as for potentially difficult or disastrous courses of action.

The *fourth* area is the effect of true artificial intelligence (AI) on objects. As of today, the goals of AI have not been realized, nor are they expected to be in the near future. Hence, considerable research must be undertaken before the presumed and actual effects on objects can be assessed using AI. One promising approach is to let complex behaviors "grow" rather than build them. Rather than rely on the programming skill of the virtual world designer, this evolutionary process supplies the intelligence. It is expected that the usefulness of this approach will continue to grow as more research is undertaken.[1]

Considerations for Standards

No matter what approach is undertaken in a virtual world, there is need for standards. As a starting point, Autodesk (best known for its CAD product AutoCAD) and VR systems supplier Division Limited (Bristol, England) are working together to develop a standard for VR systems. The two companies state that they can develop a standard that will bring VR-system design to developers working on a variety of computer platforms. Audodesk brings its expertise in existing design and modeling products and Division Limited offers its software architecture for the integration of computational and peripheral elements for the support of VR applications.[2]

The ultimate goal is to bring VR systems on to the more commonly used computer platforms. In effect, a developer of VR systems will be able to develop applications more easily and run them on a wide variety of computer platforms across the performance spectrum. Additionally, when developing standards for VR systems, there is need to consider the whole area of networking environments under which VR systems will be operating.

Regarding networking environments, sufficient time should be devoted to issues, such as privacy and security, that pervade this electronic world, on what separates electronic pranks from electronic crime, and on what it means to own data. If, for example, a company regularly transmits sensitive information between sites, encryption should be a standard part of every user's transmission procedures. Similarly, if it is possible to dial in to local area networks (LANs), there is need to take user passwords a lot more seriously. In the past, there have been cases where security is lax. As an example, a Unix shop has a root (superuser) account that has no password, the NetWare network has a supervisor account that is unprotected, or the LAN has a guest account that has access to a number of files, and the password is "guest." Networks like those are the "cyberspace" equivalents of houses with open doors. If the user community is trustworthy, that may be fine, but if it is not, a company should not be surprised to find some valuable data missing. Thus, specific standards are necessary in some type of VR networking environment.

ESSENTIAL COMPONENTS OF IMMERSION VR SYSTEMS

A total-immersion VR system, as noted in the prior chapter, attempts to bring the user completely into a computer-generated world by using the computer to stimulate the visual, aural, and tactile senses. By creating worlds of color, shapes, sounds, and feel, VR systems have the capability of amplifying the powers of the user's mind to see previously hidden relationships in complex sets of data and to absorb, manipulate, and interpret information more quickly and completely. The distinction between immersion in a VR world and analyzing the same information by using blueprints, numbers, or text is the difference between looking at fish in an ocean from a glass-bottom boat and putting on scuba gear and diving in among the fish to experience their world.

Currently, total immersion is usually accomplished with HMDs, 3-D sound systems, and pressure-sensitive gloves or bodysuits. Also, there can be use of sensors that do not result in a total immersion, which include 3-D mouses, joysticks, or force balls. As such, a VR system's essential components (as shown in Figure 2.1) comprise input and output sensors (effectors) that work in conjunction with a reality engine. Essentially, the VR closed-loop system begins when a user (or users) responds to what the individual is seeing and hearing by turning the head or moving a joystick. These signals are processed by a reality engine to create another set of sights and sounds. This continuous feedback gives the user an illusion of reality. These components are the essence of VR systems discussed below. In addition, there may be a need to utilize data from a company database as well as network the VR application to other locations. This is particularly true for VR applications found in business. The addition of a company's database and networking to other locations is found in Figure 2.1. ´

OUTPUT SENSORS

To create artificial, interactive, and computer-generated worlds in real time, there is a need for output sensors. In the discussion to follow, the focus is on current output devices that relate to a person's *visual*, *auditory*, *haptic*, *voice* and *other* output sensors. For the user to be brought completely into a virtual world, all senses must be engaged, although smell and taste have yet to be addressed.

Visual

Visual devices relate to EyePhones and headpieces that govern the eyes. Most VR companies use sight control as the starting point for creating virtual worlds. The basic item is a piece of headgear that looks like a modified Star Wars helmet and is attached by cable to a powerful workstation. Such a device is commonly known as a head mounted display (HMD). These headpieces feature two small video screens, one for each eye, for a realistic 3-D effect. Typically, there are motion or balance sensors within the headset that convey position coordinates (head turning left, head moving up) to the workstation, which then develops the appropriate scene displayed in front of the user's eyes. For example, if the user's head tilts down, as if the person is looking at the floor, the computer would generate a scene that moves upward, giving the user the sensation of looking below the horizon.

Another variation of the head enclosure device is the use of a viewing screen mounted on a boom. The user peers into the semienclosed screen while guiding it up, down, and around by using two handles. The boom allows the screen to move in the direction that the viewer wants. For relatively straightforward navigation tasks, it is very intuitive and has a high-resolution image and small sensor lag.

No matter the visual device used, most VR displays vary from 80 to 140 degrees while humans have a 180-degree horizontal field of view. In addition, when a user is wearing an HMD, liquid-crystal displays (LCDs) have between 86,000 to 110,000 colored elements. It takes three elements (1 red, 1 blue, and 1 green) to make a single pixel, or picture element. This means that the human eye receives about 30,000 to 40,000 pixels of color information. Generally, PCs and workstations have about 1,000,000 pixels of information, or thirty times as many. As far as the visual complexity of an image is concerned, the more detail there is in a scene, the more time it takes the computer to process, thereby

Figure 2.1
Diagram of the Essential Components of a VR System

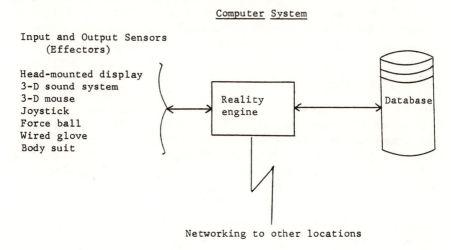

slowing down the frame rate. To achieve a sense of presence, about 10 to 12 frames per second is a desirable goal, while greater than thirty frames per second has diminishing returns. Thus, the rendering speed should occur within a blink of an eye to be useful in a VR environment.

Auditory

An important element in a virtual world is auditory where headphones and earphones regulate sound. To ensure that all sound experienced from within a virtual environment is generated by that environment, 3-D, or holophonic, headphones are used to present the user with sound. Music, sound from objects, and noise alert the user to the location of an unseen object, such as behind or overhead. In addition, sound can be used as feedback. For example, if a user hits a virtual object, the individual might hear a certain sound informing the individual of such a contact. In a similar manner, sound provides a certain feedback about the nature of the environment. If the user drops a heavy object on a hard surface, the sound will be different from that produced were the object dropped on a soft surface. These auditory cues, then, give the user knowledge about the material properties of the environment through feedback.

Recent studies have suggested that improving the quality of sound can influence the perception of image quality. For example, when people were shown the same images on two side-by-side TV sets, the one with compact-disk–quality sound consistently rated as having a better image over the one with standard monaural sound. The same effect can be presumed to increase the perceived quality of virtual images. From this perspective, sound has the ability to draw the user much further into virtual worlds than previously.

Haptic

Complementary to visual and auditory sensors in a VR environment is haptic perception, which includes tactile and force feedback. *Tactile feedback* refers to one's sense of touch or pressure applied to the skin. On the other hand, *force feedback* refers to forces acting on muscles, tendons, and joints. Haptic devices provide the user with the illusion of manual exploration or manipulation of objects in virtual worlds. They employ human tactile, kinesthetic, and motor systems for interaction with the virtual environment.

Wandering through a VR environment is described in six degrees of freedom (6DOF). The first three degrees of freedom—x, y, and z—describe the location of a single point in the familiar Cartesian space. Solid objects also need to have their orientation and motion around the x, y, and z axis. The last three degrees of freedom—pitch, yaw, and roll—represent angles away from 0, 0, 0. As such, a popular haptic device is a mouse or wand that can be combined with a 6DOF tracking system. Some of these designs allow the mouse to be used in a normal 2-D mode and then to be switched automatically to 6DOF once it is lifted off the desk. Typically, it provides a straightforward method of selecting, navigating, and interacting with objects. In contrast, some VR systems use a joystick or pointing device to select an object. No matter the device used to select an object, the user can typically scale, move, texture, or place the object on the top of other objects.

Data gloves and touch sensors (wired gloves) provide synchronous movement of the hand in a simulated mode. Usually, these wired gloves include a sensor for measuring overall hand orientation and position, known as a 6DOF, since it measures a total of six values that define an object's unique position and orientation. Using gloves outfitted with fiber-optic cables attached to a workstation, the user can place himself or herself in the virtual world via a simulated hand that mimics all movement of the real hand encased inside the glove. Pointing a finger or closing a fist are translated into the same movements for the hand on the headset screen. In this way, a user can grasp virtual objects and move them around the computer-generated world.

At this time, one problem in this area is that its tactile-feedback ability is rudimentary. It is not good enough at giving the user clues about whether something has been touched or grasped or how much pressure and force has been applied. Oftentimes, aural clues (such as a "thunking" sound or a vacuum sound) are used in place of touch sensors to aid in the grasping of objects.

Another haptic device are force balls that utilize mechanical strain gauges to measure the multiple forces or torques applied to a ball-shaped device. Generally, they include eight to nine buttons for user-defined commands. Because they provide for simultaneous input of multiple degrees of freedom, force balls are useful for object manipulation or flight control. It is recommended that the user be trained in their proper use since they are nonintuitive.

Voice

As far as voice recognition is concerned, inexpensive devices are now available that recognize an individual's words with reasonable reliability. The trade-off is between having a large vocabulary with a trainable (''speaker-dependent'') system (sometimes requiring hours of time from a single subject, so that the system has hundreds of samples) and having a small vocabulary that can usually be recognized when clearly spoken by anyone. Currently, this area is undergoing continuing development for incorporation into a VR environment.

Other

In addition, there are other devices that are currently being researched and developed. These include biosensors and eye tracking. Biosensors are special glasses or bracelets that contain electrodes that are worn next to the skin. Muscle electrical activity can be monitored by dermal electrodes. These electrodes are capable of tracking eye movements by measuring muscle movements. On the other hand, eye tracking utilizes infrared or other optical means to track whether the eye is currently looking. This approach is useful, like biosensors, for controlling view or motion and is helpful as an interface for those who have lost use of their hands or other motor skills.

REALITY ENGINE

The reality engine is software that lets a user interact with the generated world and forms the heart of a VR system. Basically, the reality engine takes a stored set of objects and landscapes and merges the ''virtualized user'' into that environment. Every time the user moves or acts, the engine updates the world and re-creates it for the user. Action is communicated by the sensors and navigation devices; the VR world is described by the user by sending signals to the displays, the sound system, and the tactile feedback devices. For a true interactive mode, the reality engine must operate in real time for sensing, recalculating, redrawing, and displaying the world at least ten times per second. The sound in a VR system has to be even more precise because gaps or broken sound can severely distract the user.

Most VR systems run on either a PC or a workstation. Even with this powerful hardware, only a finite number of items can be repositioned and redrawn ten or more times per second. Therefore, the landscape and elements of a virtual world must be described as a small number of simple polygons. For example, a landscape could be composed of (in increasing detail) 200 to 20,000 separate triangles. Each time the user moves, the perspective, location, and shadow of every triangle must be recalculated and redrawn. There is always a trade-off between the reality and resolution of an image and the speed of recalculation and redrawing. Most simulations sacrifice realism to get ten or more images per second of smoothness. However, there is a way to make a simple world look more realistic. With texturing, predetermined patterns can be overlaid on simple polygons. A square representing the side of a house, for example, could be textured with a brick pattern.

Components of a Reality Engine

To create a VR system, a user could start with a personal computer or workstation and add hardware to supplement sound and graphics creation. As illustrated in Figure 2.2, this would entail adding graphics boards since stereoscopic images require separate video images for each eye. Before the video output from the graphics boards can be used by the HMD, it generally has to be converted to the same signal that a video cassette recorder (VCR) accepts, although some HMDs accept the computer's video signal directly. In addition, special boards are required for 3-D sound along with some method of creating synthesized sounds or playing back sampled ones. Communication with sensors and VR devices, such as force balls, wired gloves, and head trackers, is performed through standard input/output (I/O) ports found on the back of every computer.

As noted in the illustration, all of these boards and I/O ports are attached to the computer interface that, in turn, communicates with the simulation manager. The simulation manager is connected to the user application and the 3-D model database so that the user can experience a VR operating mode. Because many of these pieces of hardware represent a number of additions to the original PC or workstation, there are a number of VR vendors who provide complete system integration. These vendors include some of the following: VPL Research, Sense8 Corporation, and W Industries, whose hardware platforms include Amiga, IBM RS6000, Intel PC, Macintosh, SGi, and Sun. By providing complete systems, these vendors help users avoid the problem of assembling boards, connectors, and cables that may or may not be compatible. Additional information on VR hardware is given in the next chapter.

INPUT SENSORS

In the preceding discussion on output sensors, the focus was on the user's gaining entry to a VR environment through the use of these sensors. By contrast, input sensors allow for interaction and movement once the user has entered the VR environment. Generally, input sensors can be categorized as interaction devices and tracking devices. Interaction devices provide the user with the ability to move and manipulate objects at will. Tracking devices, on the other hand, monitor various body parts in a manner that creates a presence or a feeling of being physically present in the virtual world. Each of these input sensors are discussed below.

Figure 2.2
Essential Components of a Reality Engine

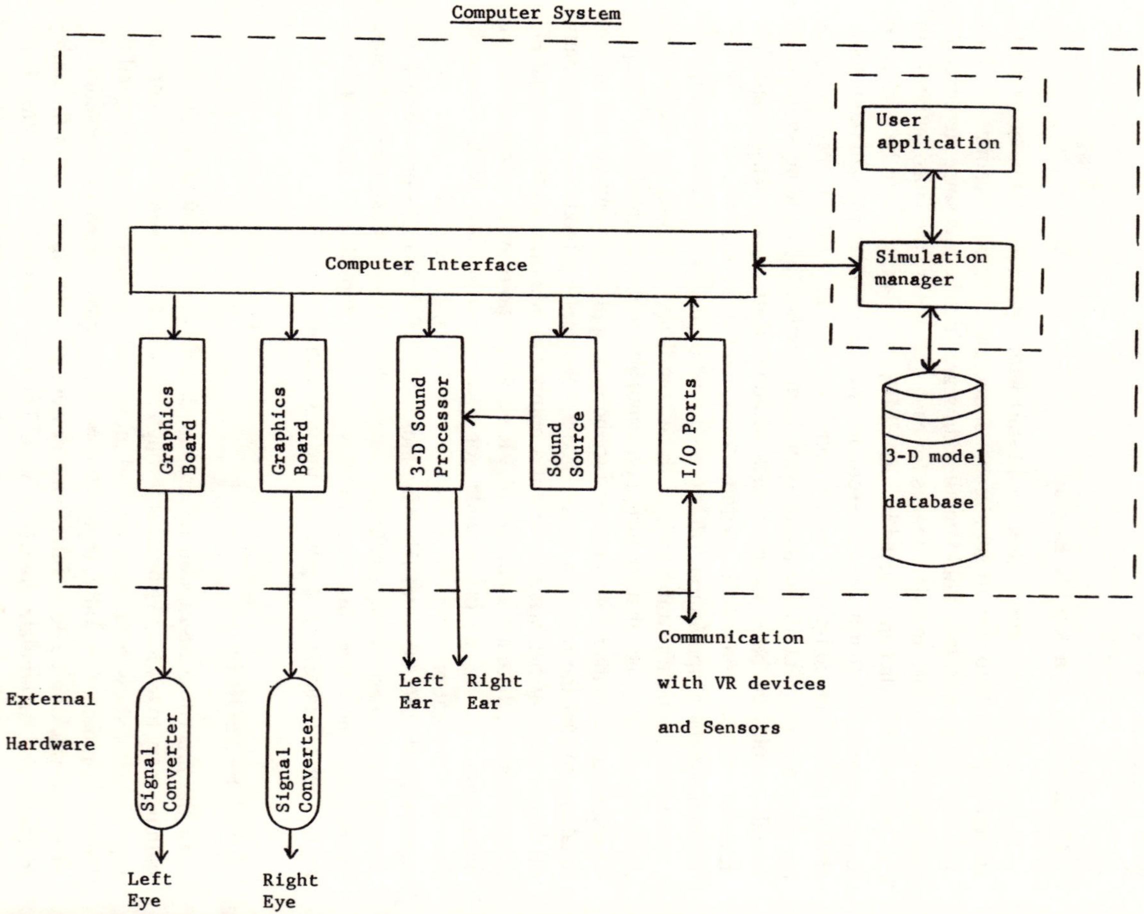

Interaction

Many of the devices that were discussed previously under output sensors fit into the category of interaction devices. They include wired-clothing devices that are worn, such as a glove or a suit. Devices that measure 6DOF simultaneously are useful for object control and navigation. Wand devices that are handheld fall into this category. A 2-D mouse and a joystick have their uses as interaction devices. Additionally, there are devices that rely on voice recognition or muscle electrical signals. For all of these interaction devices, effectiveness is determined by how well the software accesses the device's capabilities. For the most part, software more than hardware determines how the devices are used for creating a true VR world.

Tracking

Many of the devices and capabilities mentioned previously in the chapter, such as wands, wired gloves, and head tracking, center on the ability of the devices to detect an object's position and orientation at any instant. That is, no matter what the user is doing—for example, moving his or her head or raising his or her hand—the computer tracks these movements in real time so that the virtual world is synchronized to the actions of the individual. There are several important parameters that determine the effectiveness of tracking. They include lag, update rate, interference, accuracy, and range, which are discussed below.

Lag or latency is defined as the delay (in real time) between sensor movement and the resulting signal being processed for final use. It is one of the key parameters since lags above 50 milliseconds affect human performance. The *update rate* is defined as the speed at which measurements are made. Most sensors support updates at the rate of sixty per second. It should be noted that lag and the update rate are generally independent of each other. *Interference* is defined as the amount of sensitivity to environmental factors. Sensors can be sensitive to different situations, such as objects coming between the source and the sensor or extraneous sounds. Problems can occur when a sensor is used in proximity to another. *Accuracy* is another key parameter in tracking effectiveness, which is defined as the accuracy of position and orientation information. Lastly, *range* is defined as the maximum distance between the source and sensor while retaining a certain level of accuracy. Range varies with different types of sensors.

Related to these important parameters is the fact that all trackers work by measuring changes in position relative to some reference point. That is, there is a source that generates a signal, a sensor that receives the signal, and a control box that processes the signal and communicates with the computer. Once the sensor is attached to an object and both the source and sensor are properly oriented, the control box is sent an initialization signal from the reality engine. This, in turn, determines the current position as the reference point. Care must be taken when holding an HMD or a wand in a particular position at start-up.

If necessary, the device can be reset. After initialization (i.e., calibration), the tracking device can start sending information to the simulation manager of the VR system so that the user's movements can be tracked in real time.

Currently, there are several approaches to tracking technology—mechanical, electromagnetic, ultrasonic, inertial, and optical—which have evolved to detect an object's position and orientation. The *mechanical* system uses a direct mechanical connection between the object to be tracked and a reference point. Typically, this linkage is a mechanical arm with rotating joints that allow for 6DOF control. Mechanical trackers tend to be awkward but cheap, fast, and accurate. A reliable and accurate method of tracking that is popular is *electromagnetic*. For this tracking technology, a low-frequency signal that is generated by a control box sequentially stimulates three small coils of wire in the source, thereby generating three magnetic fields. When a similar set of three coiled wires is located in range of the source, a small voltage is induced in each of the coils as the three fields are created. The net result is that nine measurements are processed by the control box, yielding six values for position and orientation.

The *ultrasonic* system is a low-cost approach that utilizes three ultrasonic transducers and three small microphones. Using the same principle as before, each ultrasonic transducer emits a high-frequency sound pulse that is picked up by the three microphones. In turn, a signal processor measures the time delay, that is, the distance, between each transducer and each set of microphones. The nine distance measurements yield the resulting values. These tracking systems are slow, and accuracy is influenced by surroundings due to echoes and so forth.

The *inertial* tracking system uses a couple of miniature gyroscopes to measure yaw, pitch, and roll. These are not true 6DOF sensors because they measure only orientation, however, they can be effective as head-tracking sensors where positive information is not normally required. Lastly, *optical* tracking systems are used primarily in cockpit simulators where the range of head motion is fairly limited but where fast and accurate update rates are important. Currently, such systems are expensive.

VR APPLICATIONS THAT ARE NONBUSINESS RELATED

Areas in which businesses can make use of VR were presented in the prior chapter. These areas will be expanded at some length in the final four chapters of this text. On the other hand, there are a great number of areas that are related indirectly to businesses—more specifically, art, chemistry, disabled people, drugs, entertainment, medicine, military, and theme parks—that will be discussed below. Although not discussed below, other nonbusiness-related VR applications include allowing social researchers to push the boundaries of conventional research to solve pressing social problems, providing a means for psychologists to treat patients and study human behavior, studying weather conditions by developing simulations through VR technology, and examining the usual traffic snarls during peak rush hours through simulation. Virtual reality is also being used to bring people to places that they cannot physically enter. Specially constructed robots can be connected to VR systems to allow technicians, for example, to work inside a nuclear reactor or on Mars. These "waldos," as they are known to science fiction fans, allow users to work in dangerous places from the comfort of their workplaces.

Art

A glimpse of what the museum of the next century will be like was seen recently in New York at the Guggenheim Museum Soho. In a presentation called "Virtual Reality: An Emerging Medium," the Guggenheim demonstrated the radical changes that computers will make in the way in which people experience the art and architecture of the past. Developed by the Studio for Creative Inquiry at Carnegie Mellon University, the Temple of Horus, for example, is "experienced" by donning a special headset with built-in displays, sound, and sensors to create the sensation of movement. The result is very close to what the virtual museum will be like. The concept of the "virtual museum" might sound suspicious to many, particularly to people who relish the time they can spend every Sunday roaming the halls of their favorite museum. However, there are dozens of the most prominent museums in the United States and around the world who are studying the use of the virtual museum. Although it is not a substitute for looking at the art, it helps people to see and understand art and make room for it in their lives.

Typically, most museum officials are not worried about their Sunday regulars. Rather, they are targeting the millions of other people who do not or cannot get to a museum, but who can be reached by computer. With Carnegie Mellon's Temple of Horus, for example, two viewers in the same room can be networked into the "cyberspace" world. Ultimately, with the advent of the digital superhighway, that network could tie in viewers around the world. There is the potential to provide visitors thousands of miles away with some real experience of what a museum has to offer. Thus, the computer, far more than any other technology of the twentieth century, is helping museums fulfill their mandate, which, after all, is not just to collect, house, preserve, and display, but also to reach out and educate the public. It is no surprise that computers are a valuable educational tool. But it was not until the last few years that powerful desktop models came within the budgets of most museums. Nor, until recently, was the graphics technology—and, thus, the monitor resolution—good enough to display fine art.[3]

In addition, VR offers artists new possibilities previously unavailable and unimagined through other digital media already in use, such as video or computer graphics. Working within a VR environment, artists have the freedom to design completely new universes in which aesthetics and imagination can be combined. Furthermore, the physical laws of the material world can be altered or completely suspended within the confines of a VR environment. To obtain the sense of being in another world, an artist wears a headset that displays a computer-generated environment. With a turn of the head, a sensor on the head-set adjusts to sustain the visual illusion of being inside the environment. When the person wearing a VR headset looks at the floor, the person will see the floor of the artificial world and not the actual world. The physical sense of immersion assists in carrying great psychological power that can be accentuated by artistic intent. Overall, the interactive qualities of VR offer creative-development pos-sibilities for artists such that the individual can interact with virtual "objects" and characters and even meet a graphical representation of another viewer. The viewer of such art is not passive, but is an active participant with and within the art itself.[4]

Chemistry

Chemical and bioengineers are currently using VR to explore new ways to build molecules or splice genes. Because scientists are able to build models now, they often lack force and spatial reference. However, VR can emulate those aspects. Three-dimensional models can help biochemists better understand the shapes of complex molecules, while 2-D computer simulations of molecular structures are not as intuitive to scientists as 3-D models. Using virtual 3-D models and a force-feedback arm that responds to the nearby atomic forces, scientists can see and feel molecular structures. This system allows biochemists to see, move, bend, and twist simulated molecules to help design new drugs that fit into receptor proteins as a key fits into a lock. For example, a biochemist can test several drugs on a cancer cell to determine which is the most effective. Past studies have indicated that force feedback may cut in half the time needed to find the best fit.

As another example, a researcher at the University of North Carolina at Chapel Hill puts on special eyeglasses and utilizes a control device to work with molecular Tinkertoys. At this research facility, pharmaceutical chemists are looking into ways to design synthetic medicines. The metal device and the glasses make it possible for the researcher to manipulate 3-D computer models of real molecules that resist movements mechanically according to the molecular forces that cause the molecules to attract or repel. A researcher can see and feel the way in which certain shapes of molecules can be activated or deactivated by bonding with another molecule of a certain shape and properties. Currently, BioCad (Mountain View, California) sells "virtual chemistry" software that lets scientists create 3-D, interactive models of molecules and other chemical struc-tures.

Disabled People

Just as the military has been using VR for years to teach jet pilots and tank drivers, VR technology is also helping the disabled to navigate and communicate more effectively. For example, trying to teach children with cerebal palsy to drive motorized wheelchairs is an extremely difficult task. Children who have never moved around independently before do not understand poles, doors, hallways, and so forth. They do not have any depth perception to speak of because they have never moved themselves around and had to learn about environmental cues. In essence, they tend to be helpless because people carry them from place to place.

Today, a child can sit on a motorized wheelchair mounted on a set of rollers that wheelchair athletes use to train indoors. The individual sees through tiny TV screens mounted in front of each eye, making 3-D computer-generated images. When the child bumps into something, the wheelchair jolts to a stop. When he or she hits mud, the wheelchair goes much slower. When the child runs off the edge of the world, he or she flies through the sky until the ground is found.

In a similar manner, a quadriplegic with a virtual interface is able to engage in a wide range of physical activities, both for work and recreation. In a virtual world, a quadriplegic can walk, run, jump, play tennis, and really feel the sense of doing these things. In addition, virtual interfaces are being investigated by psychologists and psychiatrists to help patients deal with phobias. Doctors can change the amount of reality patients are exposed to and gradually wean them from their fears.

Drugs

Related to the above discussion on chemistry is the field of drugs. Drug companies around the world have formed research teams that are searching for tomorrow's drugs. Researchers are using computer models of molecules to put together all sorts of drugs tailored to lock onto disease-causing intruders and disable them. Drug designers working in a form of VR that reproduces tactile sensations are expected to benefit by feeling greatly enlarged molecules dock after they guide them through 3-D space on the screens of their computers. Currently, some wear stereo goggles for 3-D visualization of molecular structures on workstation screens. The aim is to make the molecules fit as deftly as possible. In one case, a large enzyme that contributes to cancer can be inactivated by blocking its so-called active site, where it does the damage, with a small molecule that fits that site perfectly. The first anticancer drugs developed this way by Agouron Pharmaceuticals (La Jolla, California) are now being tested.

Supported in part by Burroughs Wellcome, VR researchers at the University of North Carolina have added another approach. By using a modified remote-manipulation arm of the kind employed in nuclear power plants, and by building into the arm's grip a feel for the electronic forces that bind molecules, researchers have shown that molecules can be docked twice as fast this way compared to conventional computer graphics. It has been found in the past that a bad fit increases resistance. As the researcher moves the molecule into a better position, the individual can feel the tension relax in his or her grip of the hand. Stereo glasses allow the individual to observe the docking in three dimensions.[5]

Entertainment

Today, the entire entertainment industry embraces VR as the "wunderkind attraction," whether it be for arcade center movies, shopping centers, theme parks, or location-based entertainment. The greatest indicators of VR's progress in the entertainment area is the continual improvements in VR components, the expansion of gaming environments, and the surge of new companies involved in the design of VR attractions. One important improvement is the HMD. Often the bane of immersive VR with their bulky and unwieldy video helmets, new designs are showing up that have smaller, lightweight viewing goggles with an ease of comfort that will assist in building loyal audiences for repeat business. Likewise, improvements in computer graphic imagery are bringing forth more visually realistic and thematically compelling adventures.[6]

Many of the VR games found in today's arcades offer totally immersing experiences that give the sensation of walking, running, climbing, or flying in an alien world. In some of the games, players duck, jump, or turn to avoid obstacles they perceive as real but which are nothing more than computer bits dancing in front of their eyes. If one plays one of the games that come equipped with 3-D goggles, the world swings to the left when the head is turned in that direction. One can hear an enemy's footsteps approaching through earphones and see the weapon in one's hand move as the arm is raised to blow away the opponent. Typically, the games are a bit violent. Almost all of the VR games to date consist of variations of the standard kill-or-be-killed video games that appeal mostly to males.

The BattleTech Center (Chicago, Illinois) is the first commercial application of interactive VR to the entertainment field in that it is both interactive and social. BattleTech allows participants to exist and interact in a virtual, computer-generated world. Teams, which can include up to six players, compete against other teams. Participants command a human-shaped fighting tank, called BattleMech, which is thirty feet tall, and face a hundred square miles of alien terrain featuring obstacles, canyons, intense weather, and the enemy. The enemy is the opposing team. The primary viewing screen shows the battlefield; a second screen shows the output of the onboard computer. Controls for speed, weapons, and direction are operated by both hands and both feet.[7]

In a similar manner, VR is making inroads into TV and the movies. A recent TV series entitled *Wild Palms* and the movie *The Lawnmower Man* encapsulate the ideas of VR. Nicole Stenger is taking advantage of VR hardware advances to create a VR movie entitled *Angels*. The movie involves the interaction of the viewer, who is equipped with a DataGlove and goggles. When an angel is touched, it spins new environments and colors out of the crystals that surround it. In creating the movie, Stenger rendered original settings and eliminated some conventional DataGlove gestures. Regarding full-fledged theaters, VPL Research has formed a joint venture with a division of MCA to build a number of test theaters around the world in the next several years. If they catch on, plans call for a network of VR theaters, each the size of a large movie house. It is quite possible that VR machines will be used in the movies as plot devices.[8]

Medicine

The medical field is also utilizing VR in a big way. Doctors as well as students in medical schools, for instance, are beginning to use VR to simulate complex operations before taking scalpel to flesh. Similarly, plastic surgeons are reconstructing faces on a computer. One of the most novel medical applications combines robotic surgery with VR, thereby letting the surgeon operate without actually being with the patient. Another application, called *telepresence*, lets surgeons feel the tissue and the force exerted more effectively than they could with an endoscope or a laparoscope. Currently, VR applications also center on spinal-cord injuries, strokes, and traumatic brain injuries, among others, that allow the surgeon to manipulate virtual objects. In all medical applications, it is highly recommended that medical practitioners suit the VR application to the patient and not the patient to the technology.

To illustrate a typical application of VR to medicine, reference can be made to the "virtual clinic" developed by Ciné-Med (Woodbury, Connecticut), a small producer of medical-training videos. A surgeon-in-training watches the monitor of a powerful computer workstation while removing a gall bladder. Essentially, the Ciné-Med system mimics the approach of minimally invasive, or laparoscopic surgery, in which instruments and a camera are inserted through small incisions in the body while the surgeon works by watching a television screen. But with the virtual clinic, the instruments go into a black box where sensors interpret the movements and display them on the monitor, which also presents a 3-D moving image of the organs involved. An advanced version under development projects the operation into a pair of 3-D VR glasses.

Besides being used as a teaching tool, more advanced versions are useful for surgical planning. The software model for an actual patient could be programmed into the machine by using data from various electronic and computer-assisted diagnostic tests now prevalent in medicine. The doctor could import computerized tomography (CT) scan or magnetic-resonance-imaging (MRI) data for an actual patient and then operate in VR to determine if an operation could be performed laparoscopically or if a full incision would be required.

In the anticipation of VR tools from Ciné-Med and other companies, the National Library of Medicine of the National Institutes of Health is in the process of creating industry-standard digital cadavers. The method is one of cutting specimen bodies of a man and a woman into thousands of pieces, photographing each, and digitizing the photos to create 3-D computer images. Students will be able to use this database to study various parts of the human anatomy, in ways that are impossible with books. They will be able to fly through the body, examining the relationship of passageways with organs and other tissue. Using standard digital cadavers means that students at different schools will share what is, in effect, the same text.[9]

Going beyond these VR advancements in medicine, there are other possibilities. For one, imagine a surgeon superimposing a 3-D image on a patient and then operating on the image and patient at the same time. Even more futuristic, someday a surgeon will "walk through" the inside of a patient's body, threading between organs without disturbing them and performing precision surgery without damaging surrounding tissue. These are two of the goals of a group of surgeons from Brigham and Women's Hospital in Boston who are working with scientists at General Electric (GE) Company. In GE's Research and Development Center (Schenectady, New York), researchers are combining medicine with advanced computer graphics and VR. With a visitor seated beside him, William Lorensen, a GE graphics engineer, marvels at the 3-D image of a volunteer's brain in a screen. The picture was made by a computer from 2-D images of the brain that were taken in "slices" by GE's MRI machine. Seen through a pair of special goggles that convert images into a "stereo" format, the illusion of depth is so real that it is tempting to reach and pat the frontal lobe, stroke the occipital lobe, or run a finger through the folds of the cerebral cortex.

More exciting than the startling visuals is what scientists can do with them. With key strokes on a computer, the brain rotates and pivots on command. With more key strokes, layers of the brain peel off to reveal the inside, part by part. The cerebal cortex, the gray matter, is stripped off to reveal the whole cauliflower surface of the brain's white matter underneath, the cerebrum. It slowly pivots on the screen. With more strokes on the computer keyboard, sections of the brain responsible for assessing vision, hearing, space, senses, and motion peel off one at a time, all the way to the base of the brain. The viewer has the sensation of traveling through the brain, examining each part—its front, back, and inside—along the way. Overall, the GE researchers say the work in their lab will help the company incorporate the technology into GE's MRI and CT machines. The focus is on the importance of bringing diagnostic information right into the operating room. This could provide exciting new opportunities.[10]

Military

The U.S. military has been using real-time simulation since the 1930s and, with the advent of VR environments, is increasing its emphasis on simulation training. Flight simulators were the first such machines, and work has been performed to develop full simulation, including G forces, and to reduce simulation side-effects. Real applications of the research is in head-tracking weapons in the Cobra helicopter and on heads-up displays. However, the Army is now leading the way, funding the Defense Advanced Research Projects Agency (DARPA) development of the Simulation Network (SIMNET), a team-training simulation that generates interactive environments with hundreds of tanks, planes, and helicopters, enemy and friendly, over a network, allowing whole teams to train together. Developed from this is the $400 million to $1 billion Close Combat Tactical Training system, thereby allowing for the creation of whole virtual worlds.[11]

Essentially, then, VR and battlefield simulation are a natural combination. While one is an existing virtual world that is in need of the senses to explore it, the other is a sense in search of a world to explore. The two can be merged so as to discover what has been going on inside of simulations. The military has been creating these alternative worlds for years but has not been able to assimilate from them all that is available. A test bed can be built that captures information by using VR senses and that delivers it to a military exercise player in real time. These new eyes, ears, and hands can be plugged into a world in which information is just waiting to be seen and heard. With the growing power of computers to increase the fidelity and breath of simulations, new information can be extracted from the alternative realities that already exist. A VR environment fully involves the player's senses, mind, attention, cognition, and imagination in military training exercises as it never has before.[12]

A joint project by the U.S. Navy and the Human Interface Technology (HIT) Laboratory at the University of Washington centers on a VR simulation that will train Navy damage-control personnel in how to evaluate and respond to damage situations on *Arleigh Burke*-class destroyers. The team will use a variety of development tools, including Sense8 Corporation's Virtual WorldToolKit (WTK), and it will link the simulation to Navy databases. The simulation runs for twenty minutes and involves variable, multiple threats. Wearing standard VR goggles and gloves, the trainee will judge the accuracy of incoming information, map the damage, and act on it, fighting for the virtual ship's survival. Many controls will have tactile feedback such that a touch or the turn of a switch will translate into status changes.

Since warships cost hundreds of millions of dollars, needless to say, damage control is a high priority. Navy consultant and former Human Interface Technology Lab fellow, Bernard Vlozas, who was instrumental in launching the project, has noticed what he calls a "disconnect" between how people react in a real situation and how designers and engineers expect them to react. When watching a botched firefighting exercise on an old training ship, he has found that damage control cannot be effectively tested on most ships. Fortunately, VR is quite useful in such situations. Within a VR environment, one can simulate the mass sensory overload that the person in the damage-control center will experience.[13]

The Air Combat School (Arlington, Texas), which is a center for learning how to control high-powered jet aircraft under military operation conditions, offers three simulators: an A-4 Skyhawk, an F-8 Crusader, and an F-111 Aardvark. Each session includes full familiarity with cockpit controls, weapons training, and maneuverability of aircraft in simulated actions. This training allows the pilot to respond to other aircraft on missions ranging from Top Gun–type dogfighting to aircraft carrier landings. Typically, when a player completes one of his or her Air Combat adventures, he or she emerges with sweaty palms and adrenaline rushes. Participation at the Air Combat School is recommended by reservation, though drop-ins are able to sign up on an as-you-come basis. Each training session includes a fifteen-minute ground-school orientation and a thirty-minute follow-on mission. In less than half an hour, first-time fliers can handle their simulator well enough to perform their mission.[14]

Theme Parks

Today, attractions that combine an actual ride with visual and video effects are very popular in amusement parks. By tricking the body into thinking it is experiencing sensations like flat-out acceleration, zero-gravity free falls, and high-impact crashes, simulators can pick up where roller coasters leave off. In just the past few years, hundreds and thousands of simulators have been installed, mostly at theme parks and shopping malls. Flight simulators and amusement parks have had a symbiotic relationship for many years. Simulators work by using fancy visuals and moving theaters that fool the part of the inner ear that senses equilibrium into thinking it is hurtling through space or racing an automobile. Since amusement park simulators are not yet interactive, passengers just sit back and enjoy the ride. However, with the introduction of VR this has all changed.

The development of interactive VR technology uses computer-generated images and sound to create an illusion of reality while the user is adventuring in another world. Visitors to these theme parks are made to feel as if they are soaring in space, stepping back in time or engaging in combat—all while watching a big curved screen or wearing special headsets and electronically wired gloves. Essentially, the computer software games can be changed easily and rather cheaply, unlike the rides of traditional parks.

Virtual reality theme parks are now operating in the United States, Asia, and Europe. The technology has been too costly for public entertainment until recently. The breakthrough came when Sega Enterprises, Ltd. of Japan combined its experience in making electronic games with GE's virtual technology skills. Their joint venture moves the 2-D video games industry into a 3-D generation.

SUMMARY

The basic components of VR systems were highlighted in the chapter. Virtual reality was shown to be a highly sophisticated computer-simulation technique represented by a powerful reality engine with advanced graphics. Not only does VR render a world in "3-D," but it also recreates precisely what the data fed to it describes. For many applications, the core of this data resides in a database. Essentially, a full virtual environment gives the user the illusion of being there and permits the user to have real-time interaction with the objects. Companies that provide VR products are treated in the next chapter, followed by a chapter on VR software.

NOTES

1. Ian Andrew and Sean Ellis, "Bringing Virtual Worlds to Life," *AI Expert*, May 1994, pp. 15–17.

2. Linda Rohrbough, "Autodesk, Division Team Up to Develop VR Standards," *Newsbytes*, July 31, 1992, p. 20.

3. Montieth M. Illingworth, "Mona Lisa in Cyberspace," *SKY*, March 1994, pp. 118–26.

4. Carleen LeVasseur, "Virtual Reality on View in the Guggenheim Museum Soho," *Virtual Reality World*, January–February 1994, pp. 42–45.

5. Gene Bylinsky, "The Marvels of 'Virtual Reality,' " *Fortune*, June 3, 1991, pp. 146, 150.

6. Louis M. Brill, "Looking Glass Playgrounds Hit the Entertainment Bullseye," *Virtual Reality World*, November–December 1993, pp. 41–48.

7. Jack Grimes, "Virtual Reality Goes Commercial with a Blast," *IEEE Computer Graphics and Applications*, March 1992, pp. 16–17.

8. Michael Haggerty, "Serious Lunacy: Art in Virtual Worlds," *IEEE Computer Graphics and Applications*, March 1992, pp. 4–7.

9. John Holusha, "Carving Out Real-Life Uses for Virtual Reality," *New York Times*, October 31, 1993, p. F-11.

10. Amal Kumar Naj, " 'Virtual Reality' Isn't a Fantasy for Surgeons," *Wall Street Journal*, March 3, 1993, pp. B1, B8.

11. J. Michael Moshell, "Virtual Environment in the US Military," *Computer*, February 1993, pp. 81–82.

12. Roger D. Smith, "Current Military Simulations and the Integration of Virtual Reality Technologies," *Virtual Reality World*, March–April 1994, pp. 45–50.

13. Richard P. Greenfield, "Toward a Virtual Navy," *NewMedia Magazine*, April 1994, p. 33.

14. Louis M. Brill, "Looking Glass Playgrounds Hit the Entertainment Bullseye," *Virtual Reality World*, November–December 1993, p. 43.

Bibliography for Part I

Alexander, M. "Looking Ahead to the Next Century." *Computerworld*, March 4, 1991.
———."Virtual Reality Still Unrealistic: To Succeed, Technology Must Eliminate Physical Barriers to Everyday Office Use." *Computerworld*, June 24, 1991.
Andrew, I., and S. Ellis. "Bringing Virtual Worlds to Life." *AI Expert*, May 1994.
Anthes, G. H. "AI Makes Mark in Corporate World." *Computerworld*, May 18, 1992.
Asch, T. "Designing Virtual Worlds." *AI Expert*, August 1992.
———. "CyberTron, First Permanent Immersive VR System Installed at Disney World." *Virtual Reality World*, May–June 1994.
Bajura, M., H. Fuchs, and R. Ohbrichi. "Merging Virtual Objects with the Real World." *Computer Graphics*, July 1992.
Bandrowski, P. "Try Before You Buy: Virtually Real Merchandising." *Corporate Computing*, December 1992.
Barker, Q. "Virtual Reality Market Analysis." *Virtual Reality World*, March–April 1994.
Barlow, J. P. "Private Life in Cyberspace." *Communications of the ACM*, August 1991.
Baudel, T., and M. Beaudocin-Lafon. "Charade: Remote Control of Objects Using Free-Hand Gestures." *Communications of the ACM*, July 1993.
Benedikt, M., ed. *Cyberspace: First Steps*. Cambridge, Mass.: MIT Press, 1991.
Biral, C. "Thinking About Tomorrow." *MM*, June–July 1993.
Bozman, J. S. "AI Is Out: Objects Are In." *Computerworld*, December 28, 1992–January 4, 1993.
Brill, L. M. "Looking Glass Playgrounds Hit the Entertainment Bullseye." *Virtual Reality World*, November–December 1993.
———. "The Networked VR Museum: Where Art Meets Cyberspace." *Virtual Reality World*, January–February 1994.
———. "Home VR: Electronic Playgrounds, Living Room Style." *Virtual Reality World*, March–April 1994.
Brown, J. R. "Looking Toward the Year 2000." *Communications of the ACM*, July 1993.
Bylinsky, G. "The Marvels of 'Virtual Reality.' " *Fortune*, June 3, 1991.
———. "The Payoff from 3-D Computing." *Fortune, Special Report*, Autumn 1993.
Carlbome, J. et al. "Modeling and Analysis of Empirical Data in Collaborative Environments." *Communications of the ACM*, June 1992.
Churbuck, D. C. "Applied Reality." *Forbes*, September 14, 1992.
Clemons, E. K. "Investments in Information Technology." *Communications of the ACM*, January 1991.
Coleman, K. "The AI Marketplace in the Year 2000." *AI Expert*, January 1993.
Cook, R. "Serious Entertainment." *Computer Graphics World*, May 1992.
Coull, T., and P. Rothman. "Virtual Reality for Decision Support Systems." *AI Expert*, August 1993.
Coursey, D. "Asimov: Future Computers Will Make Work Fun." *MIS Week*, November 6, 1989.
Cringely, R. X. "Welcome to the Future." *Success*, September 1992.
Cruz-Neira, C., D. J. Sandin, T. A. DeFonti, R. V. Kenyon, and J. C. Hart. "The Cave:

Audio Visual Experience Automatic Virtual Environment." *Communications of the ACM*, June 1992.

Davenport, T. H., and T. J. Metsisto. "How Executives Can Shape Their Company's Information Systems." *Harvard Business Review*, March–April 1989.

Davidson, W. H., and M. S. Malone. *The Virtual Corporation: Structuring and Revitalizing the Corporation of the 21st Century.* New York: Harper Business, 1992.

Davis, D. D. "Reality Check: How Far Has Virtual Reality Technology Come, and Where Is It Going?" *Computer Graphics World*, June 1991.

DeGroot, M. "Virtual Reality." *Unix Review*, August 1990.

De Jager, P. "Oceanic Views and a Visit to the Holodeck." *Computing*, February 1993.

Delaney, B. "Virtual Reality Goes to Work." *NewMedia Magazine*, August 1994.

Denne, P. "Virtual Motion." *Virtual Reality World*, May–June 1994.

Dutton, G. "Medicine Gets Closer to Virtual Reality." *IEEE Software*, September 1992.

Eliot, L. B. "Reality into Virtual Reality." *AI Expert*, December 1993.

Emmett, A. "Down to Earth." *Computer Graphics World*, March 1992.

Farnham, A. "How to Nuture Creative Sparks." *Fortune*, January 10, 1994.

Fitzmaurice, G. W. "Situated Information Spaces and Spatially Aware Palmtop Computers." *Communications of the ACM*, July 1993.

Freedman, D. H. "Quick Change Artists." *CIO*, September 15, 1993.

Fritz, M. "The World of Virtual Reality." *Training*, February 1991.

Frost, N. "Outsourcing: The Right Move for Today's Virtual Organization." *The Office*, May 1993.

Fuchi, K. "Launching the New Era: ICOT Research Center." *Communications of the ACM*, March 1993.

Furness, T. "Exploring Virtual Worlds with Tom Furness." *Communications of the ACM*, July 1991.

Gantz, J. "A Virtual Market." *Computer Graphics World*, May 1992.

Gibson, W. *Neuromancer.* London, England: Harper-Collins, 1984.

———. *Virtual Light.* New York: Bantam Books, 1993.

Gigante, M., R. A. Earnshaw, and H. Jones, eds. *Virtual Reality Systems.* London, England: Academic Press, 1993.

Gray, M. "Virtual Reality: Systems Development, Predictions, Applications, Consumer Electronics." *Telecom World*, August 1992.

Green, R. "If You Think Life's Tough in General, Just Wait 'Til Virtual Reality Sets In." *Government Computer News*, October 12, 1992.

Greenfield, R. P. "Toward a Virtual Navy." *NewMedia Magazine*, April 1994.

Grimes, J. "Virtual Reality Goes Commercial with a Blast." *IEEE Computer Graphics and Applications*, March 1992.

Grygo, G. "Market Growth No Illusion for Virtual Reality." *Digital Review*, May 4, 1992.

Haggerty, M. "The Art of Artificial Reality." *IEEE Computer Graphics and Applications*, January 1991.

———. "Serious Lunacy: Art in Virtual Worlds." *IEEE Computer Graphics and Applications*, March 1992.

Hamilton, J. O'C. "Going Where No Minds Have Gone Before." *Business Week*, October 5, 1992.

Hamilton, J. O'C., E. T. Smith, G. McWilliams, E. I. Schwartz, and J. Carey. "Virtual

Reality: How a Computer-Generated World Could Change the Real World."
Business Week, October 5, 1992.

Hamit, F. *Virtual Reality and the Exploration of Cyberspace*. Carmel, Ind.: Sams Publishing, 1993.

Hamit, F., and W. Thomas. *Virtual Reality: Adventures in Cyberspace*. San Francisco: Miller Freeman, 1991.

Hays, N. "Visualization 91 Opens Eyes and Minds." *IEEE Computer Graphics and Applications*, January 1992.

Heim, M. *The Metaphysics of Virtual Reality*. New York: Oxford University Press, 1993.

Helsel, S. K., and J. P. Roth, eds. *Virtual Reality: Theory, Practice, and Promise*. Westport, Conn.: Meckler Publishing, 1991.

Hillman, D. "AI and the Intelligence Community." *AI Expert*, August 1991.

Holusha, J. "Carving Out Real-Life Uses for Virtual Reality." *New York Times*, October 31, 1993.

Hon, D. "Ixion's Realistic Medical Simulations." *Virtual Reality World*, July–August 1994.

Illingworth, M. M. "Mona Lisa in Cyberspace." *SKY*, March 1994.

———."Virtual Managers." *Information Week*, June 13, 1994.

Jacobson, L. "Virtual Reality: A Status Report." *AI Expert*, August 1991.

———. *CyberArts: Exploring Art and Technology*. San Francisco: Miller Freeman, 1992.

Johnson, R. C. "What Is Cognitive Computing?" *Dr. Dobb's Journal*, February 1993.

Kanter, R. M. "Transcending Business Boundaries: 12,000 World Managers View Change." *Harvard Business Review*, May–June 1991.

Kestelyn, J. "It's Practically, Virtually Real." *AI Expert*, August 1992.

Kowalski, R. "Imperial College." *Communications of the ACM*, March 1993.

Krueger, M. W. "The Emperor's New Realities." *Virtual Reality World*, November–December 1993.

Lammers, D. "New Japan Computing Project Set for Autumn." *Electronic Engineering Times*, July 6, 1992.

Lavroff, N. *Virtual Reality Playhouse*. Corte Madera, Calif.: Waite Group Press, 1992.

Lawton, G. "Virtual Reality on the Trading Desk." *Wall Street & Technology*, February 1992.

Lecht, C. P. "Future Considerations." *Computerworld*, March 16, 1992.

Leibs, S. "Cyberspaced." *MacWorld*, November 1991.

———. "Virtual Reality 101." *Information Week*, August 1993.

LeVasseur, C. "Virtual Reality on View in the Guggenheim Museum Soho." *Virtual Reality World*, January–February 1994.

Levy, S. *Artificial Life: The Quest for a New Creation*. New York: Pantheon, 1992.

Louderbeck, J. "Virtual Reality Emerging as Key Computing Tool." *PC Week*, January 11, 1993.

MacNicol, G. "What's Wrong with Reality? A Realist Reflects on Virtual Reality: Is It a Virtual Boon or a Boondoogle?" *Computer Graphics World*, November 1990.

Maher, K. "Developing a Market for Virtual Reality." In *Virtual Reality Special Report*, published by *AI Expert*. San Francisco: Miller Freeman, 1993.

Maynard, H. B., Jr., and S. E. Mehrtens. *The Fourth Wave, Business in the 21st Century*. San Francisco: Berrett-Koehler Publishers, 1993.

McCluskey, J. "A Primer on Virtual Reality." *T.H.E. Journal*, December 1992.

McGovern, K. T., and L. T. McGovern. "Virtual Clinic, The Future Is Now." *Virtual Reality World*, March–April 1994.

Merril, J. R. "Surgery on the Cutting Edge." *Virtual Reality World*, November–December 1993.

———. "VR for Medical Training and Trade Show 'Fly Paper.' " *Virtual Reality World*, May–June 1994.

Metcalfe, B. "What Happened to Artificial Intelligence?" *InfoWorld*, April 12, 1993.

Miyazawa, M. "Japan: 5th Generation Research Center." *Newsbytes*, July 7, 1992.

Moad, J. "Welcome to the Virtual IS Organization." *Datamation*, February 1, 1994.

Moshell, J. M. "Virtual Environments in the US Military." *Computer*, February 1993.

Moshell, J. M., and R. Dunn-Roberts. "A Survey of Virtual Environments: Research in North America, Part One." *Virtual Reality World*, November–December 1993.

———. "A Survey of Virtual Environments: Research in North America, Part Two." *Virtual Reality World*, January–February 1994.

Murphy, T. "Building a Better World." *AI Expert*, August 1993.

Naj, A. K. " 'Virtual Reality' Isn't a Fantasy for Surgeons." *Wall Street Journal*, March 3, 1993.

Nash, J. "Our Man in Cyberspace Checks Out Virtual Reality." *Computerworld*, October 15, 1990.

Newquist, H. P., III. "A Computer-Generated Suspension of Disbelief." *AI Expert*, August 1991.

———. "The State of the AI Business." *AI Expert*, February 1992.

———. "Virtual Reality's Commercial Reality." *Computerworld*, March 30, 1992.

Nilan, M. S., J. L. Silverstein, and R. D. Lankes. "The VR Technology Agenda in Medicine." In *Virtual Reality Special Report*, published by the *AI Expert*. San Franciso: Miller Freeman, 1993.

Nugent, W. R. "Virtual Reality: Advanced Imaging Special Effects Let You Roam in Cyberspace." *Journal of the American Society for Information Science*, September 1991.

Patch, K. "Virtual Reality Becoming More Real." *PC Week*, October 4, 1993.

Pausch, R. "Three Views of Virtual Reality: An Overview." *Computer*, February 1993.

Pea, R. D. "The Collaborative Visualization Project." *Communications of the ACM*, May 1993.

Pimentel, K., and K. Teixeira. *Virtual Reality, Through the New Looking Glass.* New York: McGraw-Hill, 1993.

Portante, T. "Cyberspace: Reality Is No Longer Enough." *Patricia Seybold's Office Computing Report*, October 1990.

Porter, S. "Interview: Jaron Lanier." *Computer Graphics World*, April 1992.

Powell, D. "Virtual Reality: From Infant to Adolescence." *Computing Canada*, September 2, 1991.

Ray, G. "AI: New Name, Better Game." *Computerworld*, January 11, 1993.

Rettig, M. "Virtual Reality and Artificial Life." *AI Expert*, August 1993.

Reveaux, T. "Virtual Reality Gets Real." *NewMedia Magazine*, January 1993.

———. "Let the Games Begin." *NewMedia Magazine*, January 1994.

Rheingold, H. *Virtual Reality.* New York: Touchstone, 1991.

———. "Virtual Reality: Is It Real Yet?" *Publish!*, August 1991.

———. "Virtual Reality, Phase Two." In *Virtual Reality Special Report*, published by the *AI Expert*. San Francisco: Miller Freeman, 1993.

————. *The Virtual Community: Finding Connections in Computerized World*. Reading, Mass.: Addison-Wesley, 1993.

Rifkin, G. "Packaging Some Sense Into Computers." *Computerworld*, October 15, 1990.

Rizzo, J. "Virtus Walkthrough." *MacUser*, July 1991.

Rohrbough, L. "Cyberarts: Lanier of VPL on 'Voomies' & VR's Future." *Newsbytes*, November 18, 1991.

————. "Autodesk, Division Team Up to Develop VR Standards." *Newsbytes*, July 31, 1992.

Rosenbaum, D. J. "Virtual Reality No Longer a Fantasy: Serious Interest Grows as First Commercial Applications Begin to Hit the Market." *Computer Shopper*, March 1992.

Rosenblum, L. L., and B. E. Brown. "Guest Editors' Introduction: Visualization." *IEEE Computer Graphics and Applications,* July 1992.

Rosenthal, S. " 'Virtual Reality' Isn't Virtual and Isn't Real." *MacWeek*, October 2, 1990.

Roth, A. "The ESPIRIT Initiative: AI Research in Europe." *AI Expert*, September 1991.

Rubin, S. H. "Machine Learning and Expert Systems." *AI Expert*, June 1993.

Rucker, R., R. U. Serius, and Q. Mu, eds. *Mundo 2000: A User's Guide to the New Edge*. New York: HarperCollins, 1992.

Saffo, P. "Virtual Reality Is Almost Real." *Personal Computing*, June 29, 1990.

Schmitz, B. "Virtual Reality: On the Brink of Greatness." *Computer-Aided Engineering*, April 1993.

Shandle, J. "Virtual Reality Needs Better Sensors." *Electronic Design*, September 17, 1992.

Shapiro, E., and D. H. D. Warren. "Epilogue." *Communications of the ACM*, March 1993.

Shaw, J. "99% Fat Free." *AI Expert*, May 1992.

Sinclair, M., and J. Peifer. "Socially Correct Virtual Reality: Surgical Simulation." *Virtual Reality World*, July–August 1994.

Sloane, S. J. "Close Encounters with Virtual Worlds." *Educators' Tech Exchange*, Spring 1994.

Smith, R. D. "Current Military Simulations and the Integration of Virtual Reality Technologies." *Virtual Reality World*, March–April 1994.

Stipp, D. " 'Phantom' Simulates Wielding a Scalpel, Tossing a Ball." *Wall Street Journal*, August 23, 1994.

Stix, G. "Domesticating Cyberspace." *Scientific American*, August 1993.

Stoppi, J. "The Real Thing?" *3D*, November 1990.

Sullivan-Trainor, M. L. "How Are We Doing?" *Computerworld*, May 17, 1993.

Tait, A. "Authoring Virtual Worlds on the Desktop." In *Virtual Reality Special Report*, published by *AI Expert*. San Francisco: Miller Freeman, 1993.

Tapscott, D., and A. Caston. *Paradigm Shift: The New Promise of Information Technology*. New York: McGraw-Hill, 1992.

Teixeira, K., "Behind the Scenes at the Guggenheim." *Virtual Reality World*, May–June 1994.

Thierauf, R. J. *Creative Computer Software for Strategic Thinking and Decision Making: A Guide for Senior Management and MIS Professionals*. Westport, Conn.: Quorum Books, 1993.

Thompson, J., ed. *Virtual Reality: An International Directory of Research Projects*. Westport, Conn.: Mecklermedia, 1994.

Tick, E. "The 5th Generation Project: Personal Perspective." *Communications of the ACM*, March 1993.

Toffler, A. "Technology As Weaponry." *Information Week*, January 10, 1994.

Upson, C. "Tools for Creating Visions." *Unix Review*, August 1990.

Viirre, E. "A Survey of Medical Issues and Virtual Reality Technology." *Virtual Reality World*, July–August 1994.

Warme, A. "Mandala Sport Simulators." *Virtual Reality World,* September–October 1994.

Welles, E. O. "Virtual Realities." *Inc.*, August 1993.

Wellner, P. "Interacting with Paper on the Digital Desk." *Communications of the ACM*, July 1993.

Wellner, P., W. Mackay, and R. Gold. "Computer-Augmented Environments: Back to the Real World." *Communications of the ACM,* July 1993.

Wexelblat, A., ed. *Virtual Reality: Applications and Explorations*. Boston: Academic Press, 1993.

Wexler, J. M. "Ties That Bind." *Computerworld*, June 28, 1993.

Wilder, C. "Recreating the Human Brain Cell." *Computerworld*, January 27, 1992.

Williams, P. "Applying AI to Virtual Environments." *AI Expert*, August 1992.

Woolley, B. *Virtual Worlds: A Journey in Hype and Hyperreality*. Oxford, England: Blackwell, 1992.

Zachary, G. P. "Artificial Reality: Computer Simulations One Day May Provide Surreal Experiences." *Wall Street Journal*, January 23, 1990.

———." 'Virtual Reality' Patents Gained by French Firm." *Wall Street Journal*, December 7, 1992.

Zachmann, W. F. "Simulation: The Ultimate Virtual Reality." *PC Magazine*, March 31, 1992.

Zeichick, A. L. "Virtual Editorial." *AI Expert*, August 1991.

PART II

Computer Hardware and Software in Virtual-Reality Systems for Business

3

Computer Hardware in a Virtual-Reality Environment

ISSUES EXPLORED

- To explore those problems that are basic to VR hardware as used currently
- To examine the relationship of human computer interfaces to generalized hardware and VR environments
- To look at possible developments within a VR environment some time in the future
- To explore typical current VR hardware offered by a number of vendors
- To determine appropriate criteria for the evaluation of VR hardware vendors

OUTLINE

Introduction to Computer Hardware in a VR Environment
    Problems with Utilizing Current VR Hardware
Human Computer Interfaces
    Current Direction in Interfaces
Forthcoming Developments in a VR Environment
Typical Current VR Hardware Offered by Vendors
    Ascension Technology Corporation—A Flock of Birds
    Crystal River Engineering Inc.—Audio Systems
    Digital Image Design Inc.—The Cricket and inScape
    Evans & Sutherland—Image Generators
    Fakespace Inc.—Immersive Visualization Systems
    Future Vision Technologies Inc.—SAPPHIRE

INTRODUCTION TO COMPUTER HARDWARE IN A VR ENVIRONMENT

Less than a decade ago, every computer had its place. Computer mainframes were utilized to handle large data-processing tasks; minicomputers were used to assist departmental and scientific users; and PCs were still for desktop use in handling small data processing chores. Today, those lines are blurred or gone entirely since the focus is on finding ways to enable computers of all sizes to communicate and work together. One line, however, stands firm—the separation of people and machines. Users still interact with computers primarily through keyboards, monitors, and printed output, as was done a decade ago. This is now changing with the introduction of VR in the workplace.

This chapter serves as an introduction to the hardware that can be found in a VR business- or nonbusiness-oriented environment. The combination of this hardware with software found in the next chapter has the ability to enhance all forms of human experience, especially those relating to enhancing the productivity of company employees on the job. The combination of VR hardware and software may, then, forever alter the business landscape such that nonusers of virtual worlds will lose out significantly in the marketplace.

Problems with Utilizing Current VR Hardware

Currently, there are several problems with computer hardware when employed for simulating virtual worlds. A *first* problem is the power of the desktop PC. While it enables VR systems analysts and programmers to produce systems that can operate on millions of machines, the performance of such systems is often disappointing even with some of the newer computer-chip technology. However, there is evidence that PC processors will continue to become faster and faster, while the time between new generations of chips continues to shrink.

Second, there is the relatively high cost of currently available head-mounted displays (HMDs). While there are a number of products costing several thousand dollars and more, there are indications that high-performing, low-cost HMDs will become common in the years to come. Related to HMDs is a *third* problem—the potential loss of real-world vision. However, some of the newer products, such as "Crystal Eyes" from the StereoGraphics Corporation, permit the user to maintain real-world awareness while experiencing 3-D perception of a virtual world.

A *fourth* problem is the wearing of a cumbersome headset with goggles and a data glove with fiber-optic cables connected to a computer like umbilical cords. The headset can weigh five pounds or more, too much for extended wear. A user who wants to be fully immersed in a VR world must don a data suit that envelops him or her from the neck down. For a typical business application, this type of equipment is too impractical for everyday use. Additionally, a *fifth* problem found in VR hardware relates to its technological limitations—namely, slow, limited-range, and imprecise tracking. Similarly, there is low-resolution display and crude, untextured images. Advances in the technology will reduce these problems substantially in the coming years.

Although this *sixth* problem is generally not discussed, VR software will undoubtedly lag behind in development when compared to VR hardware. That is, software development will not be up to the appropriate level to take full advantage of advancing VR hardware technology. Because of these hardware-related problems and others of VR, there is a tendency for business applications not to utilize the more conventional VR hardware. A discussion complementary to the above will be found in Chapter 6 under "Physical Considerations for the Human Element."

HUMAN COMPUTER INTERFACES

An emerging field in computer technology, called human computer interface (HCI), focuses on people and their relationships with computers. The primary purpose of HCI is to create a harmonious union between people and machines so that human desires are translated effortlessly into electronic action. Related to the development of HCI is VR, which is, in effect, a world generated by a computer. The user who experiences VR essentially steps through the computer screen into an interactive, 3-D world where many new things are possible.

Historically, the interfaces of early computers used only strings of language, such that they were *one dimensional*. Then came graphical interfaces that were icon or picture oriented, thus being *two dimensional*. The mouse, which is 2-D, was developed for more intuitive input. With increasing advances in computation power and software complexity, the *three-dimensional* interface is now possible, which will be the interface of the future. Virtual reality utilizes this 3-D approach since it is a most natural interface for mimicking the world in which we live. Moreover a human computer interface allows the user to view data in new ways not possible before.

Current Direction in Interfaces

Just recently, IBM announced that it will lead the industry in endowing PCs with the ability to understand spoken and written words. To back this claim, an IBM PC was used to demonstrate new applications for such "natural interfaces" along with the introduction of the latest versions of its speech-recognition systems and pen-based operating systems. As such, PCs are to be more natural to use. While the 1980s composed the decade of "ease of use," the 1990s will be the era of "natural computing." IBM speech-recognition software lets users create WordPerfect and 1-2-3 documents by speaking to PCs. The IBM Corporation has combined speech-recognition capabilities with a voice-synthesis program to translate English into Spanish in real time. Users can say a sentence in English and the PC generates the same sentence in Spanish. From this view, natural interfaces will enable new segments of workers to use computers. Typically, people still find computing a difficult task. They want it to be as convenient as talking.

Although this is a current direction in general-purpose computing, there are a number of interfaces that are germane to VR environments. They will be found throughout the remainder of the chapter. In fact, most of the hardware discussed centers on some type of interface when entering a virtual world. Immersion in a virtual world can take several directions. For one, the user puts on an HMD device, as shown in Figure 3.1. An HMD provides a complete and totally immersed view of the virtual world. The helmet or visor includes two small television monitors, one in front of each eye. As the user turns his or her head to examine that world further, each shifting head movement corresponds with a complementary view of the virtual world. Moreover, there can be 3-D sound. Even when using standard stereo earphones, 3-D stereophonic processing during recording and/or playback can surround the user with convincingly directional 360-degree spatial motion and support acoustics. For example, 3-D sound lets the user pinpoint a source from behind, pivot, and locate it visually.

The chief interface with a VR world is usually a hand-operated input device, such as a 2D/6D mouse that lets the user point in the desired direction of movement. A more sophisticated device is a DataGlove, shown in Figure 3.2, that lets the user "reach into" the 3-D environment; and while viewing a virtual hand corresponding to the user's real hand, the user can grasp and move virtual objects and can perform other gesture commands. Although not shown, a user can don an ankle-to-wrist lycra jumpsuit or DataSuit that includes inertial and positioning sensors. The wearer can move (either freely around a room or on a treadmill) and interact through the full range of the body's movements.

Another VR interface device, shown in Figure 3.3, is the Binocular Omni-Orientation Monitor (BOOM). The BOOM display is not head mounted. It in-

Figure 3.1
High-Resolution, Colored, Head-Mounted Display (HMD)

Source: Reprinted courtesy of Virtual Reality Inc., 485 Washington Avenue, Pleasantville, New York 10570.

volves using at least one hand to operate. This can be an advantage for most business and research applications. When working, a user typically does not want to slip off a helmet every time the phone rings and then fit the helmet into place again to return to the virtual world. Another form of VR is the cab, as shown in Figure 3.4, that involves the construction of a cockpit or control area of some vehicle, like a jet aircraft or a car, that is a complete replication of its real-life counterpart. In the position of the window are very large TV monitors or a projection screen that presents a complete computer-graphic rendering of the outside world of that simulation vehicle. Through the use of one or more display viewers, a joystick, and a throttle-type device, participants are able to navigate completely through that virtual world.

Still another way to enter an immersive VR world is to enter a chamber world, as shown in Figure 3.5. A virtual world in this environment is projected into a room surrounding all walls and ceiling. The viewer enters and by wearing specialized 3-D glasses is able to become completely immersed within the virtual world. One of the unique characteristics of this world is that many people can participate in the same virtual world simultaneously.

Going beyond the immersive aspects of VR, a virtual environment can be

Figure 3.2
CyberGlove Instrumented Glove

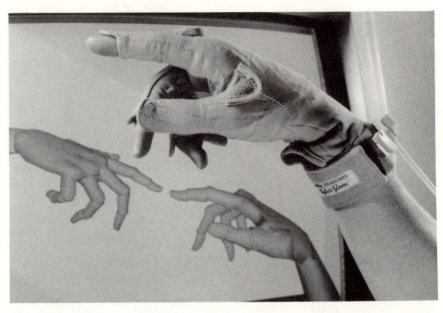

Source: Reprinted courtesy of Virtual Technologies, 2175 Park Boulevard, Palo Alto, California 94306.

created and then experienced from a desktop monitor with the assistance of a mouse, DataGlove, or space ball input device. While not very immersive, desktops and workstations have fully interactive capabilities and are found extensively in VR business applications. They allow users to navigate through whatever virtual environment they are exploring. In addition, participants in a virtual world can use a mobile binocular display that is suspended from an articulated arm that allows the participants to encounter a virtual world without the use of an HMD or a BOOM. The articulated arm is flexible enough to visually correspond to movement in any direction as well as upward or downward viewing as defined by the virtual experience.

From another perspective, viewers enter a virtual environment from a secondary position of watching themselves indirectly move through a virtual world, that is, a mirror world. Essentially, the participants create this experience by moving into a specially prepared virtual center that photographs their image and reproduces a real-time counterpart within a televised virtual environment. Participants are able to see their image within the virtual world and to move accordingly to direct their image in relation to that world.

Figure 3.3
Binocular Omni-Orientation Monitor (BOOM)

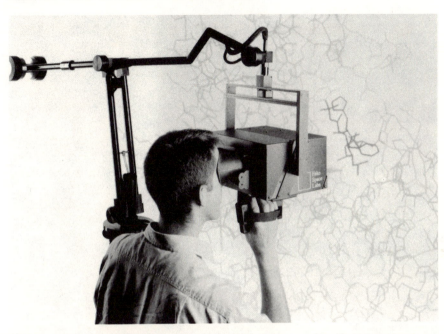

Source: Reprinted courtesy of Fakespace Inc., 4085 Campbell Avenue, Menlo Park, California 94025.

FORTHCOMING DEVELOPMENTS IN A VR ENVIRONMENT

In a typical business organization, computer technologies were developed with the idea that a computer is basically a device that will somehow find a use for day-to-day operations. This next decade of computer technologies, however, will see the microprocessors and memory technologies that power today's PCs evolve into foundations for new devices. What is called computer technology currently will merge with other innovative microelectronic and micromechanical technologies to produce a new generation of intelligent, low-cost, and often single-purpose devices that will do equal or more work than PCs do today. To understand this forthcoming development in a computerized environment, think of a person's desk. Next, remove the PC, take away the cables, the power strip, the phone connector, and the mouse and keyboard. In turn, replace all that with a blotter, just like the one a person had before a PC was placed on the desk, and tell it what to do.

Once the blotter is in place, the user needs to either take a pen and enter new

Figure 3.4
Cab Cockpit Interior

Source: Reprinted courtesy of Virtual World Entertainment, 4444 Lakeside Drive, Suite 320, Burbank, California 91505.

numbers into the cells displayed on the blotter or change old ones. Moreover, the user tells the blotter to display a graph on the virtual screen in front of the desk. If the user is sitting in a nonquiet zone, the pen can be used to tell the blotter-based environment what to do, instead of talking to it. To complete a long report, the user tells the desk to produce a virtual keyboard and then types it in. If the blotter is picked up, there is nothing underneath it, and it is just as flexible as the one used in the early 1900s. In addition, it provides a good writing surface for those rare occasions when the person needs to write on paper, using the same pen, of course. This blotter environment is an extension of pen-based computing and VR. Essentially, it enhances the computer environment used today.

Figure 3.5
Chamber World Created around the Viewer

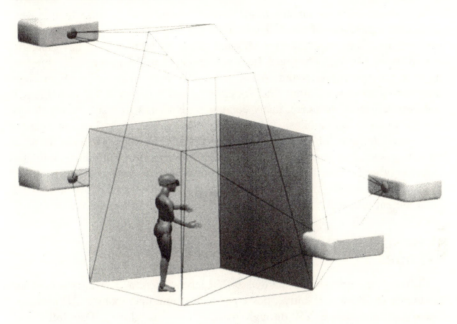

Source: Reprinted courtesy of Mr. Lewis Siegel and Ms. Kathy O'Keefe, Electronic Visualization Laboratory, University of Chicago, Chicago, Illinois 60608.

Another wave of microprocessor-based technology—not normally associated with computing—is evolving in the automobile industry, consumer electronics companies, medical research facilities, toy engineering, and many other places. This new wave uses digital technology and has already started to encroach on everyday life. The number of intelligent objects in this category has dwarfed the PC industry, that is, more microprocessors are being used in noncomputer applications than in computers. Just recently, more than 1.5 billion microprocessors and microcontrollers were shipped, but less than 10 percent were used in computers.

A good example of this new wave technology is found in today's fever thermometer. New thermometers have microprocessors and cost about $8.00, for which one gets an analog temperature sensor, an analog to digital interface between the sensor and the thermometer's four-bit processor, the microprocessor itself, enough random-access memory (RAM) to hold temperature data, read-only memory (ROM) to hold the program that senses and displays the temperature, a liquid-crystal display (LCD); and a power supply. And batteries are included in the plastic package that is barely larger than the old mercury-powered thermometer that it replaces. If today's technology can do all that for an extremely low cost of $8.00, imagine what $100.00 will do in the twenty-first century.

Silicon designers are already thinking well beyond today's PC, which is why an increasing amount of motherboard logic is being integrated onto silicon processor chips. The corporations AMD and Chips & Technologies have already put an entire PC on a chip, and Intel is committed to doing the same thing in its next generation processors. When one combines such dense levels of electronic integration with other microelectronics and microtechnical technologies and very advanced software, many computer advances will result. Many things bought today—automobiles, TVs, VCRs, clock radios, watches, or hearing aids—are intelligent objects with microprocessor technology. Who knows what tomorrow's intelligent objects will do? Surely, some sort of traditional computer technology will continue to manage a company's business needs, but it is just as certain that intelligent objects operating in a VR environment or a non-VR environment will make one's everyday chores easier on the job.[1]

TYPICAL CURRENT VR HARDWARE OFFERED BY VENDORS

Utilizing appropriate VR hardware, VR gives users a 3-D interface in an environment far more intuitive, powerful, and natural than today's 2-D desktop. Users can experience VR through devices such as gloves, DataSuits, and EyePhones. In the future, VR will incorporate newer interfaces, such as tactile and aural. Current and future VR hardware will have many business applications as will be demonstrated in Part 4 of this book.

In the prior chapter, the basic elements of a VR system were set forth. Fundamentally, a user of a VR system gains entry through sensory portals created by *output sensors*. In contrast, *input sensors* allow for movement and interaction once the user has entered the VR world. In addition, a virtual world typically includes *sound* and *haptic feedback* that is software related. This combination of hardware and software elements provides the power of interaction in a virtual world. Without these key elements, the user experiences a VR environment only passively. In the section to follow, many of the leading vendors and their hardware within a VR environment are set forth.

Ascension Technology Corporation—A Flock of Birds

The Ascension Technology Corp. makes position and orientation tracking devices that are sometimes referred to as six-degrees-of-freedom (6DOF) input devices. Measurements are made in reference to a magnetic-field transmitter. Generating and sensing magnetic fields, even in the presence of conductive metals, which distort magnetic fields, is the heart of Ascension's patents. Simply put, Ascension utilizes DC (direct current) magnetic fields—just like the earth's magnetic field—to tell where one's head, hand, or body is located, quite precisely, in free space. By placing a tiny sensor on a person's head, its location can be measured in real time. Hence, by placing thirty tiny sensors on the major joints in the human body, one can instantaneously quantify all aspects of a person's natural gait and sway. This information, in turn, can be combined with computer-graphics machines and the user is ready to solve sophisticated problems in biomechanics, computer-aided design (CAD), flight simulation, telerobotics, industrial design, 3-D visulation, medicine, and character animation in what is promised to be the next computer interface—virtual environments.

Currently, the company's products are trademarked under the phrase A Flock of Birds.™ The "Bird" signifies that Ascension sensing devices can be lifted into the air to track a human motion or to interact naturally with 3-D images on a graphics monitor. The "Bird" is a takeoff on the conventional computer mouse. In addition, the "Bird" is presently used as a head tracker in a number of VR games. The "Flock," Ascension's second product, signifies that one or more such sensing devices can be tracked at the same time. "Flock" units simultaneously track all their sensors no matter how many "Birds" are flying together. The tracking of multiple sensors in free space is especially important for VR biomechanical and animation applications. Ascension also markets a long-range transmitter—ERT (extended range transmitter). Its goal is to extend tracking over room-sized areas. (*Contact* Ascension Technology Corporation, P.O. Box 527, Burlington, Vermont 05402, (802) 860-6440, fax (802) 860-6439.)

Crystal River Engineering Inc.—Audio Systems

In recent years, an increasing amount of applied research has been devoted to reconfigurable interfaces like the virtual display. As with most research in information displays, virtual displays have generally emphasized visual information. Many investigators, however, have pointed out the importance of the auditory system as an alternative or supplementary information channel. Audio systems are currently being marketed by Crystal River Engineering. For example, Acoustetron is a complete, integrated 3-D audio workstation for use in high-end VR applications. This system is based on a fifteen-slot industrialized PC containing sound source and spatialization cards (as required for a particular application). Complex multisource models (including reflexion and Doppler) can be achieved with the modular architecture.

For PC-based applications, Beachtron is a high-speed, digital-signal–processing system capable of producing 3-D sound at a relatively low cost. The single card set can be used to simulate two independent sound sources in a virtual environment. Sound sources may be live, previously sampled, or generated from the onboard Proteus synthesizer. The Beachtron is software compatible with all of the company's products and supports the virtual audio protocol. There is also Convolvotron that delivers high quality, real-time, 3-D sound over conventional headphones. This is a very high-speed, digital-signal processing system capable of presenting four binaural sound sources in a virtual environment. A two-board set for PCs, the Convolvotron forms the basis for a range of products from high-end parallel processors to lower-cost, single-source modules. Applications of a 3-D auditory display involve any context in which the user's spatial awareness is important, particularly when visual cues are limited or absent. Examples include advanced teleconferencing environments, monitoring telerobotic activities in hazardous situations, air-traffic–control displays for the tower or cockpit, and scientific visualization of multidimensional data. (*Contact* Crystal River Engineering Inc., 12350 Wards Ferry Road, Groveland, California 95321, (209) 962-6382, fax (209) 962-4873.)

Digital Image Design Inc.—Cricket and inScape

The Cricket, which is marketed by Digital Image Design, is a 3-D interaction tool featuring upright orientation with trigger, grip, thumb, and suspend buttons. Pressure is measured on trigger and grip buttons; pressure and direction (360 degrees) are measured on the thumb button. A variable vibration provides tactile feedback. The Cricket works with 6DOF trackers by Ascension, Logitech, and Polhemus. Another product by this firm is inScape, a package of hardware and software that combines the strongest advantages of VR and a standard graphics display monitor. It can be used to display a user's data or computer model as if it were a physical object. The model is effective inside of or in front of the monitor. Unlike other VR techniques, it leaves normal work space and tools as available as they always are. InScape is a valuable tool for anyone who deals with spatial models, including statistical or financial analysts, chemical engineers, architects, and industrial designers.

Recently released is a new version of inScape, called inScape/Inventor, that provides the capabilities of inScape for Open Inventor, which is the C++ "toolkit" for 3-D graphics from Silicon Graphics that greatly increases the productivity for 3-D graphics software development. By using a special inScape camera class, users get Desktop Virtual Reality in an otherwise standard Open Inventor environment. InScape can also be used to implement immersive virtual worlds by using a large display; the larger the display, the more immersive the experience. (*Contact* Digital Image Design Inc., 170 Claremont Avenue, Suite 6, New York, New York 10027, (212) 222-5236, fax (212) 864-1189.)

Evans & Sutherland—Image Generators

The ESIG-2000 AT (Advanced Texture), which is available from Evans & Sutherland, is a low-cost image generator with capabilities previously available only in high-end systems. It incorporates the technology and architecture of another Evans & Sutherland product, the ESIG-3000, into a compact and cost-effective package. The result is an image generator with the versatility, sophisticated scene management, and image quality that characterize today's VR systems. Essentially, then, the ESIG-2000 AT is a compact, special-purpose computer image generator designed to produce imagery for VR applications. It generates photorealistic 3-D images using texturing, antialiasing, and smooth-shading techniques at the rate of sixty images per second.

In the past, realistic visual scene performance has been unavailable to many users with a limited budget. Fast update rates and high scene detail have been the domain of high-performance image generators. However, the ESIG-2000 AT provides the solution of this dilemma by delivering the speed and scene detail of today's high-end image generators in a cost-effective package. The ESIG-2000 AT can be tailored to meet a variety of real-time needs. Examples include vehicle engineering simulation; training for car, truck, tank, and high-speed emergency vehicles; mass transit operators; entertainment; and real-time visualization for architectural design. (*Contact* Evans & Sutherland, 600 Komas Drive, P.O. Box 59700, Salt Lake City, Utah 84108, (801) 582-5847, fax (801) 582-5848.)

Fakespace Inc.—Immersive Visualization Systems

Fakespace manufactures hardware systems for interaction with virtual environments, develops the software tools required to integrate these systems into visualization applications, and provides consulting services for the development of virtual environments. Among its products are the following FS², BOOM3C, BOOM3M, BOOM D3C, BOOM D3M, MEDVIEW, VLIB-SGI, Molly, and MyView along with a line of video pipeline converters. The FS² is a full-color and monochrome high-resolution cathode-ray-tube (CRT)-based immersive display integrated with a unique hands-free support structure that offers full 6DOF motion. In contrast, the BOOM3C is a full-color and monochrome high-resolution CRT-based immersive display integrated with an articulated counter-balance 6DOF of motion support structure. The BOOM3M is well suited for research-and-development (R&D) applications requiring high resolution and the ability to create "pseudo-color," including molecular modeling and VR application development. In contrast, BOOM D3C is a high resolution, full-color, CRT-based, immersive-display product. It is used in scientific visualization applications. This display's crispness and ability to show levels of shading, combined with the easy access common to all BOOM devices, also makes it extremely useful in new application areas, such as product modeling, styling, and architecture.

The VLIB-SGI software library provides a convenient interface between application programs and a BOOM device, allowing rapid integration of immersive-display capability in applications running on Silicon Graphics computing platforms. The VLIB software and drivers are now incorporated into a wide range of virtual-environment–development packages and vertical-applications products. Molly is a teleoperated motion platform designed for integration with video cameras and audio sensors. Coupled with a BOOM or an HMD, the Molly can pan, tilt, and roll in real time to approximate a user's head motion. Typically, the Molly is outfitted with MyEyes1 camera package, controlled with the MySoft-pc computer and software. Lastly, MyView is a hardware system that facilitates the superpositioning of VLIB-SGI computer-generated video together with Molly camera-generated video. This product listing gives an indication of practical immersive-visualization systems that can be used by design groups and at the desktop for research, development, and engineering applications. (*Contact* Fakespace Inc., 4085 Campbell Avenue, Menlo Park, California 94025, (415) 688-1940, fax (415) 688-1949.)

Future Vision Technologies Inc.—SAPPHIRE

The SAPPHIRE System™ is the first real-time multimedia engine to bring workstation performance to the PC. It provides a complete solution to a user's synthetic environment requirements. Built-in features, including forty-eight bits per pixel, various output, and quality sound I/O, make SAPPHIRE a complete multimedia solution on a single board. Whether the application is industrial simulation, location-based entertainment, CAD, education, scientific visualization, or immersive-synthetic environments, SAPPHIRE is easy to use. The system currently supports Audodesk's Cyberspace Developer Kit (CDK), Sense8 WorldtoolKit (WTK), and FVT's SAPPHIRE Developer Library. In addition, SAPPHIRE supports other standard software packages, such as VREAM, the Autodesk Device Interface, and Microsoft Windows.

Typically, SAPPHIRE is versatile enough to meet the user's requirements. Users can start out with monoscopic graphic environments and upgrade to stereoscopic interactivity with Stereographics CrystalEyes LCD shutter glasses. The SAPPHIRE system supports CrystalEyes directly, providing the viewer with a high-resolution display and eliminating the need for an expensive converter box. A multiboard configuration allows more than one user to participate in the same synthetic environment without adding PCs. When configuring a multiuser environment, the boards can be configured independently or in stereopairs providing maximum flexibility. (*Contact* Future Vision Technologies, Inc., 701 Devonshire Drive, Champaign, Illinois 61820, (217) 355-3030, fax (217) 355-3031.)

Ghost Dance Immersive Technologies Inc.—Helmet-Mounted Display System

Ghost Dance Immersive Technologies designs and builds VR kiosks for product and data visualization in finance, training, retail, trade-show, game-arcade, and travel applications. It offers turnkey hardware/software solutions to sales, marketing, and exhibit needs in advanced interactive displays. The interactive-immersion displays can be customized to the user's requirements, and bids for the displays are on a per job basis. In terms of digital 3-D TV, it is a high-quality, compressed-digital video in 3-D displays and has instant branching be-tween full-motion video "tracks." Digital video provides photorealism and interactivity. The hardware and software yield nearly ten times the number of pixels in current VR arcade games. Other features include 3-D sound fields, telecommunications, olfactory simulation, and kiosk design.

To illustrate these interactive-immersion displays, imagine a financial planner scanning a landscape of changing variables, color and texture coded, and dis-played as a mountainscape over which the user flies. The planner can see changes in the landscape of transactions before competitors and can act more swiftly to take advantage of changing conditions. Or imagine the increased suc-cess of personnel trained in conflict resolution, customer relations, and sales when they have virtually experienced these challenges beforehand. (*Contact* Ghost Dance Immersive Technologies Inc., 2866 McKillop Road, Oakland, Cal-ifornia 94602-1503, (510) 261-0128, fax (510) 261-7007.)

LEEP Systems Inc.—VR Interface Devices

Immersive VR systems create the illusion of being within a remote or artificial world by several means, none of which is more important than the changing perspectives caused by moving within and looking around the virtual environ-ment. From this perspective, LEEP Systems has developed a number of VR products. The CYBERFACE3 Model RS is a VR interface system comprising a table-mounted supporting arm and a head-guided display having binaural sound, LEEP binocular optics, and instrumentation of three rotational axes of head direction. Two audio channels and an RS 232 port for directional data are included. The CYBERFACE2 is a 140-degree field-of-view HMD, which, by diverging the axis of the viewing optics, provides a wide field of view.

The LEEP Standard OEM Viewing Optics comprise a very wide-angle ste-reoscopic optical assembly. Six large elements give a 90-degree field of view and 140-degree corneal and peering field. The Photographic Virtual Reality Demonstrator is a handheld demonstrator with one Model ARV-1 viewing optics assembly, a diffusing slide holder, and six photographic slides. This instrument demonstrates the immersion of very wide-field video, and the OEM optics en-able it to be used for experiments. Lastly, the Telehead Model B is a wide-angle stereoscopic remote camera platform for telepresence applications. It produces the LEEP format output for the CYBERFACE2 HMD. (*Contact* LEEP Systems Inc., 241 Crescent Street, Waltham, Massachusetts 02154, (617) 647-1395, fax (617) 647-1109.)

Liquid Image—Head-Mounted Display

An effective way for a user of VR to be immersed into a computer-generated world is through the use of HMD. The problem with using HMDs for this purpose is the poor quality of the displays that until now have been lacking in the areas of resolution, picture quality, comfort, field of view, and weight. The MRG2 was developed by Liquid Image to solve many of the problems that currently plague HMDs. This unit is a binocular HMD that uses a 5.7-inch thin-film transistor (TFT) and an active matrix LCD display. With a resolution of 240×720 and over 16 million colors, its picture quality is excellent. Its active matrix system eliminates all "ghosting" effects, flicker, and striping that appear on passive matrix LCDs. With the new cold cathode backlight, the MRG2 is not subject to breakdown or maintenance nearly as frequently as most others.

The HMD boasts a custom-built controller box that will accept video and audio inputs from a host of different sources. The MRG2 has alleviated the need to purchase any additional expensive add-ons that other companies require to operate their systems. It also has Sony digital headphones to ensure audio quality. It is well suited to game and heavy-duty applications, such as research and military/aerospace. Likewise, it accommodates Ascension Technology's "Bird" or Polhemus' FASTRAK position-tracking systems, which can be mounted either externally or internally. (*Contact* Liquid Image, 659 Century Street, Winnepeg, Manitoba, R3H 0L9, Canada, (204) 772-0137, fax (204) 772-0239.)

Polhemus Inc.—Measurement Devices

Polhemus produces a 3SPACE product line of 6DOF measurement devices. The ISOTRAK II is a 3-D position/orientation-measuring system. It replaces its predecessor, the ISOTRAK, and offers many performance improvements and a lower price. Improved accuracy and resolution, longer-range, two-receiver capability, and a high-speed serial interface are just some of the changes. The FASTRAK system represents a revolutionary new advancement in motion tracking by providing highly accurate position and orientation data with the lowest data latency available on the market. The FASTRAK is a very cost-effective system, especially when multiple receivers or longer-range capabilities are required. It is a useful solution for interfacing with VR environments and controlling simulator projectors or other applications where real-time response is crucial. It is also ideal for measuring range of motion or limb rotation in biomedical research.

The company's other products include the InsideTRAK and 3DRAW. InsideTRAK is a PC-insertable version of FASTRAK with slightly reduced specifications. The InsideTRAK master board can handle an optional second receiver. If more receivers are required, slave boards can be added. The ultimate number of receivers is limited by the number of ISA slots available. The 3DRAW is useful in capturing and archiving the dimensions of any nonmetallic object. These objects then can be brought into the user's virtual world. In the CAD and computer-graphics markets, 3DRAW can be used to develop true 3-D databases for creating 3-D wire-frame or rendered images. (*Contact* Polhemus Inc., 1 Hercules Drive, P.O. Box 560, Colchester, Vermont 05446, (802) 655-3159, fax (802) 655-1439.)

RPI Advanced Technology Group—Head-Mounted Sensory Interface

The RPI Advanced Technology Group currently markets the Head-Mounted Sensory Interface (HMSI). This easy-to-use device is light in weight (3½ oz.) and has high resolution. The product, resembling a pair of thick sunglasses, is portable and comes with its own carrying case. It offers a pivoting display option and a telescopic ear piece to place the display lenses as close to the eye as desired. Its display provides clear, clean, color images at 640 × 480 resolution (of good enough quality to be used for medical visualization). Field of view can range from 65 to 110 degrees, although there is blurring on the periphery at 110 degrees.

The RPI Group developed a hybrid VR interface that, for the first time, will allow individual infantrymen to participate in large-scale simulation exercises. The new interface will apply a wide range of newly developed VR technologies to generate a realistic battle environment and to generate realistic impacts on the environment as a result of each soldier's actions. In addition to military simulations, the new interface will provide a foundation for a wide variety of scientific, medical, and entertainment applications. The company's other products include the Personal Simulator, Pixel Pump model VGA2X, Pixel Pump model VGA3X, Cyberchair, and Cyberpod. Also, there is the Silicon Window III, which is a high-resolution simulation display system for immersive applications, such as architectural design and molecular modeling. (*Contact* RPI Advanced Technology Group, P.O. Box 14607, San Francisco, California 94114, (415) 495-5671, fax (415) 495-5124. © RPI, 1994. All rights reserved.)

SimGraphics Engineering Corporation—Collection of Libraries

SimGraphics Engineering Corp., offers a number of VR products. Its VR Workbench is a collection of libraries for building user interfaces, controlling 3-D devices, and managing information displays. Another product is the VActor Animation System that creates so-called VActors. With VActors, users wear devices for their face, hands, and body, thereby allowing them to control instanteously the movement of computer-generated characters and logos. VActors can be used in interactive entertainment or in animation production. Related products and services to VActor include VActor Performer, VActor Producer, and VActor Services. (*Contact* SimGraphics Engineering Corp. 1137 Huntington Drive, S. Pasadena, California 91030, (213) 255-0900, fax (213) 255-0987.)

StereoGraphics Corporation—Computer and Video Images

With StereoGraphics CrystalEyes family of stereo-depth-perception products from StereoGraphics Corp., computer and video images leap from the screen in true 3-D depth. Whether exploring a simulated environment, entering the abdomen during minimally invasive surgery, investigating hazardous materials sites, adding depth to a robot's vision, or creating a virtual prototype, CrystalEyes products provide a high-resolution and realistic stereo view. CrystalEyes VR is a lightweight, electronic eyewear that provides high-resolution, full-color, and stereoscopic viewing of virtual worlds. The CrystalEyes Video System is a self-contained, 3-D, video system that includes view, record, and playback capabilities. The CrystalEyes Projection System is a high-resolution, large-screen, 3-D system that, in conjunction with CrystalEyes eyewear, permits mass viewing of 3-D spatial information on screens from five to twenty-five feet.

To illustrate the use of this hardware, consider the following. Combining VR and AI technology, vrTrader is Avatar's VR visualization system for stock-market analysts and traders. Through a live link to real-time quotes on cable television or FM radio, vrTrader provides a dynamic, up-to-date 3-D picture of what is happening in the market. Level alerts, news reports, and other significant events trigger stock symbols to blink, drawing the user's attention immediately to a market, industry group, or particular stock where activity is occurring. Users can "fly" through the system by using a standard mouse or can use CrystalEyes VR's head-tracking capabilities to look around and change the perspective of the image on the screen—all in true 3-D. In combination with the CrystalEyes Projection System, vrTrader can also be used for presentations, both real-time or prerecorded, at corporate presentations and other large events. (*Contact* StereoGraphics Corp., 2171 E. Francisco Blvd., San Rafael, California 94901, (415) 459-4500, fax (415) 459-3020.)

VPL Research Inc.—Comprehensive VR Systems

VPL Research Inc. has developed a wide range of products for creating virtual worlds. It offers the EyePhone, a headset vaguely reminiscent of the infrared night goggles used by the military. The EyePhone contains two small eyepiece-size monitors mounted into a scuba mask- or helmetlike enclosure to limit peripheral vision. The color LCD monitors each show slightly separate images to accomplish the illusion of depth and three dimensions: a kind of visual stereo. The EyePhone works in tandem with VPL's AudioSphere headphone sound system. The stereo system provides two different audio feeds to the wearer from as many as four simultaneous sound sources; the user can then hear omnidirectional sound coming from front, back, side to side, and even from above and below. This sound aspect of VR is necessary to create the illusion of a complete environment as well as to prevent extraneous and distracting noise from the room where the wearer is working with the VR gear.

Another part of the VPL system is the DataGlove, which serves as an input device that converts hand movements into computer readable form. Unlike other devices, such as trackballs or joysticks, the user's hand is inside this interface, which has fiber-optic sensors mounted on the glove that provide the computers with data about such hand movements as finger pointing or clutching. Used in tandem with the EyePhone, the DataGlove lets a user move his or her hand into the field of virtual vision and see virtual, hand-making movements identical to the ones that are being performed in real life. A specific tracking mechanism called Polhemus, which is the same one used to track the head's motion, provides the computer with continuous information on movements that are translated into virtual elements.

All of this is programmed and controlled via a computer language called The Body Electric, which is not only the language and environment in which worlds are created but also the methodology by which users interact with that world. Taken together, all of these components form a comprehensive system known as Reality Built for Two, commonly known as RB2, which provides a complete VR environment for one or two individuals by incorporating the EyePhone, AudioSphere, DataGlove, Silicon Graphics workstations, and The Body Electric.

VPL Research Inc. is also involved in the marketing of VR software systems. It markets RB2 (a multi-$100,000 VR software system) as well as Microcosm, an entry-level VR system costing much less (under $50,000). Though the Microcosm will be much lower in performance than the RB2 systems, VPL states that Microcosm takes advantage of advancing VR technology and will be close in performance to the original RB2 systems.

Recommended uses for Microcosm include any application in which lower graphics rendering is suitable. This includes a range of applications, including education, as a development station for the RB2 and for VR industrial applications. Microcosm comes in two models, one based on the Apple Macintosh and the other the Iris Indigo workstation of Silicon Graphics. Both come with special peripherals and software including the EyePhone XVR for virtual world viewing, the DataGlove XVR for controlling the user's movement in a virtual world, and, for the Indigo only, the Swivel XVR. Microcosm also comes with the RB2 authoring tools and libraries. (*Contact* VPL Research Inc., 3977 E. Bay Shore Road, Palo Alto, California 94303, (415) 988-2550, fax (415) 988-2557.)

Other VR Hardware

In addition to the above, there are a number of other products that are available from VR hardware vendors that are given below.

The Immersion Probe™ is a 3-D human interface tool for natural manual interaction with 3-D computer environments. This low-cost desktop system includes a stylus mounted on the end of a series of mechanical linkages. The stylus is held between the fingers like a pencil, allowing the user to dexterously convey spatial position (x, y, and z) and orientation (roll, pitch, and yaw) information to a host processor. (*Contact* Immersion Human Interface Corp., P.O. Box 8669, Palo Alto, California 94309, (415) 960-6882, fax (415) 960-6977.)

The Datavisor 10X is a full-color, high-resolution, wide-field-of-view HMD. The 10X video control unit allows resolutions of up to 1280 × 960 pixels per

eye in full color, and is also capable of monochrome resolutions up to 1600 ×
1200. Employing advanced optical, electronic, and display components, it is
designed to exploit the capabilities of today's high-performance graphics workstations and simulation hardware to the fullest extent possible with current technology. (*Contact* n-Division Inc., 7915 Jones Branch Drive, McLean, Virginia
22102, (703) 506-8808, fax (703) 903-0455.)

The ADL-1 is a low-cost 6D tracking system that converts position and orientation information into computer-readable form. It calculates head/object position
with 6DOF by use of a lightweight, multiple-jointed arm. Sensors mounted on the
arm measure the angles of the joints. The micro-based control unit uses these angles to compute position-orientation information in a user-selectable coordinate
system that is then transmitted to the host computer using an RS232 line. (*Contact*
Shooting Star Technology, 52023 Yale Road, R. R. 1, Rosendale, British Colum-
bia, Canada V0X 1X0, (604) 794-3364, fax (604) 794-3139.)

The Cyberscope is an optical hood that attaches easily to a computer monitor
and transforms a flat screen display into a true-to-life 3-D image. Combining
high-quality front-surface optics with an innovative new visualization technique,
the Cyberscope provides full-color stereoscopic 3-D without flicker, eye strain,
or ghost images. (*Contact* Simsalabim Systems Inc., P.O. Box 4446, Berkeley,
California 94704-0446, (510) 528-2021, fax (510) 528-9499.)

The Personal Immersive Display (PID) 131 has a wide field of view and has
good clarity and resolution of display (up to 1280 × 1024). An inner plastic
shell surrounding rigid aluminum supports the optics. The display can be quickly
fitted and adjusted for any size head. In order to facilitate natural head balance
and movement, the center of gravity is positioned nearer to the pivot point of
the head. A miniature cathode-ray tube and glass relay lens are fixed on each
side of the head. The lens relays the real image to the focal length of the
eyepiece combiner, which then provides an infinity image to the wearer. (*Contact* Virtual Reality Inc., 485 Washington Avenue, Pleasantville, New York
10570, (914) 769-0900, fax (914) 769-7106.)

The CyberGlove™ uses the latest in high-precision joint-sensing technology
and is state-of-the-art in instrumented gloves. It is the driving element of
CyberCAD™ virtual design environment of Virtual Technologies and is used to
create, edit, and position 3-D virtual objects. The CyberGlove is an 18-sensor
instrumented glove with 0.5-degree resolution, two bend sensors and one ab-
duction sensor per finger, and sensors to measure thumb and pinkle rotation and
wrist pitch and yaw. (*Contact* Virtual Technologies, 2175 Park Blvd., Palo Alto,
California 94306, (415) 321-4900, fax (415) 321-4912.)

CRITERIA FOR THE EVALUATION OF VR-HARDWARE VENDORS

To assist the typical user in the evaluation of VR-hardware vendors, it is
suggested that the individual visit the vendor's office, talk with their personnel,

Figure 3.6
Key Questions Useful in the Evaluation of VR Vendors

Does the VR vendor have

• A good corporate reputation for reliability?
• Long-range plans for support of their product(s)?
• A reputation as a producer of quality hardware?
• Financial stability?
• A high credibility rating in the industry?
• A staff with an in-depth industrial knowledge and experience?
• An intimate knowledge of its VR product(s)?
• Commitment to its product(s)?
• An effective training program?
• Accessibility and availability to clientele?
• An effective implementation program?
• Additional services as needed to support its product(s)?
• Effective communication with users?
• A policy and product that encourages user interaction and involvement?
• A well-designed maintenance plan?

and get a feel for the organization. Next, there is need for vendor evaluation criteria to assist the user in analyzing VR-hardware vendors. In addition, the criteria help the user examine the vendor's background, support, and plans for the future. Key questions to evaluate VR vendors are found in Figure 3.6.

An incorrect evaluation of these key questions could harm the typical company's VR systems development and implementation efforts. Generally, there are no clear-cut answers to these questions since each VR installation is unique. What benefits one installation may not benefit another. Hence, the user must be actively involved in the vendor evaluation process for best results. A comparable list will be set forth in the next chapter for VR software.

SUMMARY

The main thrust of this chapter is that the computer is more than an autonomous piece of equipment if it is supplemented by appropriate VR hardware to make virtual worlds possible. The utilization of HMDs, synthetic 3-D audio, and 6DOF position trackers, to name a few, are designed to work with a computer to make business applications possible. As noted in the chapter, many VR business applications do not require the extensive use of VR headgear or suits, but only a PC and the appropriate VR software. Although this is the present mode of VR operations, this may not be true tomorrow. It may well be that computers operating in virtual worlds will be embedded in walls or possibly square-inch tabs that can be carried easily. Or, as mentioned in the chapter, the utilization of a blotter environment is possible. Thus, the evolving world of VR technology may well be quite different from that of today and much less costly.

NOTE

1. John Dickinson, "A New Generation of Intelligent Objects Will Enhance Our Daily Lives," *PC Computing*, March 1992, p. 74.

4

Computer Software in a Virtual-Reality Environment

ISSUES EXPLORED

- To examine the potential problems with current VR software that can hamper its successful implementation
- To explore the utilization of object-oriented technology and the C++ Language by current vendors
- To set forth reasons why it is preferable to purchase VR software rather than get involved in custom-made software
- To explore typical current VR software offered by a number of vendors
- To set forth appropriate criteria for the evaluation of VR software vendors

OUTLINE

Sense8 Corporation—WorldToolKit Release 2.1

StrayLight Corporation—Photorealistic VR Engine

Superscape Ltd.—Superscape VR Software

Telepresence Research—Products and Services

Virtuality Entertainment Ltd.—VR Systems

Virtus Corporation—Virtus WalkThrough Pro 2.0 for Windows

VREAM Inc.—VR Creator

Worldesign Inc.—Industrial and Commercial Applications

Other VR Software

Criteria for the Evaluation of VR Software Vendors

Summary

INTRODUCTION TO COMPUTER SOFTWARE IN A VR ENVIRONMENT

The creation of virtual worlds by systems analysts and programmers requires the utilization of the appropriate VR software tools. For the most part, virtual worlds change with every user and with every new application. Virtual-reality software tools must support the user's varied design needs. In some cases, the visual elements consist of geometrical shapes of the objects in the virtual world and the appearance of texture, color, lighting, and other specific characteristics. In other cases, the accent is on comparison of items or figures that trigger some type of reaction that is visible to the user "flying over" the area under investigation. In still other cases, the virtual world consists of the exploration of new concepts and ideas that are difficult to understand within a traditional approach to modeling.

As a starting point in the development of virtual worlds, computer-aided–design (CAD) software can help create visual elements. That is, CAD software begins the process with the actual design of objects in 2- and 3-D space. However, this software does not allow the user to walk through a 3-D model just created and look around for further design improvements. This is where VR software comes into play, whereby the systems analyst or programmer can prototype a number of virtual environments until the best one is found for the situation. As such, VR software can perform a wide variety of virtual world tasks. Hence, there is need for a diversity of current computer software in a VR environment for meeting the needs of many personnel in a typical company. This is the subject matter of Chapter 4.

Problems in Utilizing Current VR Software

Currently, there are a number of problems in utilizing VR software. *First*, an important problem is directly related to the number of requests for new applications throughout an organization. Typically, today's computer-department manager is facing an almost daily problem of having many more requests and requirements from an organization's end-user community than can be met by his or her department. For example, the most frequent requests are for single-use, complex-analysis reports that require some time for their proper development and implementation. For the most part, it is simply a lack of available manpower within a given time frame for undertaking a variety of projects, including VR systems. In today's downsized environment, the majority of computer departments are simply operating below budgeted staff and have been for several years, because of a shortage of qualified personnel.

Second, the complexity of the VR applications generally require programmers who have the required skills for successful VR development and implementation. There is a definite learning curve involved in VR systems. Not only must programmers learn C, C++, or a comparable language, but they must also rethink how a system will operate within a 3-D virtual world. Hence, there is a need for programmers to rethink their traditional approach to programming and implementation which may not be to their liking whether they are new or experienced programmers.

Third, systems analysts and programmers may not be knowledgeable about what types of VR software are currently available. Although this topical area will be covered in this chapter, current systems analysts and programmers are lacking the necessary skills for the successful development and implementation of such systems. Thus, they tend to downplay the need for VR systems no matter what valid arguments can be made in their favor.

To help overcome these obstacles, some of the newer VR software packages now provide end users with the ability to satisfy a significant percent of their own requests. They provide a means of lessening end-user requests by encouraging functional end-unit managers to utilize the microcomputer as a solution to needs that might have been considered to be inappropriate in the past. With a flexible, human-oriented command structure, VR software packages allow end users to operate at a high level of development with minimal investments by the computer department. Overall, effective computer management centers on providing end users with the appropriate software and training to meet their VR processing needs in lieu of developing the applications for them.

UTILIZATION OF OBJECT-ORIENTED PROGRAMMING

Object-oriented programming (OOP) has distant ancestors in Simula, a programming language created in Norway in the late 1960s, and Smalltalk, developed soon after at Xerox's Palo Alto Research Center in California. But it has really caught on in only the past two or three years. The reason is that PC software is now becoming far more complex as programmers try to exploit the potential of today's powerful new machines. The basic idea of OOP is to build programs out of self-contained modules, or "objects." Rather than reinventing the wheel every time they create a new program, programmers can borrow prewritten modules from a library and put them together as a program.

In a sense, OOP software design is going back to the past. The large software projects of the 1960s—AT&T's national phone-switching network or IBM's operating system for its landmark 360 mainframe—took a basically modular approach. The latest PCs are more powerful than the old mainframes, and there are now literally millions of computer programmers and end-user programmers, many of whom have never written a large computer program. Object-oriented programming helps them grapple with all that complexity for a successful programming project.

The WorldToolKit (as discussed later in the chapter) follows an object-oriented style, wherein functions are grouped by classes. The following are a couple of the primary classes: *universe*, the "container" of all entities, and *objects*, the dynamic entities in the simulation. Many functions can act upon objects (i.e., tasks, hierarchies, sensors, appearance, and collision detection). As such, each object performs a *task* per frame. Objects can be linked together in *hierarchies* and objects can be attached to *sensors*. The color, texture, or size of an object can be changed in *appearance*, and there is *collision detection* between objects and polygons. Polygons can be dynamically created and texture mapped by using various sources of image data. Rendering is performed in either wire-frame, smooth-shaded, or textured modes. Lights can be dynamically created or loaded from a file; they are updated with every frame. The user can have multiple viewpoints, and they can be attached to multiple sensors. Sensor devices, such as a 2-D mouse, can be connected to lights, objects, viewpoints, and so forth. Objects or viewpoints can follow predefined paths that can be dynamically created and interpolated. The terrain can be either randomly generated or based on actual data. Terrain following of objects and viewpoints is supported. New worlds are automatically loaded when the user passes through a user-defined portal. As can be seen, an object-oriented approach is quite feasible within a VR-software environment.

Object-Oriented Programming with the C++ Language

The new C++ language is derived from the popular C programming language. It has emerged as the predominant OOP language. As noted above, object-oriented methods of program development have become popular because they are used to support greater reusability of code. In addition, they provide greater support for abstraction and encapsulation and are supposed to correspond more closely to the way in which human beings think. The growing popularity of C++ can also be linked to VR-software environments.

Within a VR environment, for example, object-oriented programmers who use C++ can combine and control polar or *x-y* style coordinate objects in a single program by having two coordinate classes. This is done by defining the interface in a special class and then having each of the coordinate classes inherit from it. This involves the initialization of the member functions of the coordinate class to zero and the deletion of the private-member function, thereby creating pure virtual functions. A *virtual function* is one that can be implemented in every class of objects that supports the function. Pure virtual functions cannot be implemented in the class in which they are defined but only in the classes derived from their class. To get a real object, a coordinate *x-y* class, derived from the coordinate class, must be created. Finally, a third class that contains the polar-coordinate objects is created. Both derived functions contain private sections where coordinate values are stored in their appropriate forms. As can be seen, OOP with C++ is a viable approach for use in virtual worlds.

PURCHASED VERSUS CUSTOM-MADE VR SOFTWARE

Many organizations, especially the small ones, do not have the capability of developing their own VR-software programs—in particular, very complex VR environments. Even companies that have such capabilities may find that costs involved in the internal development of VR software are high. This is partially due to the shortage of trained VR-software-development personnel, which is forcing organizations to pay very high salaries for qualified personnel. As a result of this problem, demand has increased for ''off-the-shelf'' software. The move to buy or use VR-software packages developed by specialized software firms will accelerate. It is wasteful, even impractical as far as dollars and lead time are concerned, for organizations to develop VR software that already exists and that can be easily tailored for specific organization needs. Hence, the decision to buy software is dependent on time, cost, off-the-shelf suitability, and necessary expertise.

When VR software is purchased off the shelf, the user receives several benefits, including (1) the choice of a variety of offerings, (2) reduced risk by buying the expertise and experience of the vendor, and (3) curtailment of expenses by buying a VR-software package that includes maintenance. In the future, business organizations will reap even more benefits from packaged VR software because many vendors are beginning to direct more attention as well as R&D expenditures to this area. Because organizations are computerizing more and more applications, more and more sophisticated VR-software products are in demand. In the near future, a virtual flood of packages is expected to be offered by a wide range of vendors.

Relationship of VR Software to Hardware

Some of the key elements of business applications that use VR software are the real-time graphics, the high level of interactivity, the simulation of object behavior, and, optionally, immersion. Although much of VR technology has been present in professional aircraft and other training simulators for years, the swift advances in computing hardware have brought interactive, 3-D graphics simulations of virtual worlds within the reach of PC and workstation users. The emergence of off-the-shelf development packages and authoring systems now makes it possible to develop virtual-world applications without developing all the supporting software in house.

Currently, developers are looking to this technology to provide new markets and methods for dealing with information. Conventional computer graphics have long been used for CAD and visualization. Virtual reality now offers these users the ability to interact with and immerse themselves within their creations before any real construction is done. The simulation and training benefits of VR can now be applied more widely. The combination of VR software and hardware (as set forth in the prior chapter) provides a means for business to deal with the large amounts of information to which modern business managers must attest.

It should be noted that the technology of VR is still in its infancy. As examples, the head-mounted–display (HMD) helmets, used for creating the sense of immersion within the VR environment, generally offer much poorer resolution than monitors. Gloves and other devices are sometimes cumbersome and prone to problems. However, this does not diminish the benefits that 3-D visualization and simulation can provide. As will be seen in Part 4 of the text (Chapters 7–10), the "window-on-a-world"– or desktop-VR–style of synthetic environments is quite adequate for many users since they and their associates often prefer to view the simulation on a conventional monitor or projection video.

TYPICAL CURRENT VR SOFTWARE OFFERED BY VENDORS

In this section, the essentials of typical current VR software offered by vendors are set forth along with their tie-in with computer hardware. As will be evident in the discussion, many of these software packages differ from more conventional 3-D imaging in two important ways. The user is effectively placed inside the simulation and can directly manipulate objects within the simulation. In some cases, this is accomplished through the use of a head-mounted, 3-D–viewing apparatus with a separate display for each eye and through the use of a special glove equipped with sensors that allow the computer to respond to any movement of the hand. In other cases, there is no need for special VR hardware to experience simulated virtual worlds. No matter the requirements of the VR software, what is needed to trigger the expansion of VR worlds is a set of useful software for business applications that justify the cost.

To help place the following discussion on software in perspective, popular VR packages are summarized in Figure 4.1. Currently, there is a full range of VR-software packages available to fit just about every major computer platform and workstation environment. Acquiring VR software runs from about two hundred dollars for Virtus WalkThrough (Virtus Corporation) and Virtual Reality Studio 2.0 (Domark Software, Inc.) to as much as several thousand dollars for

Figure 4.1

Overview of Popular VR-Software Packages

Vendor	Autodesk	Domark	MicronGreen	Sense8	StrayLight	Virtus	VREAM
Software Package	Cyberspace Developer Kit	Virtual Reality Studio	Virtual Environment NAVIGATOR	WorldTool-Kit	PhotoVR	WalkThrough	Virtual Reality Development
Type of Software	Toolkit	Authoring system	Authoring system	Toolkit	Authoring system	Authoring system	Authoring system
Input Devices	Keyboard, mouse, 6D freedom of input devices, tracking devices	Keyboard, mouse	Keyboard, mouse, Polhemus, Logitech, 6 DOF sensors	Mouse, space-ball, Ascension Bird, joystick, Polhemus ISO-TRAK2, and FASTRAK	Mouse, space-ball, Logitech mouse, tracker	Mouse	Mouse, 3-D mouse, space-ball, Logitech mouse, Head Tracker, Matell power glove
Features	Simulation of physical properties, compatible with Auto-CAD and 3D Studio, built-in networking support	Clip-Art Catalog, Sound Effects editor, VCR style playback feature	Runs inside of AutoCAD, user programmable, extensive in-environment tools	Library of 600C++ functions, real-time texture mapping, portability (C/C++)	Photo real-istic, Auto-desk. com-patible, 30 frames per second video	Path replay, object orient-ed modeling, real-time rendering	Graphic inter-face, no pro-gramming skills required, tex-ture support
Platform	386/486, requires 8MB RAM, 80MB HD, MS-DOS 3.1 or greater	286 or above, requires 640K minimum RAM, minimum 4MB HD	386/486, requires 8MB RAM, 10MB HD, MS-DOS 4.1 or greater	486 PC AT with 8MB RAM, minimum 8MB HD, SUN Sparc, SGI	386 or 486 PC AT with 4MB RAM, minimum 100MB HD	386 or 486 PC AT/4MB RAM, minimum 4MB HD, Windows 3.1	386 or 486, Pentium, PC AT with 4MB RAM, minimum 10MB HD, DOS and Windows

the WorldToolKit Release 2.0 (Sense8 Corporation). Acquiring VR-software packages, as with other types of software, is defined by the user's needs, applications, and budget. Once there is a clear definition of how VR can be applied to one or more business or nonbusiness projects, any number of VR-software packages can be considered.

As an example, if immersion and photorealism are very important, the PhotoVR (StrayLight Corp.) is a good candidate. If interactivity and cross-platform migration are important needs, Virtus WalkThrough is equally at home either on the Macintosh or in a Windows environment. If one is visually oriented and wants to see the creation in VR, the Virtual Reality Development System (VREAM) or the Virtual Environment NAVIGATOR (MicronGreen) is a good candidate for the VR application. For sophisticated VR worlds, the World-ToolKit is a good candidate since it integrates a simulation manager, a real-time rendering pipeline, an object manager, lighting, animation sequences, input sensors, and graphic-display devices all together.

The above VR-software packages can be divided into two categories: (1)"toolkits" and (2) authoring systems. Essentially, "toolkits" are composed of certain high-end programming codes that are combined to form the substance and content of a virtual environment. Typically, most code is written in C++. In contrast, authoring systems are point-and-click, graphic-design editors that allow users to construct dimensional worlds by arranging a series of geometric primitives into buildings, vehicles, and assorted landscapes. While "toolkit" users are assumed to be intermediate to advanced programmers capable of transforming C++ codes into equivalent virtual worlds, authoring-system users are generally nonprogrammers and visually oriented users who are mouse literate.

Although not stated per se in the following discussion, current VR software offered for sale can change the way in which company personnel work in the remainder of this century and in the next century. Going to work may mean going into a room at one's home and logging into a virtual office. Once at a virtual desk, the individual can access corporate data and virtual colleagues around the world. However, there is a word of caution, that is, there can be psychological and possibly physical damage for those who get too involved in VR. People may use it as an escape mechanism to avoid dealing with "actual reality." Hence, there is a need for a balanced perspective when utilizing virtual worlds in business or otherwise.

Autodesk—Cyberspace-Developer Kit

Autodesk's Cyberspace-Developer Kit (CDK) is a complete and low-cost "toolkit" for 3-D visualization and simulation. Developers working in such diverse fields as architecture and medicine can use the CDK on their desktops to develop 3-D, interactive worlds quickly and easily. The CDK is a comprehensive set of object-oriented libraries of the C++ class that solve many of the problems faced by developers of these kinds of applications. It offers functionality for creating and manipulating 3-D objects. The CDK classes make it easy to import and export geometric models from popular programs, such as AutoCAD and 3D Studio software (products of Autodesk) and bring them to life. A built-in, solid-modeling package also lets the user create 3-D solid geometry. And once created, objects are easily manipulated and changed within a 3-D space.

The CDK lets the user develop real-time, interactive simulations of the real world. The user can assign physical properties, such as mass and density, to 3-D objects and can simulate reactions to physical phenomena, such as gravity and friction. And to facilitate real-time interactions, CDK provides extensive event-handling, scheduling, and collision-detection support. The CDK works with today's displays, graphics cards, and input devices as well as with tomorrow's.

As far as output devices are concerned, drivers for many current devices are built into the CDK, so run-time display is easy. And with the CDK open architecture, integrating the displays of tomorrow is straightforward. In addition to standard displays, a variety of HMDs are supported. Standard VESA 1.2- and Autodesk Device Interface 4.2-rendering specifications are supported, as are additional board sets. An interface provides sound effects support; specialized devices offer 3-D-sound support. Interactive models can be controlled with many of the input technologies, which include scalar devices; 2-D–input and mouse devices, digitizers, joysticks, and trackballs; and 6-D–input (X-Y-Z, roll, pitch, and yaw) and 6DOF mouse devices and HMDs with tracking. The CDK operates in an open architecture. The product requires a 386- or 486-based PC with 8 megabytes (MB) of RAM and an 80MB hard-disk drive. In addition, the CDK supports a number of graphics-accelerator boards and displays.

More recently, the CDK Release 2 for Windows reflects new additions. Although much of the architecture and capabilities of the original product are present in the new release, several important enhancements have been added. First, a range of new rendering solutions are supported, including both fast renderers as well as accelerated solutions. Second, the CDK has been closely integrated with 3D Studio to allow not only geometry and textures to be seamlessly transferred to the CDK but also lights, cameras, and animation key-frame data. With Release 2, motion that is defined by using the key-frame module of 3D Studio is readily established in the CDK. To create dynamic virtual worlds, it is no longer necessary to define motion paths with code. Even the definition of complex, hierarchical motion can be readily handled with 3D Studio for interactive consumption using the CDK. (*Contact* Autodesk Inc., 2320 Marinship Way, Sausalito, California 94965, (415) 332-2344, fax (415) 491-8303.)

Avatar Partners and Data Broadcasting Corporation— vrTrader for Windows

One of the most interesting VR packages is the vrTrader for Windows, developed by Avatar Partners and marketed exclusively by Data Broadcasting Corporation (DBC). The vrTrader software uses DBC's Signal receiver box to receive real-time data from one of three DBC networks: (1) FM radio, (2) direct satellite, or (3) the vertical-blanking interval of several cable TV networks. The software presents stock-market data as 3-D objects with graphics and text around them. Stocks are projected onto a matrix that resembles a 3-D football field, with each security represented by a color-coded pole coming out of the ground. The color and behavior of each stock object quickly indicates a buying or selling opportunity. Each pole can grow, spin, blink, or emit a sound that indicates the movement of that security. The overall scene is a startling visual picture of a subscriber's portfolio in action at any given moment of the trading day. The software further updates related factors, like the existence of recent news reports.

Using vrTrader under Windows, a subscriber can view up to 300 stocks from a choice of over 9,500 from the NYSE, AMEX, and NASDAQ exchanges. Avatar has expanded the ability to visualize market data by combining several advanced technologies, including VR, voice recognition, sound synthesis, and AI. Both real-time and delayed (fifteen minutes) quotes are supported by vr-Trader. The user can assign visible thresholds and auditory alerts to monitor each stock's volume, price, and fundamentals. The vrTrader is adaptable to a trading room or exhibition environment through the use of projection TV and stereo sound.

The vrTrader for Windows will run on a 386- or 486-based PC or on a Pentium-based system equipped with Microsoft Windows. Audio alerts require a Creative Labs Soundblaster–compatible sound card. A minimum of 4 MB of memory are recommended. Data Broadcasting Corporation's signal box and subscription service are also necessary. Additional information on the vrTrader will be given in Chapter 9. (*Contact* Data Broadcasting Corp., 1900 South Norfolk Street, P.O. Box 5979, San Mateo, California 94402-0979, (415) 571-1800, fax (415) 571-8507. Avatar Partners is located at 13090 Central Avenue, Suite 3, Boulder Creek, California 95006.)

Domark Software Inc.—Virtual Reality Studio 2.0

Using Virtual Reality Studio 2.0 from Domark Software, almost anyone who uses a computer can design, explore, and share virtual worlds. Developed alongside professional products, this software package now offers a range of features that make design and playback of virtual worlds even more simple and comprehensive. Included in this package are the following: 3-D shape designer/manipulator, sound-effects manipulator, animation program, computer VCR Playback Function, clip-art library with a full-color catalog, spheres and flexicubes, 2-D bit maps (including sprites and animation cells), and in-depth video tutorial. This new version can be run on IBM PCs and compatibles as well as on the Commodore Amiga.

A user can, for example, design a house, then walk through it or fly over it. Once a user has designed an object, coloring it is simple with this software package's complete paint program. The ''Create'' panel allows a user immediate access to otherwise complicated programming commands. A user can instantly create or edit any object. Spheres can be created by simply pointing and clicking. Using the VCR Playback Function, a user can create a movie. In turn, the user can move through it in slow motion, can fast forward, or can fly through it from any perspective. In addition, the user can create and animate limitless scenarios from cars on raceways to men in space. (*Contact* Domark Software Inc., 1900 S. Norfolk Street, No. 110, San Mateo, California 94403, (415) 513-8929, fax (415) 571-0437.)

MicronGreen Inc.—Virtual Environment NAVIGATOR

MicronGreen markets the Virtual Environment NAVIGATOR, a product built with the CDK from Autodesk. This software is the result of a collaborative effort with the Institute for Simulation and Training and the University of Florida. The NAVIGATOR is a real-time tool for experiencing, altering, and interacting with 3-D models. It has benefited from the classic open architecture of Autodesk's CDK libraries, which follow the tradition of AutoCAD software's integrated problem-solving solutions. The functionality available in the CDK is substantial, and the integration with AutoCAD and 3D Studio is one of its most important features.

It should be noted that the Virtual Environment NAVIGATOR differs from Autodesk's CDK in the level of programming. While the power of the object-oriented design and C++ vehicle is very good for creating good simulations, the CDK requires an experienced technical programmer. However, Micron-Green's software is a complete VR-authoring tool that requires much less sophisticated programming experience. For those who want access to the CDK's simulation capabilities without becoming C++ experts, the NAVIGATOR has such capabilities. (*Contact*: MicronGreen Inc., 1240 N.W. 21st Avenue, Gainesville, Florida 32069, (904) 376-1529, fax (904) 376-0466.)

Sense8 Corporation—WorldToolKit Release 2.1

The WorldToolKit (WTK) Version 2.1, which is available from Sense8 Corporation, is a set of C functions that lets a programmer build real-time graphics simulations. It supports input and output devices, such as HMDs, and is used for building VR applications. WorldToolKit makes interactive, 3-D graphics applications prototypical, while providing the functionality required to build complex applications. Currently, it is a library of over six-hundred function calls that simplify the process of creating real-time, interactive 3-D simulations. Though WTK is intended for C programmers, it is shipped with several complete applications that can be compiled and used as is.

Since WTK is not a 3-D-modeling program, 3-D objects are created by using familiar tools like AutoCAD, 3D Studio, Swivel 3D, or any other 3D modeler that generates DXF or 3-DS files. This package reads these files and allows the user to interact and explore the models in real time with existing PC hardware. The WorldToolKit does contain functions for interactively creating spheres, cubes, cylinders, polygons, and the like. The user can use these functions to dynamically create shapes within a virtual environment.

Sense8 has continued to develop and enhance the range of features and rendering capabilities of WTK. Release 2.1 contains over six-hundred function calls, double the number found in WTK 1.0. The following is a list of features: support for new input/output devices; interfaces to more modelers, that is, 3D Studio, MultiGen, and Wavefront; object, polygon, and vertex constructors; 24-bit color; use of Performer libpr for faster rendering on Silicon Graphics Workstations; antialiasing filter for improved image quality; wire-frame, flat, Gouraud-shaded, and texture-mapped polygons; transparent, shaded, and perspective-corrected textures; support for multiple windows that display different viewpoints; runs with Windows; and improved terrain generation and rendering.

WorldToolKit 2.1 provides high-level function calls to make application development as rapid as possible. It has no restrictions on the functionality that can be built into an application. It is not only power driven but also solutions driven. This means it provides low-level access as well as high-level calls. A sample WTK application is

```
/* create the robot arm components* /
upperarm=WTobject_new ("upperarm.nff), . . . );
gripper=WTobject_new ("gripper.nff, . . . );
/* assemble the robot arm* /
WTobject_attach (upperarm, gripper);
/* assign gripper behavior* /
WTobject_settask (gripper,followcursor);
```

The user is never limited by the system, no matter the level of task required. In addition, WTK 2.1 is extremely flexible, which means there is often more than one way to develop a particular feature in an application.

The WTK Release 2.0 provides very intuitive function calls to make application development as easy as possible. After using WTK for a short while, it is often possible to guess a function call without having to look it up. As an illustration of how straightforward and intuitive application programming is, the call

```
WTuniverse_new(WTDISPLAY_CRYSTALEYES, WTWINDOW_NOBORDER)
```

constructs the universe container object and sets up the computer-graphics device appropriate for StereoGraphics CrystalEyes 3-D glasses.

Currently, real-time, 3-D-graphics development tools are available for Windows 3.1. This new capability combines the flexibility and features of Sense8's

WTK with the powerful environment of Windows 3.1. Now, any computer that can run Windows 3.1 can run a Virtual Reality application built with WTK for Windows. This development opens up a whole new class of applications, that is, a user can create a stand-alone Windows application that extracts data from an Excel or Lotus 1-2-3 spreadsheet and then links it to physical attributes in the virtual world. Or Visual Basic can be used to create an application that combines a 2-D interface with WTK for Windows's virtual 3-D environment.

There are a number of potential applications using this VR software. For architectural walk-throughs, a 3-D DXF model of one's new house or remodeled kitchen is loaded and then used for exploring. Using a mouse, the user selects a cabinet surface and applies a different wood texture or paint color. By linking the 3-D model to an Excel spreadsheet, the user can change the height or width of a wall from Excel. For educational simulations, a world could be built in which various laws of physics apply or in which the user's own rules apply. In the area of research, the effects of two molecules docking can be simulated or a wired glove can be used to dock one of them. Additionally, this software is helpful for data visualization whereby stock-market data from a remote database is extracted by using SQL queries, and a virtual world is created whereby stocks are represented as virtual rooms containing additional price and trend information on the walls. (*Contact* Sense8 Corp., 4000 Bridgeway, Suite 104, Sausalito, California 94965, (415) 331-6318, fax (415) 331-9148.)

StrayLight Corporation—Photorealistic VR Engine

PhotoVR, marketed by StrayLight, is a photorealistic VR engine that is used to create and explore highly realistic 3-D virtual environments. Users create 3-D designs that utilize popular CAD or animation software. PhotoVR is then employed to import these designs and move interactively around the 3-D environment in real time. Scenes may be of virtually unlimited complexity without any reduction in interactive performance. PhotoVR directly imports 3-D designs from Autodesk's 3D Studio, as well as AutoCAD with AutoShade. Moreover, designs can be directly imported from AT&T's Topas Animator. In each class, these designs are imported with all shading settings intact.

PhotoVR's unique feature is that its interactive speed remains constant regardless of scene complexity. Speed is measured in frame rates, that is, the number of new views generated per second. Typically, PhotoVR delivers eight frames per second for changing the user's direction of view and three to four frames per second for motion within a scene. This remains constant whether a scene has 10 polygons or 100,000 polygons. The company also markets CyberTron, an immersive VR arcade game, based on a gyroscope. (*Contact* Straylight Corp., 150 Mt. Bethel Road, Warren, New Jersey 07059, (908) 580-0086, fax (908) 580-0092.)

Superscape Ltd.—Superscape VR Software

Dimension International, the author of the VR product Superscape, has changed its name so that it is synonymous with its product, and has opened a North American headquarters office in Palo Alto, California. Currently, Superscape is divided into four sections. The first section, Superscape VRT3, which contains the complete Virtual World creation and editing system, is all that most users will ever need. The second section, Superscape Networks, is an optional addition and allows unlimited worlds to be visualized on up to eight run-time systems. A third section is the Superscape-Developers Kit, which is aimed at serious third-party developers. Finally, a fourth section is the Visualiser program, which is a cut-down version (no editing facilities) that supports Virtual Worlds created in Superscape.

Getting familiar with Superscape's interface is relatively easy. The start-up menu comes in two portions: an iconic tool bar and an optional menu that displays a text explanation of each of the icons. Once familiar with the package, the text menu can be turned off. There are no less than seven editors on offer: Textures, Sound, Key, Layout, Shape, Resource, and World. Other commands offered allow the import of DXF files (Autodesk's Drawing Interchange Format) into the Shape editor, and software scripts can be created and assigned to objects. The quickest method of creating a new Virtual World in Superscape is by entering the World Editor from the main menu. The package then presents the user with an empty virtual plain containing only a reference square, blue sky, green ground, and a dithered horizon. Any objects or set pieces from the library can then be placed in the virtual landscape.

Other menus allow for the creation and editing of sounds, color pictures, and 3-D models for Virtual World creation. Sounds and models can be distanced, that is, the further away the user's viewpoint, the quieter the sound and the less detail that can be seen. Objects can be easily created in the Shape Editor and then placed into the new "world." A little software-programming knowledge will go a long way here, especially when attributes (like morphing and automated movement) need to be applied. Objects can also be linked together by using the parent-child links provided in the World Editor.

There are many uses for Superscape, such as fire-escape analysis, submarine simulation, and Army-combat analysis. Included with the software come twenty or more demonstration worlds, each one highlighting specific features of the package. Novice users learn the basic techniques of world creation by analyzing the various implementations: simulators, office layout, training, product design, and architecture. (*Contact* Superscape Ltd., Zephyr One, Calleva Park, Aldermaston, Berkshire RG7 4QZ, England, (44) 734-810077, fax (44) 734-816940.)

Telepresence Research—Products and Services

Telepresence Research is devoted to the design and development of virtual-environment and remote-presence technologies and applications. The company's basic goal is to create compelling immersive experiences in remote or synthesized environments. Its primary objectives are to design forms of interactive experience that are engaging, accessible, and immersive; to design integrated systems and applications that provide both short-term product potential and long-term innovation for the telepresence medium; and to develop telepresence technologies with new capabilities and techniques in hardware, software, design strategies, and tools. The products that Telepresence Research offers include consulting and prototype services, technology development, and integrated installations. Development is focused on five application areas: entertainment, learning and exploration, training and simulation, scientific visualization, and remote presence.

Contract R&D services for Telepresence Research include concept development, product design and prototyping, and system integration for virtual-environment and remote-presence experience. Vitual environments are computer-generated worlds that users enter and take action in via telepresence technology. For example, a person might directly explore a molecular model or an imaginary planet and its inhabitants. On the other hand, remote presence utilizes such technologies as head-coupled video cameras, other remote-sensing technologies, and robots to enable people to experience and take action in real places that are physically distant, hazardous, or inaccessible. Examples include a space station or a nuclear reactor.

In addition, the company markets the telepresence mobile robot. This integrated system consists of a boom-mounted, monochrome or color, stereoscopic viewer, a wireless communications package, and a self-powered mobile platform carrying a telepresence camera system and range sensors. The 3DOF camera mechanism tracks the user's head in real time, allowing the user to feel that he or she is actually present in the remote location. (*Contact* Telepresence Research, 320 Gabarda Way, Portola Valley, California 94028 (415) 854-4420, fax (415) 854-3141.)

Virtuality Entertainment Ltd.—VR Systems

Virtuality Entertainment markets the IBM Immersive Virtual Reality (IVR) Development System. This is a complete, integrated system designed specifically for creating IVR application software. This system represents the culmination of a cooperation that brings together the IVR know-how of Virtuality and the experience, technology, and resources of IBM. In addition, Virtuality markets V-SPACE, which is an interactive, 3-D-modeling and VR-world-creation system running under Microsoft Windows. The V-SPACE is an innovative way to develop 3-D content rapidly in applications such as architectural design, engineering design, medical training, and 3-D animation.

Project Elysium is a low-cost range of VR computer systems that have been jointly developed by Virtuality and IBM. The range comprises Virtuality's "V-SPACE" application development "toolkit," "V-PC" operating system, VR PC Accelerator Cards, and "Visette2" HMD. These two companies offer a range of portable VR computers intended for VR applications, with an entry-level price of $9,900. This has been made possible by integrating IBM's ValuePoint PC with Virtuality's mass-produced VR technologies into a wide range of VR computers.

Virtuality manufactures the world's best-selling VR entertainment systems, called Series 2000. As with its entertainment division, the company is the leading developer of VR entertainment software that has contracts with Sega and Universal Studios. As the company develops its new VR standard called V-PC within the emerging entertainment industry, it is seeking to capitalize on its development expenditure by broadening its market into the nonentertainment sectors. (*Contact* Virtuality House, 3 Oswin Road, Brailsford Industrial Park, Leicester LE3 1HR, United Kingdom (44) (0)116 2337000, fax (44) (0)116 2471855.)

Virtus Corporation—Virtus WalkThrough Pro 2.0 for Windows

Virtus WalkThrough Pro 2.0 for Windows is a 3-D-modeling program available from Virtus Corporation. It requires no special hardware such as goggles, joysticks, or DataGloves, often necessary for many VR applications. In its simplicity and straightforward operation, WalkThrough Pro 2.0 for Windows more closely resembles a presentation graphics or 2-D-modeling package than a complex CAD package. To create a "world" or model, the user works in 2-D and 3-D views simultaneously. An object placed in the 2-D view is rendered in 3-D automatically in the Walk View. The user can then manipulate the object's position, size, color, and other characteristics.

Since the program comes with dozens of premade items, including home furniture and office equipment, the user can copy and paste these into models. The program also incorporates perspective-correct texture mapping for added realism. With a mouse, the user can navigate around and through objects in the 3-D Walk View. In addition, WalkThrough Pro 2.0 allows the user to "record" a particular path through a model for later demonstration. WalkThrough Pro 2.0 ships with the Virtus Player, a utility that enables the user to open, view, and navigate within his or her own Virtus model. The program has import and export facilities that allow it to work with other design applications, and users can integrate both 2-D and 3-D views into drawing, word-processing, and page-layout programs. WalkThrough Pro 2.0 for Windows requires an IBM PC or compatible with a 386 or better processor, 8 MB of RAM, a VGA or SVGA color monitor (recommended), and Microsoft Windows version 3.1 or later. For the Macintosh version, the system requirements include any color Macintosh, Macintosh System version 6.05 or later, and 8 MB of RAM.

Virtus WalkThrough Pro 2.0 for Windows has the following features. It has simultaneous drawing and rendering as well as real-time rendering of drawings that allow for instant intuitive feedback. Its industry-segmented 3-D libraries cut user's design time dramatically by offering readily available objects. With object-oriented drawing capabilities, a user can prototype ideas faster by drawing familiar shapes with a single click and drag. Its import options allow the user to combine 3-D models with other graphics packages, view objects created in other packages, and speed design by tracing over drafts to create 3-D drawings. On the other hand, its export options eliminate the need for reinput of design, speed up the project completion, and combine 3-D models with other graphic and CAD packages. Moreover, output of both Design and Walk View from any perspective can be printed.

Virtus WalkThrough Pro 2.0, whether the Windows or Macintosh version, is useful for a number of applications. A bank, for example, could put it to work to show management what proposed branch layout changes would look like. In advertising, producers are using Virtus WalkThrough Pro 2.0 to determine the best setup and positioning for photo shoots and commercials, minimizing expensive time with photographers, camera operators, and models. In another example, a fire department could use Virtus WalkThrough to preview a rescue attempt in a towering inferno. Subway workers could monitor and explore underground tracks. Other applications will be given in Part 4 of this text. (*Contact Virtus Corp., 118 MacKenan Drive, Suite 250, Cary, North Carolina 27511, (919) 467-9700, fax (919) 460-4530.*)

VREAM Inc.—VR Creator

The VR Creator from VREAM lets users develop and execute fully interactive, textured VR worlds on a PC. The VR Creator gives users the ability to create stand-alone or networked VR worlds. In a networked world, multiple users may enter a virtual world and interact with each other across a network. This networked aspect of the software is consistent with the company's goal of making high-quality VR accessible to the consumer marketplace. The price for a networked VREAM system depends on the number of nodes in the network.

The VR Creator is a complete VR development and execution environment in a single, low-cost, and easy-to-use package. The software is an ideal entry point for those who are just getting started with VR. Nonprogrammers can easily create complex, interactive, textured, and, now, multiuser virtual worlds through the point-and-click, pull-down menu graphical user interface. Equally important, only a PC, mouse, and keyboard are required for each of the users in a networked world, so that the investment to get started with VR remains minimal.

Currently, advanced users or those who are programming inclined can use the VREAM scripting language with its user-defined variables, in conjunction with external programs if desired, to build sophisticated functionality into VR worlds and applications. These may be multiuser in nature. For those advanced users who are interested in using specialized interface hardware, the VREAM system continues to support an ever-expanding list of devices, including HMDs, 3-D tracking systems, 3-D mice, gloves, and 3-D ball controllers. Multiuser functionality enhances both of the major components of the VR Creator: the VREAM 3D World Editor and the VREAM Runtime System. The VREAM 3D World Editor allows the user to draw the 3-D objects that comprise the virtual world, define the characteristics of the objects in the virtual world, and define the action-triggered behavior of those objects. The multiuser feature extends this simple paradigm, letting the world creator define behavior links between the objects and the multiple users who will inhabit the virtual world.

Once the virtual world is defined, the VREAM Runtime System allows the user to enter the world immediately and interact with it in real time. The user may walk through the virtual world, objects may be grasped and moved with the user controlled hand, and all of the defined world behaviors become active. With the multiuser enhancement, the user is able to interact fully with others within a virtual world, grasping, holding, or pushing other inhabitants of the world, throwing objects back and forth between users, or otherwise interacting with the active users in the world. The VREAM VR software requires a 386-, 486-, or Pentium-based, IBM-compatible running MS-DOS; four MB of RAM; a math coprocessor, and a standard graphics board.

The VREAM contains many advanced features found in more expensive VR software. The VR-development system can be interfaced with specialized hardware for fully immersive VR experiences. Photorealistic textures may be applied to surfaces within a virtual world, thereby providing greater realism, that is, a wood grain on a table, a brick pattern on a house, or an animated image on a television. Monoscopic and stereoscopic images may be generated from an active virtual world. There is a comprehensive link structure that allows complex logical operations to be incorporated into virtual worlds. Moreover, there is the capability of dynamically creating, changing, saving, and deleting objects while experiencing a virtual world. The VREAM incorporates pop-up windows, timers, and counters into VR applications. External PC applications may be launched, thereby allowing a virtual world to serve as a front end to other systems. Import and export DXF 3-D object files, along with import PCX bitmap files, are a part of the software's advanced features. (*Contact* VREAM Inc., 2568 N. Clark Street, No. 250, Chicago, Illinois 60614, (312) 477-0425, fax (312) 477-9702.)

Worldesign Inc.—Industrial and Commercial Applications

Worldesign is a spin-off of the Human Interface (HIT) Laboratory at the University of Washington. It is an important information-design studio that uses virtual-worlds technology for industrial and commercial applications. Its first major contract was a consulting agreement with Evans & Sutherland, Simulation Division. Evans & Sutherland, a veteran manufacturer of high-end, computer-graphics engines for simulators, hired Worldesign to study the application of VR in industrial and commercial markets. The company's other contracts include Japanese companies as well as European companies. The company's information designs include projects that develop an interface between operators and complex machinery and that show how the next generation of utilities might function. Robert Jacobson, founder and president of Worldesign (as well as of HIT Lab), knows that the company has entered uncharted waters with its concept of information design. He recognizes that there is a lot of education to be undertaken since people have taken for granted the media environments in which they live.

Worldesign performs custom software design and development of virtual-worlds applications on a contracting basis. It also help its clients integrate and install the applications developed for them. Worldesign has developed a product called the Virtual Environment Theater (VET), which is an effective way to interact with virtual worlds. Additionally, a software product is being developed that acts as a visual front end for geographic information systems (GISs). The electric-power utility industry and its environmental, logistics/dispatch, and public-presentation applications compose the initial market targeted for the new GIS product.

Worldesign favors a collaborative approach to design and technology and will pool the best available resources for projects. Essentially, the company focuses on custom-built VR applications where there are implementations of high-end hardware and software, which meet specific customer needs. Its WorldSpace Object Libraries make up a comprehensive library of physical and abstract objects, behaviors, and relationships that work with and enhance the performance of existing VR "toolkits." (*Contact* Worldesign Inc., 5348 1/2 Ballard Avenue N.W., Seattle, Washington 98107, (206) 781-5253, fax (206) 781-5254.)

Other VR Software

There are several other VR-software products on the market. They include the following.

The Lightscape Visualization System is an advanced visualization system for CAD, commercial animation, and VR applications. It incorporates radiosity and ray-tracing techniques. In addition, it has a physically based lighting interface and an ability to produce 3-D–rendered simulations that users can walk through and explore interactively. (*Contact* Lightscape Technologies, Inc., 4030 Moorpark Avenue, Suite 219, San Jose, California 95117, (408) 246-1155, fax (408) 246-0255.)

Research Triangle Institute provides a full range of VR solutions within specific application areas, including environmental sciences, systems engineering, chemistry, architecture, aerospace, defense, transportation, manufacturing, and human physiology. The institute's tools involve rapid modeling, detailed texturing, integration with sound, speech recognition, and the addition of simulation dynamics. (*Contact* Research Triangle Institute, P.O. Box 12194, Research Triangle Park, North Carolina 27709-2194, (919) 541-6951.)

Vistapro 3.0 is a 3-D landscape program that lets users re-create and explore landscapes on earth or Mars. Features include twenty-four–bit color, buildings, waterfalls, roads, 3-D trees and vegatation, clouds, fractal texturing, and the ability to generate left and right images for 3-D viewing. Vistapro 3.0 includes a user-defined color palette that delivers a PC recreation of landscapes, real and imaginary. (*Contact* Virtual Reality Laboratories, Inc., 2341 Ganador Court, San Luis Obispo, California 93401, (805) 545-8515, fax (805) 781-2259.)

Virtual Reality Studio is a dedicated facility for the production of VR simulations, computer graphics, 3-D audio, and video transfers. Comprised of SGI workstations, PCs, Macintoshes, special design, audio software, and the like, it is capable of integrating and programming systems to create real applications by evaluating real-world objectives and applying creative designs and production skills. (*Contact* Virtual 'S' Ltd. The Limes, 123 Mortlake High Street, London SW14 8SN, England, (44) 81-39-29000, fax (44) 81-39-22424.)

The Parallel Universe is a dial-up, multiuser, real-time 3-D environment enhanced by spatially relative voice communications. It requires standard telephone lines for access. Its primary applications are concurrent engineering and multiplayer games. (*Contact* Virtual Universe Corp. 700 4th Avenue, Suite 510, S. W. Calgary, Alberta, T2P 3S4, Canada, (403) 261-5652, fax (403) 237-0005.)

The Well is an on-line service of more than two hundred public-discussion areas, each containing twelve to two hundred topics. It includes a VR conference discussion area. In addition, it provides access to worldwide E-mail, USENET, and the Internet. (*Contact* The Well, 1750 Brideway, Sausalito, California 94965-1900, (415) 332-4335, fax (415) 332-4927.)

As time passes, the glamour and opportunities afforded by VR will entice a number of start-up companies as well as entry by the well-established hardware and software vendors, like IBM and DEC. Thus, it is expected that there will be a number of important players in the VR software market in the years to come.

CRITERIA FOR THE EVALUATION OF VR SOFTWARE VENDORS

In the preceding chapter on VR hardware, reference was made to the availability and quality of software. Although software can be purchased, sometimes it does not meet the user's needs. Hence, it is necessary to inquire about software available from other sources. No matter what sources are used for acquiring VR software many questions must be asked. They are found in Figure 4.2 and cover a wide range of important areas.

SUMMARY

Although VR software in the past produced cartoonlike worlds which tended to be less than realistic, nevertheless, these initial software efforts have dem-

Figure 4.2
Key Questions Useful in the Evaluation of VR Software

- *How much does the VR software cost?* What options are offered, at what cost, and how are they installed? To say the least, it is important to get a clear statement initially on the options, particularly on the cost of desirable options if they are incorporated into the delivered package versus how much the same options would cost if tacked on after installation.

- *Is there a trial period?* Some software vendors customarily allow their software to be installed at a prospective purchaser's site for trial use. A nominal preacquisition investment could short-circuit many future problems by helping the user to decide on options, training, and other costly variables.

- *What are the costs for installation assistance and training?* Costs tend to vary from one vendor to another.

- *What is the cost of a maintenance contract?* The fee is generally about 10 percent of the then-current, one-time license fee of the package, beginning in the second year. Because fees are being pressured upward toward the 15-percent level, rather than let the rate float at the vendor's discretion, a fixed rate at the front end of an agreement should be contracted.

- *How are newer versions or updates handled?* Newer versions or updates can be built into the maintenance fee, although newer versions, or updates, can often be purchased separately if the purchaser does not take a maintenance contract.

- *How are fixes handled?* Fixes are usually free as long as the user has not tampered with the package.

- *What support will be provided?* Support should be received during the installation phase.

- *Is the VR software package flexible and easy to use?* The VR package should provide the capability of meeting the company's changing virtual-world requirements. In a similar manner, the package should assist the user by being easy to use.

- *Does the VR software package have the performance capabilities needed?* If the package can only handle certain aspects of virtual worlds, then the purchaser should beware.

- *What is the operational status of the VR software package?* The focus here is on when it was written, by whom, and for what users?

- *Is the source code available?* Given the source code and perhaps a couple of other listings, the purchaser knows as much about a package as the vendor. The vendor invariably charges a one-time fee for the code, and the purchaser usually then assumes all maintenance responsibilities.

- *What arrangements have been made for ongoing maintenance if the vendor goes out of business?* The answer to this question and the next one should be tied to the availability of the source code.

- *What are the charges for custom modifications?* These are generally expensive, but possibly beneficial in the long run if the modifications substantially improve the VR-software package's utility to the purchaser.

- *What penalties can be levied on the vendor for late delivery?* The same comment can be made regarding nonperformance.

- *Is there adequate documentation?* Documentation can be a key issue when many end users are involved.

onstrated the practicality of VR in business. As discussed in this chapter, the state of the art in VR software has progressed to the point where various functional areas in a typical business organization can benefit from virtual worlds. For example, physical worlds can be sketched by creating shapes with AutoCAD. In turn, developers can create virtual objects and link them to those shapes. The objects would then be linked into multiple systems. Next, developers can load and link the "classes," or properties, needed for the space and can place the objects in their initial position. Finally, sensors can be linked to objects through reactors—the rules governing movement through virtual worlds. The net result is that a number of functional areas in a typical business can benefit from the employment of VR software in developing virtual worlds.

5

Computer Databases and Data Communications in a Virtual-Reality Environment

ISSUES EXPLORED

- To rethink the whole area of databases and data communications such that VR applications can really profit the typical company
- To examine the current direction in databases such that VR applications can build upon these current successes
- To explore the management and organization of data within a typical VR environment
- To set forth important present and future directions in data communications and networking
- To build upon these important directions in data communications and networking as they relate to VR

OUTLINE

Introduction to Computer Databases and Data Communications in a VR Environment

Need for New Directions in Computer Databases and Data Communications for VR

Current Approach to Computer Databases

Internal On-Line Database-Management Systems

    Four Organization Models for Database-Management Systems

    Distributed Database-Management Systems

    Current Movement to Object-Oriented Database-Management Systems

External On-Line Databases

    Timely External Information for Business

Need for New View of Data in a VR Environment

INTRODUCTION TO COMPUTER DATABASES AND DATA COMMUNICATIONS IN A VR ENVIRONMENT

To place this chapter's material in its proper perspective, present developments of computer databases and data communications are treated first so as to serve as a background for a discussion of the requirements needed for VR applications throughout a typical company. Although R&D on VR is centering on such items as product design and troubleshooting, an important goal of the technology is to enable users to gain the ability to interact with complex information via their senses. As such, VR enables users to enter computer-generated environments that include three-dimensionality through sound, sight, and touch. Some researchers in the VR field are examining how VR technology can provide users with the ability to view data in various ways in databases and network environments. Other researchers are saying that the most important thing happening is the networking of VR worlds. No matter the viewpoint, it is expected that VR applications for business will depend heavily upon computer databases, data communications, and networking.

NEED FOR NEW DIRECTIONS IN COMPUTER DATABASES AND DATA COMMUNICATIONS FOR VR

Although the past two chapters presented the current state of the art of hardware and software for VR applications, there is need to go one step further and integrate computerized databases and data communications with these developments. That is, hardware and software of virtual worlds are not islands unto themselves but may require extensive use of computer databases that may be found anywhere in a company's far-flung global operations or even outside the company. From this viewpoint, there is a need to rethink how VR applications operate to meet user needs, especially such that there is a natural tie-in with computer databases and data communications and networking. In this way, the growth of VR applications for business is assured.

As an example of this rethinking process, database-management-system vendors have positioned their database products as multimedia repositories since companies view digital multimedia as complementary to their database investment. It makes sense for companies to attach multimedia information, such as an image or an audio segment, to a record (row) in a relational table. Accounting records, personnel records, and the like can be enhanced by multimedia information. A comparable rethinking is necessary for databases as well as data communications and networking before the full potential of VR applications for business can be realized. Because of the importance of this subject matter, it will be discussed at the appropriate times in the material to follow for computer databases and data communications as well as networking.

CURRENT APPROACH TO COMPUTER DATABASES

In a typical company today, there is a considerable amount of data being stored, whether it was generated internally or acquired externally. For the most part, these data are helpful to company personnel whether they be executives and their staff or operating personnel throughout the company. For example, to answer ''what-if''-type questions on a timely basis, stored data have to be accessible to company personnel. For this mode of operation, the database must be on-line. Essentially, the information that must be available on an immediate demand basis should have been predetermined by systems analysts when developing data-file (i.e., computer databases) requirements. Important data required by the system should be stored on-line in data-storage devices, and less important data should be stored on other low-cost storage media.

Data that must be stored on-line must be thoroughly evaluated by systems analysts, who must determine the following: (1) the amount of space needed for storing important data records in the database, (2) the time required to find and retrieve a data record, and (3) the time needed to transfer the proper record from the terminal device to the main computer memory as well as from the computer to the device after the record is processed. Intensive review and analysis of these factors is necessary to evaluate the on-line storage capacity needed. Hence, storage capacities, speeds, and transfer rates are of utmost importance when stating equipment specifications.

Several types of data storage can be categorized as off-line or on-line storage. *Off-line storage* involves data that are not under the control of the computer. These data files can be used as input for a computer system to permit the updating and retrieval of information, or they can be used to produce various types of reports. Generally, data needed to be referenced weekly or less frequently are good candidates for off-line storage. In contrast, *on-line storage* involves data under the direct control of the computer. When access to certain data is needed frequently, on-line storage is appropriate. On-line data files are commonly referred to an organization's database; information is centrally located in one or several databases. Another way of viewing storage is in the way in which the data are accessed. Must the data be accessed (while under the control of the computer) in sequential order? If so, magnetic-tape files are most appropriate for storage. If the data can be accessed directly and randomly as needed, they require direct-access storage devices (DASDs).

INTERNAL ON-LINE DATABASE-MANAGEMENT SYSTEMS

Because data is of great importance to a typical organization, there is a need to provide on-line access to database elements for immediate processing by using direct-access–file storage devices. One method of maintaining a large, complex database and managing relationships among the database elements is to employ a database management system (DBMS). Thus, management-information-system (MIS) managers should employ DBMSs to their fullest capacity to satisfy present and future needs of users, whether they be within or outside the MIS department.

Typically, the reach of a DBMS extends beyond the individual-file–management systems, such as inventory files and accounts receivable files of the past, to an entire database (or databases), consisting of corporate planning, marketing, manufacturing, accounting, personnel, and other data elements. Furthermore, a DBMS allows *procedure independence* of the database for a large number of data elements. This means that the programmer does not have to describe the data file in detail, as is the case with procedure-oriented languages like COBOL, but has only to specify what is to be done in a *data-management language*.

Four Organization Models for Database-Management Systems

Although vendors offer a variety of DBMSs, models that provide for the creation, access, and maintenance of data to aid organizations in the effective management of databases fall into four categories: (1) hierarchical, (2) network,

(3) relational, and (4) object. All of these organizational models are discussed below. Emphasis is placed on the current movement to object-oriented DBMS.

A *hierarchical* database system uses a tree structure to distinguish relationships between records in a file. Every data item or field is "owned" by a higher-ranking item, and access to it must be routed through that hierarchy. In other words, items are arranged according to a parent-child relationship whereby each parent may have many children, but each child may have only one parent. A fixed relationship between the data elements in the hierarchy is established, and data are retrieved by the DBMS moving along the hierarchy in a manner dependent on the request from the user.

A *network* database system establishes individual files for each major element of data. "Pointers" in the records are used to link these elements together. Pointers are the disk addresses where each record in a file is stored. In effect, the network model allows "children" to be related to many "parents," and very general interdependencies can be expressed. As such, a network database tends to be more flexible than a hierarchical database.

A *relational* DBMS is simply a collection of 2-D tables (called relations) with no repeating group. In the tables, the rows constitute records, and columns constitute fields. The term *relational* comes from the clearly defined relations that data within a field have, which orders the records in the database. For example, numeric fields can be ordered from least to greatest, alphabetic fields can be in alphabetical order, and so forth.

The relational model, which is found currently in DBMS models, offers many advantages over hierarchical and network models. It is based on a logical rather than a physical structure and shows the relationships between various items. Data are represented in tabular form, and new relations can be created. Searching is generally faster than within the other schemes, modification is more straight-forward, and the clarity and visibility of the database are improved. Because the relational database-management system (RDBMS) is based on a flexible row-and-table format, this approach is appropriate for most business applications, from the simplest ones built by end users to high-volume applications involving millions of transactions per day built by computer personnel.

An RDBMS also processes records one set at a time. The computer will search for and identify all members of the sought-after set; for example, all past-due accounts. By contrast, hierarchical DBMSs examine each record and identify whether it is past due. If it is not, the system goes to the next record. If overdue, the system sends out a notice. In addition to these time and money-saving attributes, the RDBMS has a formal theoretical foundation which provides rules for structure, maintenance, and integrity (preserving the data against unauthorized changes). More important, organizations can add new data fields, build new access paths, and split tables without disturbing other programs or data stored in the database.

Distributed Database-Management Systems

The RDBMSs increasingly are being pushed from corporate mainframes to department-level computers and local area networks as organizations evolve toward distributed database-management systems (D-DBMSs). The advantages of a D-DBMS is its ability to present information in a transparent manner and in the most appropriate format. A D-DBMS manages data physically located on a number of networked computers, with the logical appearance to the user or applications programmer of a single database. Essentially, a D-DBMS enables users to access information regardless of the hardware or application software used and without having to know where it resides or how to access it. A truly D-DBMS allows users to split up data tables horizontally or vertically and put the fragments on different nodes at different sites. Queries are made exactly as if the information were local.

In a D-DBMS–operating mode, integrity is maintained throughout the database during transactions and during recovery and backup. Control protocols such as two-phase commit provide locking mechanisms that assure that data remain constant. Global-query optimization features automatically select the best means of carrying out complex transactions over local- and wide-area networks, and on-line performance monitors give users a view into the distributed process to allow troubleshooting and system tuning.

Current Movement to Object-Oriented Database-Management Systems

Although RDBMSs have been popular, they are being replaced or supplemented by object-oriented technology. Essentially, the simplicity of the relational model of data and the acceptance of the relational Structured Query Language (SQL) as an industry standard have contributed to its popularity. Even as the acceptance of RDBMSs has spread, their limitations have been exposed by the emergence of various classes of new applications, including design, engineering, multimedia, geographic, scientific, and, more recently, VR. These highly complex applications do not always lend themselves to RDBMS. However, object-oriented database management systems (OODBMSs) are a more universal approach to a multitude of applications that extend beyond the business community.

Currently, *object orientation* is a term whose meaning changes in different situations. End users encounter *objects* in their graphical user interface in the form of icons or other graphical representations of parts of an application. Programmers use object-oriented programming (OOP) languages to write highly modular applications. In an OODBMS developers use *objects* to store complex data, say for CAD/CAM (computer-aided design/computer-aided manufacturing) or geographic information systems (GISs). Object-oriented analysis and design (OOAD) allows programmers to apply design methodologies and use CASE (computer-aided software engineering) tools to create object-oriented programs. In addition, distributed object management provides a way for distributed, heterogeneous applications spread across a wide-area network to communicate and share data. Typically, OODBMSs are interwined with computing activities throughout an organization.

The first users of OODBMSs tended to be engineers who found that relational databases were unable to handle the storage requirements of complex scientific data or CAD drawings. While RDBMSs can store straightforward, predefined, alphanumeric data types, a system for storing scientific data might require the use of a variable-dimension array. A database for CAD drawings would need to preserve the relationships between the lines and angles of the vector graphics within each file. As noted in the prior chapter, CAD drawings are the initial stage of a VR environment.

In a somewhat similar manner, businesses have begun to consider OODBMSs as ways to centralize and simplify the storage of a wide range of complex data, such as text files and mapping data. Some of this information is stored in file systems with the applications that created them; much is still on paper. Business organizations are also expressing interest in OODBMS products for their ability to cut application development backlogs by reducing development time through the reuse of code. As organizations move toward a unified, organization-wide system, they will be able to take a lot of disjointed systems that have been built on an application-by-application basis and will be able to create a single, local perspective on customers or products and services using OODBMSs.

EXTERNAL ON-LINE DATABASES

To assist company personnel in carrying out their duties, a new industry has emerged from vendors focusing on on-line databases. Large banks of information are processed, stored, and delivered electronically. What is provided is not so much additional information (most of it has been around in printed form for a long time), but an improvement in the ease with which information can be retrieved. From this perspective, timely external information is now available for a typical company to meet its daily needs, including its VR needs.

The on-line industry had its roots in small, privately owned bulletin boards, which now number in the thousands. But it is evolving toward a more structured business with a few big mass-market services. Four leading commercial services alone account for over four million users. Both large and small services allow customers to communicate with friends or fellow hobbyists, join discussions, or download sample software programs. But the large networks, including America Online, CompuServe, Prodigy Services Company, and GEnie (run by General Electric), offer a variety of other services, from shopping to travel arrangements to stock trades.

Additionally, there is the Internet, which is the largest computer network in the world, consisting of thousands of smaller regional networks that are interconnected. Hence, the name given is the Internet. Every computer on the Internet has its own unique Internet address. This ad hoc group of private and public networks shares a common computer code and backbone network. To the uninitiated user, Internet travel can be a difficult process because the user must know the correct codes to find his or her way to the right database or electronic library. There are numerous companies that specialize in making this access easy. Still, everything that moves over networks connected by Internet codes travels at a fraction of the cost of traditional carriers. This is due partly to a subsidy from the federal government. Access is low in cost since institutions pay a flat fee and there is no charge per message, though in some cases there is a minimal hourly charge for being hooked up to the network. People who want to buy products, enter an "electronic community," or search a database do not have to do so through Prodigy, CompuServe, or some other commercial service. If they know the right codes, they can enter an Internet address and gain direct access to the service of their choice.

Timely External Information for Business

For timely external information that is oriented toward business firms, the field is crowded with competing companies. Consider just the traditional publishers of financial data. Dow Jones & Company already has several offerings available via computer terminals, including a package that enables investors to learn the value of their portfolio every five minutes or so. Dun & Bradstreet sells on-line some of the printed information that was formerly distributed by mail. McGraw-Hill owns Data Resources, probably the preeminent company in the on-line information field. Other companies with on-line database offerings include ABC, Boeing, Chase Manhattan, Citicorp, Control Data, General Electric, G.T.E., Mead, Time, and Xerox.

A typical service is the Global Report, which is Citibank's round-the-clock information service for executives and their staffs. It specializes in international news, rates, background information, and analysis. Global Report focuses on international business and carries world, country, and regional news; market, industry, and company news; and extensive market coverage, including bonds (corporate, Treasury, European, international, and mortgage-backed municipal), commodities, foreign-exchange rates, funds and trusts, futures, money markets, options, and time-delayed stock prices.

Of all the on-line databases, one of the most widely used by business as well as by government and education is Dialog. The Dialog Information Retrieval Service gives users immediate access to the world's largest and most comprehensive computer storehouse of information. No matter what is needed, useful answers can be found among the more than 100 million references, abstracts, or statistical series from published material that can be searched on-line with Dialog. With an inexpensive terminal or PC (connected via the telephone), users search quickly for the desired information, describing the topic in their own words and using simple English commands to get the results wanted. No programming knowledge is needed to access more than 150 Dialog databases that cover all major disciplines—science, chemistry, technology, medicine, law, business, finance, social sciences, humanities, the arts, public affairs, and general news. In turn, this information may be useful for typical VR business applications.

NEED FOR NEW VIEW OF DATA IN A VR ENVIRONMENT

To handle massive amounts of data needed in a VR environment, forward-thinking companies are exploring new ways to do so. For example, Apple Computer, Hewlett Packard, and IBM are exploring VR systems that require a certain amount of data in the area of scientific visualization by using head-mounted displays (HMDs), DataGloves, speech recognition, and advanced graphics capabilities. In addition, executives, researchers, and scientists at American Express, AT&T, Caterpillar, Electronic Data Systems, Kodak, Nynex, Reuters, and Texas Instruments are exploring the potentials of VR from a viewpoint that is different from the past. As such, data of some type is required to create virtual worlds.

Data Management for VR

The problems found in handling massive amounts of data are not entirely new. Going back to the mid-1970s, MIT's Architecture Machine Group developed the Spatial Data Management System to address the issue in a new and different way. This system projects a wall-sized video image called Dataland. The viewer sits next to two touch-sensitive monitors: one shows an overview of Dataland, the other displays a table of contents of Dataland's "ports of information." By manipulating joysticks and touch pads, the viewer flies above Dataland and drops into those ports. In contrast, almost twenty years later, in the Aerospace Human Factors Research Division of the NASA/Ames Research Center (Mountain View, California), researchers work with their multimillion dollar Virtual Interface Environment Workstation (VIEW). The system incorporates a head-mounted visual display, DataGloves, speech recognition, 3-D and speech synthesis, computer graphics, and video-imaging gear. The workstation was developed mainly for planning space missions. Although astronauts spend much of their time monitoring a spaceship's many electronic systems, VIEW is also an information-management interface. It is used by NASA to research advanced data display and manipulation concepts.

In effect, VIEW expands the Spatial Data Management System's 2-D "dataspace" concept to a 3-D one, in which the viewer flies through "dataspace." NASA uses VIEW to concoct a display environment in which the operator manipulates data and monitors systems organized in the surrounding virtual-display space. Operators enter the virtual environment, verbally announce which data windows they wish to see, use the DataGlove to move those windows around in 3-D, press "buttons" on virtual-control panels, and reconfigure systems. The objective is to develop a workspace with an interface tailored to the operator's skills that can be reconfigured easily for various tasks. In conjunction with this system, NASA is developing technology that allows insertion of live-video windows in the virtual environment to present a mixture of computer-generated backgrounds and video from a remote camera, videodisk, or tape. This could provide a foundation for presenting large informational databases. Since VR is a computer interface, and interactive multimedia, or "hypermedia," incorporate desktop computers, CD-ROM drives, and video and audio technology to provide interfaces to large databases, this technology probably will serve as front end for these databases.[1]

Data Organization for VR

In addition to handling very large amounts of data, VR technology also helps to organize data. Researchers are studying the visualization of database queries and responses in addition to developing models for browsing information spaces. Since organization personnel around the world each day input data in a method modeled after completing paper forms (a nonintuitive task that requires selecting from on-screen menus and that thus invites working by rote), it would be quite helpful to develop new ways of working with computers and their databases. Currently, some desktop VR systems present 3-D carousels to keep track of directories, subdirectories, and files on a disk. Many persons imagine taking this technology further, but the main problem lies in choosing a metaphor for "dataspace." Is there need to put on a DataGlove and goggles to visit a virtual library and walk through that library and among its stacks? Why not, for example, extend the office metaphor. That is, if there is a need to figure the benefits of a retiring employee, one could put on the data goggles, open a virtual file cabinet, retrieve the employee's virtual folder, and touch the data field containing the retirement data, thereby allowing a spreadsheet program to calculate final pay. Would a company employee rather work in a forest, where each tree represents a file and its branches hold records, or in a playground where giant blocks represent batches of files and monkey bars represent data distributed on a 3-D matrix?

Although it is interesting to speculate about VR, it is more important to develop applications that use VR technology and that cut costs and boost productivity than to merely automate tedious tasks, such as record filing. Many company personnel who use a desktop or window environment know how to discard a file or move a window, even if they have not used that particular system before. But there is no metaphor for working in 3-D. There is no interface to match the cognitive structure that people use before they can move to another metaphor. This does not mean that graphic constructs cannot be developed to chart the flow of information, representing that flow with a 3-D matrix of values expressed in position, amount, and color. Hence, VR companies are studying how computers and telecommunications mediate human-interaction patterns.[2]

As can be seen from the above discussion, the issues are new and complex relating to databases necessary within a typical VR environment. To assist the reader in better understanding the database aspects of VR, the next section will present more of their intricacies as they relate to data communications and networking. First, I will present the current state of the art in data communications and networking that utilizes an open-systems architecture and client/server technology—the basic framework for a company's day-to-day operations.

CURRENT ENVIRONMENT FOR DATA COMMUNICATIONS AND NETWORKING

In order to realize the full potential of VR (as discussed in this text), it is necessary to look beyond its technology and data requirements by establishing a fundamental framework that will facilitate the development of virtual worlds. Such a framework is found in *open systems*, which allows users to retrieve data locally that may be found halfway around the world. In addition, *client/server technology* is helpful since it is the next step in the way in which computers and networking technologies are applied. Because both are important, they are discussed below.

Open-Systems Architecture

Today, computer managers are being asked continually to manage more and more of the information technology—that is, hardware, software, and networks—in their organizations. They must develop the ability to reach beyond the mainframe-oriented data center, into an end-user domain filled with a diversity of PCs, departmental systems, and networks, as well as a mélange of software tools and applications. And they must be prepared to make the elements of this mixture work together. No longer can computer managers think of a single vendor or hardware or a single operating system. Currently, they need to find ways to integrate an expanding assortment of computing products and services, including VR, to meet the demands of enterprise-wide and even interenterprise information in a competitive environment that has expanded to a global scale. Such an approach is found in an open-systems environment.

Open systems implement specifications for interfaces, services, and supporting formats that enable properly engineered application software to be ported across systems, interoperate with other applications, and interact with users in a consistent manner. To place open systems in perspective, large retailers, such as Wal-Mart, Kmart, Dayton Hudson, and Sears, manage inventory by linking them to manufacturers as if in a single network. While this open-systems approach eliminates the advantages of a supplier's proprietary network, it also gives manufacturers valuable information. These retailers provide manufacturers with updated sales and inventory information electronically so that they can plan production. With such data arriving in a standard format from so many customers, a manufacturer like Levi Strauss or Vanity Fair can easily estimate aggregate demand weeks in advance and produce sales forecasts to help manufacturers plan production even further in advance. This capability can be very helpful to a company desiring to take the analysis one step further by using VR technology.

From another perspective, system vendors previously dictated how the pieces were put together in a data-communications and networking structure. However, open systems is a change in the power relationship between the user and the vendor. Open systems is about users controlling their destinies, being in charge of what gets purchased and installed, and mandating that the vendors make sure it works together well. Thus, companies are more in the driver's seat in an open-systems environment.

Client/Server Architecture

A client/server is a computing architecture in which any device in a network can request information or processing services from any other. When a device is asking for data or processing power, it is a *client*. When it is supplying information or services, it is a *server*. As such, client/server architectures provide users transparent access to file servers, database servers, print servers, and other devices, thereby maximizing user options and network throughput while minimizing operating costs and response time over the network. The client/server model is a powerful method for writing applications that partition the program into pieces installed in two or more separate network stations. Tools built for implementing applications in this way allow program parts developed independently to interoperate over a network.

In reference to improving payoff for information and VR technology, client/server makes sense because it helps organizations maximize their extensive investments in processing power—from the desktop to the mainframe. Client/server architecture only makes sense if it is appropriate for all organizational applications. There are a number of factors for the shift to client/server computing. The most important ones are networks, standards, and the tremendous power and versatility of today's desktop devices. Currently, no single vendor can supply all the pieces to make client/server computing a reality. A good test of how well a vendor is positioned to meet an organization's client/server needs is to examine how open the company's product line is. Open-computing, software, and network tools are the plug-and-play components that are the foundation of client/server architecture.

CURRENT APPROACH TO DATA COMMUNICATIONS AND NETWORKING

As information technology is moving in the direction of networks to support mission-crucial as well as VR applications, it has raised the importance of managing data communications and networking. The complexity of tools, information, people, and processes needed to build, operate, and monitor networks has become visible to more and more users throughout the organization. The way an organization approaches the design, implementation, and operation of data communications and networking can make or break the quality of its network services. More than ever, networks of all types—whether they be local area networks, metropolitan area networks, or a combination of these (which are discussed below)—are at the very heart of a company's operations. They must be managed with greater levels of reliability and service quality today as well as in the future.

LOCAL AREA NETWORKS

Local area networks (LANs) meet the increasingly vital need to interconnect computers, terminals, word processors, facsimile and other office machines within a building, campus, or a very small geographic area. A LAN may be designed to support only one vendor's terminal equipment, or it may be designed for multivendor support. Network logic may be embedded in the terminal equipment, in bus/network interface units, or in central controllers. Overall, LANs are flexible and cost-effective tools, compared to computer mainframes, that greatly expand the variety of services that can be performed by PCs and workstations. A model based on the International Standards Organization's Open-Systems Interconnection (OSI) helps explain the software and hardware characteristics of LANs. Fundamentally, the OSI model describes the seven layers of activity for typical LAN communications.

Wiring of Local Area Networks

Underlying any LAN is the physical wire connecting computing devices. Some LANs use either coaxial cable or twisted-pair wire. Each has advantages and disadvantages, depending on the particular application. A LAN that uses coaxial cable—Ethernet, for example—can link more than one thousand devices in a single network. It can carry data transmission with a bandwidth of up to 100 megabits per second (Mbps). Generally, the greater the bandwidth, the more information that can be sent through a system in a given amount of time. The high bandwidth offered by coaxial cable, therefore, is a safe choice for a LAN that may be required to perform many transmission functions among many users. A high bandwidth is also needed to accommodate video signals or to transfer very large files, such as extensive spreadsheets.

Fiber-optic cable is a somewhat newer alternative to both coaxial and twisted pair. It offers higher bandwidth than both. Not only is the fiber-optic cable used for LANs, but it is also often used to connect separate LANs that are located at some distance from each other. Moreover, fiber optics are useful for LAN situations where there are data security problems with electromagnetic interference. Compared to copper-wire and coaxial cable, fiber cable is relatively immune from tampering and interference from electromagnetic radiation.

Fiber-optic networks are typically used as backbone links connecting islands of office networks, minicomputers, or shared peripherals. Fiber links are also employed as point-to-point data highways connecting computer mainframes to distributed systems or other LANs. In such applications, high bandwidth and distance—fiber links can stretch as far as four kilometers unrepeated—are the prime considerations. Even in office applications, fiber is preferable to copper wires because it suffers no bandwidth degradation owing to signal reflection and is easier to maintain.

Wireless Local Area Networks

Today, wireless LANs are emerging as an important addition to present-day offerings of wired LANs because of cost, compatibility, and ease-of-use issues. Although wireless networks are unlikely to replace wire-based systems (as set forth above), they offer an attractive alternative for those persons who are looking to add new users to corporate LANs and to support mobile workers who telecommute from far-flung locations. Within a wireless-network operating mode, there are two kinds. Wide-area wireless networks, like cellular and public packet-switching wireless networks, cover relatively long distances (metropolitan areas) with modest data-communications performance. On the other hand, local-area wireless networks cover a shorter distance (a floor of a building or a corporate campus), but offer a much higher bandwidth.

GLOBAL NETWORKS

Going beyond the confines of a LAN that exists within a building or several buildings in proximity to one another, there are metropolitan area networks (MANs). A MAN is of limited geographic range, generally defined as within a fifty-mile radius. In the past, a number of small companies have begun business by installing fiber-optic cable in metropolitan business areas. Their primary customers are companies of all sizes that need to communicate within the metropolitan area. The customer is usually responsible for providing equipment. The primary market is the customer that needs a lot of high-speed digital service. The MAN providers typically offer lower prices than the telephone companies and offer diverse routing as well as backup in emergency conditions. Because of the pressing need to link a typical organization with other organizations locally, nationally, or internationally, the discussion below takes this important direction into account.

Today, wide-area networks (WANs) are generally considered to be those that cover a large geographic area, require the crossing of public right-of-ways, and use circuits provided by a common carrier. Wide area networks may be made up of a combination of switched and leased, terrestrial and satellite, and private microwave circuits. The WAN for a large multinational company may be global, whereas the WAN for a small company may cover only several cities or counties. General Electric, for example, has a private global network to transmit voice, data, and video signals to its offices in twenty-five countries. If there is a need to tie in with a MAN provider, a LAN-MAN-WAN link can be provided for a typical organization.

To overcome difficulties experienced by users in WANs, there is a need for a new approach, that is, the farther the computer is from the data, the harder it is for the user to get to it. This is especially true if the computer is found in another city or across the nation. Trading the security and relative speed of a LAN for the sluggishness and uncertainty of a WAN creates unforeseen data bottlenecks and administrative headaches. A new universal network transport mechanism, called asynchronous transfer mode (ATM), gives the user easier access between a Token Ring or Ethernet LAN and such wide-area mechanisms as T1 and X.25. By providing a common infrastructure that is suitable for everything from desktop and LAN applications to campus, metropolitan, and global networks, ATM offers a new direction in network technology.

Until recently, LAN and WAN technologies have approached data transmission differently. The driving force behind ATM is a new class of applications involving voice, video, multimedia, imaging, and client/server functions. These broadband applications demand much higher network capacity than the traditional personal-productivity, on-line–transaction-processing, and database programs. The disparity between LAN and WAN transport protocols makes it difficult to create broadband enterprise networks. Regarded as a universal protocol for high-speed networking, ATM has been chosen by the CCITT (Consultative Committee of International Telegraph and Telephone—the international data communications standards organization) as the transport-layer protocol for emerging broadband integrated-services digital networks (BISDNs). The basic integrated-services digital network will be discussed later in the chapter.

Wireless Wide Area Networks

Wireless WANs are being put to use in a variety of applications although current technology limitations make wireless WANs unsuitable for many applications now common on LANs and internetworks. That is, wireless services are well suited mainly for applications that involve short, burstlike messages. Wireless data networks already have become a crucial advantage in many industries. An example is the courier industry. In the late 1970s, Federal Express Corporation revolutionized the overnight delivery business by building a private wireless network to track its packages. The Federal Express network was not low in cost. It cost the courier hundreds of millions of dollars but helped propel the company to the front of a very competitive industry.

Although wireless WAN services are found in organizations of varying sizes, the next few years will be crucial in deciding how important such services become in corporate networks. One of the most important issues that must be resolved is the matter of standards. Today's wireless WANs are based on proprietary technology even though several carriers have thrown open their systems to third-party developers. Until standards are in place, many organizations will be reluctant to make major commitments to wireless WANs. As is the usual case with all standards, progress is slow toward the development of standards for wireless WAN systems and equipment.

INTEGRATED-SERVICES DIGITAL NETWORKS

One way of bringing together the preceding discussion on data communications and networking is to think of total communications for a typical organization. Although this can take many directions, only one is discussed below because of space limitations. The focus is on integrated-services digital networks (ISDNs) that can provide users with a total network in which compatible voice, data, and video configurations will be transported on a single pair of wires, eliminating leased-line and digital circuits for data, voice lines for telecommunications, and cable services for video. It can offer users a multifaceted communications network to transmit and receive information worldwide. The concept of ISDN is that of a standard protocol that is used for linking private and public networks in order to receive and transmit digital information. Compatibility stems from predetermined standards, allowing all types of equipment to interface provided that they are manufactured to accepted standards.

The ultimate goal of ISDN is to combine all of the telecommunications services that are currently being provided by different networks into one large-scale network. Services to be offered through ISDN include telephone services (call forwarding, transferring, conference calling, automatic wake-up calling), data services (closed user groups, called- and calling-line identification, multi-address calling), teletext services (delayed messages, multiple addressing, Telex access, and a graphic mode), facsimile services (delayed delivery and multiple designations), and video-text services (transactions, such as reservations and shopping, and special-character sets). In preparing for ISDN, companies need to consider whether their current data-communications decisions are compatible with an evolution to ISDN-based communications. In addition, companies should examine their internal structure for planning voice, data, and office facilities to ensure that internal conflicts between separate voice and data departments are minimized.

In summary, ISDN is an international network architecture that offers a standard universal interface for voice, data, and video, thereby allowing highly efficient, interactive use of the public telephone network. In contrast, Open-Network Architecture (ONA) is a regulatory development that will allow specialty information services, such as messaging, E-mail, security, and answering services, to take place over a local telephone network. Although the implementation time of ISDN and ONA technologies is uncertain, it would depend in large part on public demand. But their impact on the PC user throughout the 1990s will be felt. One probable effect of this implementation will be increasing numbers of at-home workers, including executives. Without immediate access to the workplace, *telecommunicating* on a widespread basis was not possible before now; but this will change as network communication from the home, without special cabling or transmission facilities, will enable a person to function as if in a company-owned office. Thus, a home computer will begin to assume the importance of an essential storage and communications device, much like the telephone. The public telephone network will be asked to transport this information.

OTHER IMPORTANT DATA-COMMUNICATIONS AND NETWORKING TECHNOLOGIES

Complementary to the preceding discussion are E-mail systems, voice-messaging and speech-recognition systems, video conferencing, and the information highway, which are discussed below. If fast and accurate communications are needed and overnight couriers and telexes are too expensive in volume, there is need to consider E-mail. Because E-mail distributes messages from one computer to another, transactions are very fast, are cost effective, and run twenty-four hours a day. This is especially helpful across time zones. Some E-mail systems even offer the ability to transfer entire desktop publishing programs, recalculable spreadsheets, revisable word-processing documents, and updatable databases—something a facsimile (fax) machine will never do. To use E-mail, the user enters the system and types a message. Tagged with an electronic address, the message is then transmitted to a ''mailbox''—a point in the main computer's memory where it is stored until called up. The message can be funneled into the PC of a specified system user or sent to a middle person who can print and deliver the message. Because a typical E-mail works through PCs, a user can work up a document on a PC and send it instantaneously without the hassles of couriers or post-office schedules.

Currently, there are over 6 million E-mail subscribers in the United States. Communication is increasingly available for companies with as few as six locations through public E-mail systems, such as Western Union's EasyLink, Dial-com, and MCI Mail. All of these firms are integrating E-mail with other telecommunications methods, enabling the computer to transmit via fax, telex, or cablegram—almost unlimited information- and communications-delivery-capabilities. Electronic-mail subscribers can often get access to a variety of public databases, financial-reporting services, news-clipping services, and news wires. Western Union, for instance, offers FYI News, a service that provides up-to-the-minute reports on business, finance, politics, entertainment, and more.

For company employees wishing to receive, use, and distribute calls and messages, *voice messaging* can be helpful for meeting that need and can dramatically speed up the communication process and make it more accurate. Essentially, voice-messaging technology eliminates intervention between a caller and the intended message recipient. Messages incorrectly taken, lost, or forgotten are becoming a thing of the past. With a high-quality voice-messaging system, company employees have to make only one telephone call to retrieve all their messages. In essence, voice messaging can be at the hub of all potential communication centers: business, home, car, pager, E-mail, telephone answering service, fax machine, and push-button telephone. Voice messaging connects all of these spokes into one central message system, thereby saving the executive time, money, and energy.

A related area to voice-messaging systems is *speech-recognition systems.* Speech-recognition software packages have two basic purposes: either accepting voice commands to streamline the operation of the computer or taking verbal dictation that can be saved as a text document. The former class basically accepts verbal input to activate macros, many matching spoken words to a list of menu commands. For example, Voice Blaster from Covox automatically creates a list of an application's menu items; the user trains the software to respond to his or her voice as commands are spoken. The program requires a sound card, yet supplies a microphone-and-earphone headset. All in all, it is expected that speech products in the coming years will be mature enough to warrant serious consideration for everyday business use.

Videoconferencing, which is available for business units that are widely dispersed geographically, is designed for use as a business tool to assist in overseeing dispersed operations. There are two distinct types of videoconferencing. The first type, ''person-to-person,'' links one PC to another, thereby allowing two people to share moving pictures and some type of shared work space. Usually these systems transmit postage-size images over ISDN, regular phone lines, or Switch-56 via a little video camera mounted on the monitor. The second type is ''group-to-group'' videoconferencing that tries to merge two or more conference rooms. Large monitors, multiple microphones, and dedicated transmission lines are usually required for this type of sharing, resulting in better picture and sound quality than person-to-person videoconferencing. Of course, the cost is much higher.

In group-to-group videoconferencing, there can be an exchange of ideas that involves company personnel of distant operations. The accent may be on a free exchange of potential answers to specific questions that arise in the normal course of conversation. From this perspective, the interaction of participants at distant points from one another may signal the need to develop specific computer programs for answering the questions posed. At the next videoconferencing meeting, a presentation can be made that focuses on potential answers to the important business questions posed earlier.

Currently, several vendors are offering public rooms or sharing their private rooms with others. The public-room concept, pioneered by AT&T, is offered under the name of Picturephone Meeting Service (PMS). Offered from a number of public rooms, PMS can be rented on an hourly basis. Besides having its public PMS, AT&T also installs private rooms that are compatible with the public ones. For instance, AT&T works cooperatively with companies such as Hilton Hotels and the World Trade Center in New York to provide videoconferencing rooms, and US Sprint supplies for-hire videoconferencing rooms for companies that are not ready to install their own facilities. Many large corporations are currently making use of private broadcasts by satellite directly into their own facilities or into hotel meeting facilities to deliver corporate communications or training to employees. As they have gained experience with the use of corporate video, companies have installed their own private networks of satellite receiver dishes, located at their corporate facilities, that enable employees to watch regularly scheduled company programs.

There are many benefits from utilizing videoconferencing. First, there is a reduction in travel costs. By eliminating many trips, a company cuts out the unproductive time people spend on traveling, thereby resulting in increased productivity. The ability to hold a meeting almost instantly in a relaxed atmosphere, with less time away from office and home, has removed a lot of stress often involved with meetings. In addition, videoconferences enable the company to involve more people in meetings. These individuals might include experts or scientists, who would rather be at work in their labs than traveling to a meeting.

EMERGENCE OF THE NATIONAL INFORMATION HIGHWAY

At this time, the Internet is the closest network that the United States has to a national information highway (i.e., the National Information Infrastructure), sometimes referred to as the electronic highway, the digital expressway, or just plain "cyberspace." This ad hoc computer network was started in the late 1960s by the Defense Department. Fundamentally, two events converged to create the Internet: technology and necessity. The technology was the packet-switched networking. The necessity was the perceived threat of thermonuclear war, that is, the U.S. Air Force was interested in building a computer network that stood a chance of surviving a major attack. Therefore, the Air Force built a network without a central control point so that it could lose one, or several, computers and the computers remaining could still communicate with each other. This led to the creation of the ARPANET, the progenitor of today's Internet.

The Internet, which was briefly noted earlier in the chapter, has basically become the postal service, telephone system, and research library of the electronic age, thereby allowing millions of people to exchange information virtually anywhere in the world and at any time, usually in a matter of minutes, using available data-communications and networking technology. The source of the Internet's appeal is that anyone on the Internet can post and retrieve information, but the practical result, which is often frustrating to businesses accustomed to logical hierarchy and ordering, is that there is no defined or enforced structure for posting that information. As a result, experienced Internet users generally have difficulty when trying to retrieve information.

Although establishing a direct connection to the Internet is difficult, it is becoming easier as more commercial Internet service providers spring up to meet the growing demand from businesses and as increasingly powerful computers and software make it possible to hide the Internet's Unix command system behind graphical, point-and-shoot interfaces like Mosaic (a free software program developed with federal financing by the National Center for Supercomputing Applications) or even Microsoft Windows. The catch is that one cannot use such graphical tools with a simple Internet gateway, like CompuServe or MCI Mail. It requires a direct Internet link, which adheres to the special Internet communications rules, or a dedicated high-speed phone line that can cost hundreds of dollars a month. At this time, the Internet is not the final national information highway, but a forerunner or prototype of the futuristic superhighway that is being proposed by private industry and the federal government.

The ultimate goal of the national information highway in the twenty-first century is to develop an information infrastructure that will enable all Americans to access information and communicate with each other easily, reliably, securely, and cost effectively in any medium, whether it be voice, data, image, or video, at anytime and anywhere. The net result is that this capability will enhance the productivity of work and will lead to significant improvements in education, social services, and entertainment. While Europe and Japan have government-subsidized programs to advance existing and future communications modernization, the United States has a long-standing course of marketplace-driven technology development by private industry. Current thinking is that there should be a cooperative relationship between private industry and the federal government to develop the national information highway of the next century.

Today, the technology exists to get started on this intended goal of the national information highway. Many of the enabling technologies for such a venture are emerging across a wide range of products and services. Fiber-optic systems, for example, are finding their way into millions of homes as cable operators and telecom providers race to upgrade their services. New technology ventures are realizing the power of multimedia data as well as cellular and wireless communication. The established hardware and software vendors along with information providers themselves, from entertainment and publishing firms to government agencies and universities, are encouraged by the possibilities of using the new technology to meet the challenges of the national information highway. An overview of the national information highway infrastructure is found in Figure 5.1.

In the area of data communications and networking, the cable and telecommunications carriers' laying of fiber-optic cable coupled with the utilization of so-called broadband services such as ATM, Synchronous Optical Network (SO-

Figure 5.1
Linkage of Suppliers of Information to the Home within a National Information Highway Environment

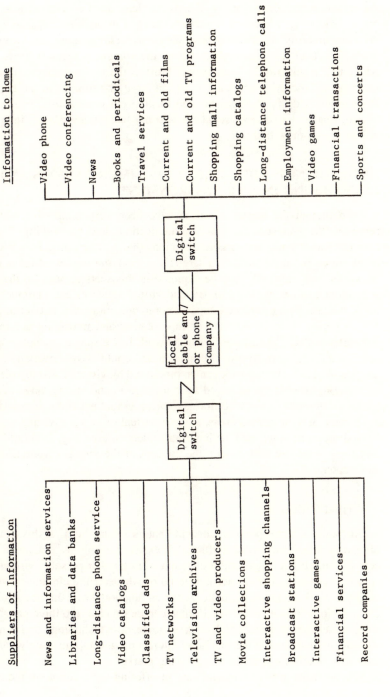

Suppliers of Information

- News and information services
- Libraries and data banks
- Long-distance phone service
- Video catalogs
- Classified ads
- TV networks
- Television archives
- TV and video producers
- Movie collections
- Interactive shopping channels
- Broadcast stations
- Interactive games
- Financial services
- Record companies

Digital switch

Local cable and/or phone company

Digital switch

Information to Home

- Video phone
- Video conferencing
- News
- Books and periodicals
- Travel services
- Current and old films
- Current and old TV programs
- Shopping mall information
- Shopping catalogs
- Long-distance telephone calls
- Employment information
- Video games
- Financial transactions
- Sports and concerts

NET), ISDN, and Switched Multimegabit Digital Service (SMDS) will supply the infrastructure for a variety of new services, such as video-on-demand and on-line shopping. Moreover, a renewed interest in satellite transmission and the growing maturity of wireless technology will complement the terrestrial network. However, as important as all of the foregoing technology is, it is the whole that counts on the bottom line. Most of these providers are forming partnerships, alliances, agreements, and even large investments in the hope of creating industry de facto standards and locking out competition. Hence, the true bottom line is the issue of standards and not technology per se since the technology exists or will shortly.

NEED FOR NEW VIEW OF DATA COMMUNICATIONS AND NETWORKING IN A VR ENVIRONMENT

Even though the above advances have been very impressive, they do not represent the end state in data communications and networking. Newer data communications and networking directions that will be useful in a VR environment are on the near horizon. There is a current and important focus on virtual networks. Not only will they be explored in this section, but also the problems with them will be investigated. Beyond virtual networks are a number of newer areas that are being explored by data-communications and networking experts. For example, there is the idea of representing and managing communication networks in 3-D ''dataspace.'' The network has a spatial metaphor that could provide a framework to move around in and could show flows and switch situations. As such, the network can be monitored by virtually visiting the network, recognizing trouble spots as red flashing objects and seeing ways of rerouting traffic as alternate tunnels.[3] Before exploring virtual networks, it would be helpful to look at their related areas, namely, virtual offices and virtual workgroups. This discussion concludes with virtual videoconferencing. It should be noted that these areas are tied in with the concept of the virtual corporation set forth in Chapter 1.

Virtual Offices

Currently, a very popular concept that is taking hold in this country and abroad is called the ''virtual office.'' It exists, but only as a concept. One person's virtual office is generally different from another person's virtual office. It is whatever the individual needs it to be or whatever the circumstances warrant it to be. Working in the virtual office is as functional as using the equipment in the traditional office. The virtual office can be divided into three parts: telecommution, self-employment, and work at home. The technology and a number of vendors are supporting the increased interest by developing widely varied products specifically targeted to this growing market.

Several firms are now specializing in offering the technology required for a virtual office. For example, Digital Telemedia (New York City) has figured out how to make money from the merger of telephone and computer technologies. This consulting firm helps companies set up high-speed communication lines to their clients' computer centers. Essentially, this can be called computer engineered VR. This, then, is Telemedia's virtual office, run with pocket pagers, laptop computers, and phone services. And Telemedia is showing other companies how to use digital-communications technology to replace old, paper-based ways of doing business. Some clients now process in hours what takes some other companies days to finish.

The concept of a virtual office can be found at the corporate headquarters of Chiat/Day, one of the world's leading full-service advertising agencies. A virtual office was implemented as part of a corporate emphasis on continually enhancing client service, improving staff satisfaction and creativity, and boosting bottom-line results. Essentially, the company has created a "team architecture" by taking 125,000 square feet of space that used to be subdivided into conference rooms and cubicles and compartmentalizing it by activity. Within these activity areas, separate project rooms are established for each of several entrepreneurial strategic business units that now service individual clients. While the team architecture that underlies Chiat/Day's virtual office idea is not new, its full implementation had to await the arrival of appropriate office technology required for success. In the final analysis, the key to successful implementation of team architecture is the availability of technology tools that expedite remote access to corporate computing and telecommunications resources. Staff members are no longer assigned to a department but to a client. And rather than work in specific offices assigned to any given department, each strategic business unit is assigned a project room where staff in that specific unit can work.[4]

Virtual Work Groups

Virtual work groups were somewhat of a dream years ago until the arrival of data communications and networking on a widespread basis. The idea is simple since true work groups do not necessarily sit together at adjacent desks but are often spread across the building, across the country, and sometimes across the world. And many true work groups are so "virtual" that some members of the groups are on the move much of the time, visiting corporate branches, making customer calls, attending executive retreats, and going on vacation. To accomplish this task, many companies utilize Notes (from the Lotus Corporation). Essentially, virtual work groups are people who might, in fact, be quite distant from one another, not all of whom can be found in the same seat every morning. In other words, people are bound into a group that is defined, not by geography, but by the task at hand. The life of these groups can be very short or very long, depending on the task undertaken. For example, firms like Texas Instruments and Boeing are building the virtual work group with the information network, thereby pulling their engineers around the world into computerized meetings.

On the other hand, the Chrysler Corporation engineers automobiles twenty-four hours a day, that is, eight hours in Detroit, eight in Asia, and eight in Europe. The engineering project moves by computer from place to place.

Virtual Networks

The virtual LAN started as a far-out concept associated with ATM networks of the future. Now it has evolved into a technology that is implemented in traditional LAN internetworking products. Essentially, virtual LANs (VLANs) are logical groupings of network addresses organized independently of the physical networks they reside on. In other words, a VLAN is the ability to make the network configuration transparent so that users can communicate freely without knowledge of the network. The objectives of VLAN technology are threefold: (1) to provide and manage scarce bandwidth for the high-performance applications like graphics, CAD/CAM, and multimedia that are seen on current networks; (2) to separate the logical-network management from the physical-network infrastructure; and (3) to facilitate network node moves, adds, and changes. At their best, VLANs transcend both physical networks and geography, thereby allowing network administrators to change logical configurations and manage bandwidth as needs dictate.

Some vendors are promoting hubs that permit the creation of VLANs. For example, Alantec and Ungermann-Bass sell hubs that support VLANs. With this new generation of hubs, network managers can design LAN work groups that are determined by software rather than by the physical connection of cables or wires. The hubs make it easier to move a user from one LAN segment to another. The older alternative was to physically unplug and move wires within the hub—a time-consuming and tedious task.[5] As shown in Figure 5.2, switched hubs allow for the creation of VLANs whereby networks of users are grouped by function rather than by physical location and are derived from software tables rather than from regular physical connections.

Currently, there are networks in operation that fit the definition of VR. For example, two people are connected via some type of network and can display anything they like, thus interacting with each other. The Sense8 Corporation has a networked version with Ethernet connectivity. With it, the same worlds are on both machines and information is sent between them. Within such a network, information can be exchanged between countries around the world. The NEC corporation has been internally demonstrating transfer of virtual world information between sites equipped with DataGloves and 3-D glasses and at speeds of at least 56 kilobits per second. And ATR's (Advanced Telecommunications Research, located near Osaka, Japan) Tele-existence project plans to send gigabits of information to very large databases by the end of the century in order to provide true "telepresence." Essentially, the person sitting across from you is not really there but at some other place in the world.[6]

Researchers at the Virtual Universe Corporation have developed a prototype

Figure 5.2
Switched Hubs and the Creation of Virtual LANs

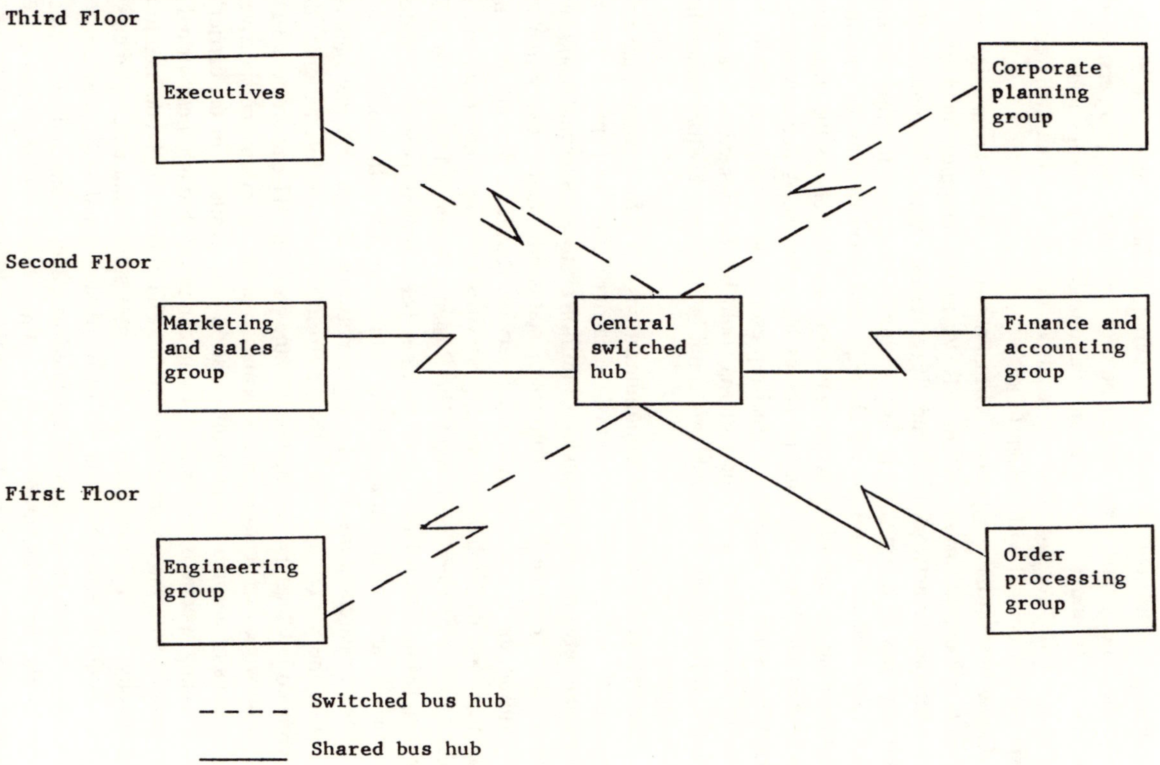

Third Floor

Second Floor

First Floor

Corporate
planning
group

Finance and
accounting
group

Order
processing
group

Central
switched
hub

Executives

Marketing
and sales
group

Engineering
group

- - - Switched bus hub

——— Shared bus hub

of a network hub that employs VR technology. The device, housed in a Sun workstation running on the Unix operating system and supported by a pair of 486-based PCs, is expected to have immediate implications for CAD applications. Using the Virtual Universe system, designers will be able to perform modeling functions in virtual space, avoiding the cumbersome clay-modeling process. Other prime users would be architects and city planners, who would be able to simulate city streets and the designs of buildings and other aspects of urban infrastructure. The net result is that the product will reduce travel expenses associated with design tasks.[7]

Going beyond these aspects of virtual networks, a most promising use of VR is *network management*. Using VR to model complex networks may be considerable for network managers. It serves as a way of communicating complex services in a way that is easy to understand, and it helps the network's staff to model the ways in which requested services may be provided. The customer has an idea of the services needed, and this shows the customer a view of how a telephone company perceives the network. A network manager, for example, could fly around a virtual representation of a global WAN. Network trouble spots and even traffic patterns could be represented as colors, hues, or sounds. It is possible that problems could be anticipated before rather than after they happen.

Researchers at British Telecommunications (BT), for example, are using VR to simplify network management of the carrier's complex network. The national telephone network of BT includes 25 million customer lines and 6,000 switching centers that generate five megabytes of status information every five minutes. In addition, the voice, data, and video services that BT offers are growing more complex, and its Global Networking Services for corporate customers involve links to other carriers' networks. The Systems Research Division at BT Laboratories (Martlesham Heath, England) has been looking at ways to reduce that complexity and has found a potential solution in VR software.

These researchers are developing a network design and management tool based on the Superscape VR software (from Dimension International) that was referenced in Chapter 4. Using this desktop package, BT can create a 3-D model of its network that lets engineers visualize status from any perspective, using the masses of net-management information now available in the carrier's databases. Using special input devices, users can move through these virtual worlds and interact with the objects they contain. The objects can be defined to behave realistically, thereby responding to either user stimulus or external-data sources.

The model is arranged in layers of increasing detail and complexity. At the upper layers, the network is represented as cubes connected by lines. At the lower levels, the cubes can represent buildings, rooms, or single pieces of equipment. An operator navigates through the model by using a trackball. Moreover, Superscape offers "emotional cubes," that is, cubes that indicate how they should be treated by users. Cubes, for example, that represent failure-prone parts of a network can be made to shake nervously, while "shy" cubes containing sensitive data can be made to shrink away from users as they approach. British Telecommunications says visualization is a big improvement over its current graphical user interfaces, which often require users to shuffle and expand pop-up windows. In fact, the carrier thinks VR could prove helpful whenever very complex issues must be addressed.

An important aspect of this VR-modeling technique used by BT is its ability to integrate a multitude of real external-data sources into the virtual world. Another feature of the network model is the ability to find optimal routes by selecting beginning and end points on the network. The system also has the potential for collaborative problem solving, that is, as many as eight users can simultaneously inhabit the network model. Each can observe different aspects, or one user can guide another's view so that both see the same thing. In addition to BT, researchers at Bellcore (Livingston, New Jersey) are trying out VR technology to help analyze problems with Signaling System No. 7 that have crashed whole sections of public networks in the United States and other countries.[8]

In the military, a most important virtual network is SIMNET (Simulation Network). The Defense Advanced Research Projects Agency (DARPA) and the U.S. Army initiated a project in 1984 to construct a large prototype of a low-cost, networked, team-training environment. Completed in 1989, SIMNET consists of over two hundred tanks, personnel carriers, and aircraft simulators with four-person crews, at approximately ten sites in the United States and Europe. These four-person simulators are linked via high-speed telecommunications and interact with the same simulated battlefield in real time. Crews of the M-1 see their own instruments and, through the tank's viewpoints, see the ever-changing terrain of the battlefield, including other tanks controlled by other simulator-based tank crews. Furthermore, planes, helicopters, and other military hardware can participate from other simulators. What results is a full-scale war game like no other—hundreds of soldiers training and playing against each other in a simulated battle on an open and changing terrain without ever leaving a building.

The hardware of SIMNET is mostly off-the-shelf, with the exception of the fiberglass simulator shells and the image generators. Standard Ethernet was used as the communications system. The software was the innovative part. Essentially, SIMNET is a large arcade game whose graphics and sound system are surpassed in most commercial arcade games. There is no motion base. The databases are large but without much detail. The unique feature of SIMNET is the networking, that is, the synergy of having several hundred people playing the same game at the same time. Its success is a human-interface phenomenon more than a purely technical one.[9]

Virtual Videoconferencing

Virtual reality, as discussed as some length in this text, is a man-machine symbiosis in which computer-generated reality senses the user's movements and changes accordingly. From this view, VR applications might include VR videoconferencing, in which participants attend meetings without leaving their homes. From one perspective, users could put on a VR helmet and use the 6DOF tracking ball to meet other participants in "cyberspace." The user would be presented with an image of a conference room; moving the head would be similar to looking around an ordinary conference room. The participants would be able to see each other. They would be able to converse as though they were in the same room as well as view slides, videos, animations, and recordings. Users would be able to establish their own parameters for their personal appearance and sound.

Today, a system could be developed to fit a company's needs by using the above VR approach. However, current software is available to users who desire a low-cost alternative to a full-blown VR version. Such an approach is found in the Virtual Meeting System (VMS) package. This software (from RTZ Software) is a set of four programs that synchronize a presentation and permit participants to ask questions or illustrate their points using Apple-events-aware applications or VMS's own white-board-like draw program, which lets everybody in the conference see what the presenter draws.

Conference participants install a conference application, a QuickTime movie-and-slide player, and the white-board program, along with presentation files (which must be distributed before each conference takes place). A conference server on a separate computer manages and broadcasts the presentation and can be controlled by any participant. The Virtual Meeting System requires System 7 and costs several thousand dollars for the first ten users and several hundred dollars for each additional user.[10]

SUMMARY

Because VR technology gives users direct experience rather than just information, there is need for more than just hardware and software to effect viable business applications. In this chapter, I not only discussed the fundamentals of databases, data communications, and networking, but also those factors that are essential to developing a VR environment. In turn, this background will be helpful in gaining an understanding of how to build VR systems in the next chapter as well as the VR applications set forth in the remainder of the text.

NOTES

1. Linda Jacobson, "Virtual Reality: A Status Report," *AI Expert*, August 1991, pp. 26–30.

2. Ibid., pp. 31–33.

3. Ibid., p. 32.

4. "Virtual Office Runs on Telecommunications," *Managing Office Technology*, June 1994, pp. 57–58.

5. Andrew Collier, "Virtual LAN Strategy," *Communications Week*, September 27, 1993, pp. 1, 59.

6. Thomas J. Hargadon, "Network Virtual Reality and Other Visions," *The Office*, May 1992, p. 24.

7. Nattalia Lea, "Calgary Researchers Start Work on Virtual 'Hub,' " *Computing Canada*, September 28, 1992.

8. "A Virtual Reality Check for Net Management," *Data Communications*, June 1993, p. 13.

9. J. Michael Moshell and Richard Dunn-Roberts, "A Survey of Virtual Environments: Research in North America, Part Two," *Virtual Reality World*, January–February 1994, pp. 27–29.

10. Carolyn Bickford, "The Virtual Power Lunch," *Macworld*, June 1993, p. 77.

Bibliography for Part II

Alesandrini, K. "Voice Messaging Can Improve Productivity." *The Office*, September 1992.

Alpert, M. "CD-ROM: The Next PC Revolution." *Fortune*, June 29, 1992.

Anonymous. "Virtual Reality: Spreadsheets for Industry." *Release 1.0*, October 8, 1990.

———. "Create with Sense8." *AI Expert*, May 1992.

———. "Virtual Reality as Videoconference." *Digital Media: A Seybold Report*, August 17, 1992.

———. "VR Design Becomes Craft at Worldesign." *Digital Media*, November 10, 1992.

———. "Multimedia: Autodesk Ships Cyberspace Developer Kit; C++ Toolset Provides Object-Oriented Framework for VR Applications." *EDGE: Work-Group Computing Report*, March 1, 1993.

———. "A Virtual Check for Net Management." *Data Communications*, June 1993.

———. "Virtual Office Runs on Telecommunications." *Managing Office Technology*, June 1994.

Appleton, E. L. "Thinking Machines." *DEC Professional*, November 1993.

Baker, S. "Internet Navigation Tools." *Unix Review*, June 1994.

Barr, C. "Virtual Reality Goes Mainstream." *PC Magazine*, April 28, 1992.

Benedikt, M., ed. *Cyberspace: First Steps*. Boston: MIT Press, 1992.

Bickford, C. "The Virtual Power Lunch." *Macworld*, June 1993.

Biedny, D. "High-End 3-D Lands on the Desktop." *Newmedia Magazine*, September 1994.

Binda, L. A. "3 Pioneers on the Information Superhighway." *Open Systems Today*, June 6, 1994.

Bragg, T. "Together/C++." *Software Development*, July 1994.

Brill, L. M. "Facing Interface Issues." *Computer Graphics World*, April 1992.

———. "Kicking the Tires of VR Software." *Computer Graphics World*, June 1993.

———. "Virtual Reality: Designing, Authoring, and Toolkit Cyber Software." *Virtual Reality World*, May–June, 1994.

———. "Designing, Authoring, and Toolkit Cyber Software." *Virtual Reality World*, July–August 1994.

Brown, M., and L. Sherman. "Multimedia Databases: Image Is Everything." *NewMedia Magazine*, April 1993.

Bylinsky, G. "At Last! Computers You Can Talk To." *Fortune*, May 3, 1993.

Caruso, D. "Stepping Into Virtual Reality." *Digital Media: A Seybold Report*.

Colin, J. R. "Mercury on the Rise at HIT Lab: Software Pulls Together Virtual Reality Hardware." *Electronic Engineering Times*, January 18, 1993.

Collier, A. "Virtual LAN Strategy." *Communications Week*, September 27, 1993.

Coull, T., and P. Rothman. "Virtual Reality for Decision Support Systems." *AI Expert*, August 1993.

Coyne, J. P. "Virtual Reality and Relational Databases." *Virtual Reality World*, November–December 1993.

Damore, K. "A Virtual Reality Developers' Kit Is Coming from Autodesk." *InfoWorld*, February 8, 1993.

Davydov, M. M. "Logical Data Base Design in a Relational Environment." *Data Base Management*, April 1992.

————. "From Model to Database." *Database Programming & Design*, March 1994.

Deutschman, A. "The Next Big Info Tech Battle." *Fortune*, November 29, 1993.

————. "Scramble on the Information Highway." *Fortune*, February 7, 1994.

DeWitt, D., and J. Gray. "Parallel Database Systems: The Future of High Performance Database Systems." *Communications of the ACM*, June 1993.

Dickinson, J. "A New Generation of Intelligent Objects Will Enhance Our Daily Lives." *PC Computing*, March 1992.

Drummond, R. "E-Mail Integration: Forging a More Perfect Union." *Data Communications*, February 1994.

Durr, M. "The Virtual Reality of Switched Networks." *Datamation*, May 1, 1994.

————. "Managing the Switch to Virtual Networks." *Datamation*, June 1, 1994.

Dutton, G. "A Virtual Operating System to Handle Virtually Anything." *IEEE Software*, May 1992.

Dworetzky, T. A. "Roadmap to the Information Highway." *MM*, February–March 1994.

Dyson, E. "Virtual Reality: Spreadsheets for Industry." *Forbes*, September 17, 1990.

Eckel, B. "Exception Handling C++." *Unix Review*, February 1994.

Edelstein, H. "DBMSes: Playing by the Rules." *Open Systems Today*, July 19, 1993.

————. "All the Right Data in All the Right Places." *Open Systems Today*, December 6, 1993.

Eliot, L. B. "Reality into Virtual Reality." *AI Expert*, December 1993.

————. "Data Highway Needs Fuzzy Logic." *AI Expert*, January 1994.

Eliot, L. B., and F. Holiday. "C++ for Business Applications." *Software Development*, September 1993.

Emmett, A. "An Operating System for Virtual Reality." *Computer Graphics World*, January 1993.

Faison, T. "Object-Oriented State Machines." *Software Development*, September 1993.

Ferranti, M. "Multidimensional Spreadsheets on the Rise." *PC Week*, April 12, 1993.

Ferrara, R., and P. A. Naecker. "The Data Warehouse: A Giant Step Forward." *DEC Professional*, November 1993.

Fiorito, T. "Mirror, Mirror." *DEC Professional*, November 1993.

Fitzsimmons, J. "Autodesk Releases Virtual-Reality Development Kit." *Computer Shopper*, May 1993.

Ford, R. "Push Buttons Are Not Only Interface Option." *MacWeek*, February 3, 1992.

Francis, B. "CD-ROMs Drive Toward New Standards." *Datamation*, February 15, 1993.

Garner, R. "Walkthrough Offers Real-Time 3-D." *MacWeek*, December 4, 1990.

Gasparro, D. M. "Moving LAN E-Mail onto the Enterprise." *Data Communications*, December 1993.

Glitman, R. "Bringing the Cyber Office to Corporate America." *PC Week*, January 14, 1991.

Gold, E. M. "PCs Rewrite the Rules for Videoconferencing." *Data Communications*, March 1994.

Gomes-Casseres, B. "Group Versus Group: How Alliance Networks Compete." *Harvard Business Review*, July–August 1994.

Greenstein, I. "Driving Toward the Digital Highway." *Oracle Magazine*, Fall 1993.

Haeckel, S. H., and R. L. Nolan. "Managing by Wire." *Harvard Business Review*, September–October 1993.

Hargadon, T. J. "Network Virtual Reality and Other Visions." *The Office*, May 1992.

Hayes, N. "Lanier 'Rants' About New VR Issues." *IEEE Computer Graphics and Applications*, May 1993.

Hayes, T. "Virtual Reality." *Unix World*, August 1990.

Heck, M. "3D Studio Makes PC a Smart 3-D Platform." *InfoWorld*, November 29, 1993.

———. "3D Studio Offers Exceptional Customization." *InfoWorld*, February 20, 1995.

Heisel, S. K, and J. Jacobson, eds. *Virtual Reality Market Place 1994*. Westport, Conn.: Mecklermedia, 1994.

Heywood, P. "Users Get a Closer Look at Virtual Private Networks." *Data Communications*, June 1994.

Isdale, J. "Cyberspace Development." *Software Development*, December 1993.

Jacobson, L. "Virtual Reality: A Status Report." *AI Expert*, August 1991.

Johnson, J. T. "Wireless Data: Welcome to the Enterprise." *Data Communications*, March 21, 1994.

———. "The Internet: Corporations Worldwide Make the Connection." *Data Communications*, April 1994.

Kalman, A. "Virtual World for Windows." *Newsbytes*, January 25, 1993.

Keizer, G. "How Spreadsheets Changed the World." *Lotus*, June 1992.

King, J. "Network Tools of the Virtual Corporation." *Network World Collaboration*, April 4, 1994.

King, S. S. "Switched Virtual Networks." *Data Communications*, September 1994.

Kosko, B., and J. Dickerson. "Fuzzy Virtual Worlds." *AI Expert*, July 1994.

Kovsky, S. "Virtual Reality Technology Inspires Solid Research." *Digital Review*, July 16, 1990.

Kramer, M. "Object-Oriented DBMSs Moving into Mainstream." *Client/Server Computing*, February 1994.

Krol, E. *The Whole Internet User's Guide and Catalog*. Sebastopal, Calif.: O'Reilly & Associates, 1992.

Kupfer, A. "The Race to Rewire America." *Fortune*, April 19, 1993.

———. "Look, Ma! No Wires!" *Fortune*, December 13, 1993.

———. "Augmenting Your Desktop with Telecom." *Fortune*, July 11, 1994.

LaPlante, A. "Multidimensional Spreadsheet Simplifies Operations." *InfoWorld*, September 6, 1993.

Lea, N. "Calgary Researchers Start Work on Virtual 'Hub.' " *Computing Canada*, September 28, 1992.

Leibs, S. "The Ultimate Office." *Information Week*, June 25, 1990.

Long, G. G. "Voice Mail Improves Employee Productivity and Customer Satisfaction." *Office Systems*, April 1992.

Louderback, J. "Go Boldly Forward in 3-D with Virtus WalkThrough." *PC Week*, August 2, 1993.

Lowe, R. "Three UK Case Studies in Virtual Reality." *Virtual Reality World*, March–April, 1994.

Luzi, A. D., and R. K. McCabe. "Harnessing the Power of Databases." *Journal of Accountancy*, July 1993.

Mahabharat, C. T. "India—Autodesk Plans to Source Software." *Newsbytes*, May 21, 1993.

Marcus, B. "Feedback Devices: The Human Machine Connection." *Byte*, April 1992.

Marshall, P. "Smaller E-Mail Packages Come On Strong." *InfoWorld*, December 6, 1993.

Martinez, C. D. "Interactive 3-D Modeling, Virtus WalkThrough 1.1.3." *MacWorld*, July 1993.

———. "Depth-Defying Design." *Macworld*, August 1993.

Mattison, R. "An Introduction to Object-Oriented Data Bases and the Data Management Review Object-Oriented Data Base Survey." *Data Management Review*, July 1993.

———. "The Data Management Review Object-Oriented Survey Continues." *Data Management Review*, August 1993.

McConnell, J. "Getting a Management Handle on Virtual LAN Infrastructures." *Network World*, May 23, 1994.

McDowall, I. "3D Stereoscopic Data for Immersive Displays." *AI Expert*, May 1994.

Morency, J., N. Lippis, and E. Hindin. "Virtual LANs Promise Big Gains, Pose New Risks." *Network World*, May 2, 1994.

Morgan, C. "Federal Projects Taken to New Dimensions with Virtual Reality." *Government Computer News*, August 3, 1992.

Morse, S. "Distributed Databases." *Network Computing*, November 15, 1992.

Moshell, J. M., and R. Dunn-Roberts. "A Survey of Virtual Environments: Research in North America, Part Two." *Virtual Reality World*, January–February 1994.

Murphy, T. "Applications as Objects." *Software Development*, September 1993.

Nash, J. "Our Man in Cyberspace Checks Out Virtual Reality." *Computerworld*, October 15, 1990.

Newquist, H. P. "Virtual Reality's Commercial Reality." *Computerworld*, March 30, 1992.

Norris, S. "Division Ltd. Outlines the Potential Posed by Virtual Reality." *Computergram International*, September 4, 1991.

O'Brien-Martz, E. "ISDN Deployment Moves Slowly But Surely." *TE&M*, August 15, 1993.

Oshi, J. A. "Internet Connections May Be Hazardous to Your Data." *MacWeek*, May 9, 1994.

Pantelidis, V. S. "Virtual Reality in the Classroom." *Educational Technology*, April 1993.

Pausch, R. "Three Views of Virtual Reality." *Computer*, February 1993.

Purdy, J. G. "Look, Ma, No Wires." *Computerworld*, May 24, 1993.

Radosevich, L. "Wireless Nets Gaining Ground." *Computerworld*, June 21, 1993.

Rea, P. "Innovative Network Structure Displays." *Virtual Reality World*, January–February 1994.

Reed, D. R. "Writing Reusable Classes in C++." *Unix Review*, February 1994.

Rettig, M. "Virtual Reality and Artificial Life." *AI Expert*, August 1993.

Richter, M. J. "Virtual Networks, Virtual Reality." *Communications Week*, April 19, 1993.

Rizzo, J. "Virtus WalkThrough." *MacUser*, July 1991.

Rohrbough, L. "Autodesk, Division Team Up to Develop VR Standard." *Newsbytes*, July 31, 1992.

Romkey, J. "Whither Cyberspace?" *Journal of the American Society for Information Science*, September 1991.

Rosenbaum, D. J. "Virtual Reality No Longer a Fantasy: Serious Interest Grows as First Commercial Applications Begin to Hit the Market." *Computer Shopper*, March 1992.

Rosenthal, S. "Virtual Reality Isn't Virtual and Isn't Real." *MacWeek*, October 2, 1990.

Saffo, P. "Virtual Reality Is Almost Real." *Personal Computing*, June 29, 1990.

―――. "Virtual Reality Is More Than Goggles, Gloves, and Fantasies." *Computerworld*, September 16, 1991.

Saracco, C. M. "Object and Relational Data Base Management Systems." *Data Management Review*, November 1993.

Sherman, L. "New Systems Provide Virtual Meetings at Your Desktop." *NewMedia Magazine*, November 1994.

Sherman, S. "Will the Information Superhighway Be the Death of Retailing?" *Fortune*, April 18, 1994.

Silverstone, S. "Virtus Automatically Builds 'Walk Through' Models." *MacWeek*, June 5, 1990.

Smith, H. C. "Dependency Modeling for Relational Database Design." *Database Programming & Design*, September 1990.

Smith, L. B. "Hitch a Ride on the Digital Highway." *PC Week Special Report*, November 1, 1993.

Spring, M. B. "The Virtual Library." *Virtual Reality World*, November–December 1993.

Stedman, N. "Field of Dreams." *Video*, May 1991.

Stevens, R. T. *Object-Oriented Graphics Programming in C++.* Boston: Academic Press, 1994.

Stewart, T. A. "The Netplex: It's a New Silicon Valley." *Fortune*, March 7, 1994.

―――. "Managing in a Wired Company." *Fortune*, July 11, 1994.

Stokell, I. "Autodesk Intros Cyberspace Developer Kit." *Newbytes*, March 8, 1993.

Strattner, A. "VREAM Bringing Virtual Reality to a PC Near You." *Computer Shopper*, December 1992.

Strauss, P. "Virtual LANs Pave the Way to ATM." *Datamation*, August 15, 1993.

―――. "LAN Boom Paves the Way for Client/Server." *Datamation*, November 15, 1993.

Streeter, A. "VPL Brings Virtual Reality to Mac." *MacWeek*, January 27, 1992.

Strom, D. "Hitching a Ride on the Data Superhighway." *Communications Week*, May 2, 1994.

Tansy, T. "Virtual LANs No Longer a Fantasy." *LAN Times*, March 28, 1994.

Tetzeli, R. "The Internet and Your Business." *Fortune*, March 7, 1994.

―――. "Is Going On-Line Worth the Money?" *Fortune*, June 13, 1994.

The, L. "Scaling E-Mail for the Enterprise." *Datamation*, April 15, 1993.

―――. "Synchronize Your E-Mail Directories." *Datamation*, November 15, 1993.

Tolly, K., and D. Newman. "Wireless Internetworking." *Data Communications*, November 21, 1993.

Van Brussel, C. "Virtual Reality Is Real." *Computing Canada*, September 28, 1992.

Van Name, M. L., and B. Catchings. "Virtual Reality Represents New Level of Communication." *PC Week*, October 15, 1990.

Vennaro, N. "The Future of Data Base Management Systems: Object-Oriented or Relational?" *Data Management Review*, October 1994.

Waldo, J. "Virtual Reality." *Unix Review*, July 1992.

―――. "The Virtue in Virtual." *Unix Review*, June 1994.

Watkins, C. D., and S. R. Marenka. *Virtual Reality Excursions with Programs in C.* Boston: Academic Press, 1994.

Wexler, J. M. "AT & T Casts Virtual Net." *Computerworld*, April 26, 1993.

White, J., and J. R. Brown. "Computer Graphics Today and Tomorrow." *Communications of the ACM*, July 1991.

Wilder, C. "Discovering the Hidden Computer." *Computerworld*, November 25, 1991.

———. "Virtual Reality Seeks Practicality." *Computerworld*, April 27, 1992.

Zachary, G. P. " 'Virtual Reality' Patents Gained by French Firm." *Wall Street Journal*, December 7, 1992.

PART III

Building Virtual-Reality Systems for Business

6

Development of Virtual-Reality Systems for Business

ISSUES EXPLORED

- To explore the need for creativity in a typical VR-system project
- To examine those items that evolve around getting started on a VR-system project
- To set forth those design principles that are appropriate in developing VR applications
- To examine in detail those steps that are generally undertaken by end users and computer professionals in developing virtual worlds
- To look at those factors that pertain to a periodic review of VR systems

OUTLINE

Introduction to the Development of Successful VR Systems

Builders Who Are Essential to the Development of VR Environments

Getting Started on a VR-System Project

    Identifying the Management Sponsoring the VR Project

    Establishing a VR-Project Team

    Determining the Scope of the VR Project

    Justifying the Time and Cost of the VR Project

Utilizing Design Principles That Are Appropriate to the VR Application

Physical Considerations for the Human Element

Modeling Considerations for the VR Application

VR-Systems-Development Methodology for End Users

    Training End Users in VR Software

INTRODUCTION TO THE DEVELOPMENT OF SUCCESSFUL VR SYSTEMS

Virtual reality as discussed in this text is a computer simulation that lets one see, hear, feel, and/or manipulate a synthetic universe. Users, in effect, experience a sense of presence in a virtual world, many times interacting with other participants and modifying one or more aspects of the world itself. Virtual worlds have simplified access to important information. As demonstrated in the prior chapter, access need not be hindered by geography since remote participants and databases are as easily accessed as local sources. An important goal of VR environments, then, is to make access to information as easy as seeing or breathing and, likewise, to make control of that information just as easy.

Because virtual worlds provide users—in particular, business people—with a new way of accessing information (that was previously buried in numbers or were presented graphically in a superficial way), there is a need to take a look at those factors that focus on initially getting started on a VR-system project. What makes a VR-system project a special case is the high visibility of the project. Although the risks involved in developing a VR project can be high, so can the rewards. In this chapter, the methodology that can be used by a typical end user who is working outside of the computer department is set forth, followed by an appropriate methodology to be employed by a computer professional. In either case, there is a need to incorporate total-quality-management (TQM) requirements that are found in typical computer programs. From this perspective, final VR systems are viable ones that meet the user's information needs.

BUILDERS WHO ARE ESSENTIAL TO THE DEVELOPMENT OF VR ENVIRONMENTS

In virtual worlds, there are three types of builders that are essential for success. They are world, tool, and system builders. The first group, or *world builders*, consists of the creative people who put together virtual worlds for potential application. They dream up specific worlds that are the main focus of tool and system builders. For example, the Department of Defense is involved in an ambitous effort to standardize geographical databases. Although much of the world is currently available as map data at the Defense Mapping Agency, transforming that data into a form suitable for graphical simulation is, needless to say, a challenge of the highest order. Researchers who are basically working in the territory of world builders find that no amount of central planning will suffice. They have found that major efforts involving top-down design of virtual worlds may be counterproductive. They find it is better to populate a preliminary world with VR users and then observe their needs. In turn, tools are provided to these users whereby they build the virtual worlds they desire.

The second group, or *tool builders*, consists of the engineers and computer scientists who develop the tools that are helpful in the development of particular VR applications. These tools are specific to interactive modeling building and simulation. An examination of the current virtual tool-building efforts range from one-person entreprenurial operations to major research efforts. For example, one of the oldest is the Virtual Environment Operation System (VEOS) Project at the University of Washington's Human Interface Technology Laboratory (HIT Lab). The Institute for Simulation and Training (IST) is presently working with the HIT Lab to develop PolyShop, an Army-sponsored, shared, networkable, virtual environment that is optimized for world building from the inside. Current commercial tool builders include Autodesk's Cyberspace Developer's Kit and Sense8's WorldToolKit.

The third group, or *system builders*, consists of the designers or developers of present-day VR applications that will be found in Part 4 (Chapters 7 through 10) of this text. The current VR business applications are being developed internally for most of a company's functional areas, that is, marketing, engineering, manufacturing, purchasing, finance, accounting, and human resources, to name some of the most important areas. In a similar manner, software vendors are beginning to sell VR packages that can be used by a wide number of customers. One such example is the vrTrader for applying virtual worlds to the stock market. Because of the importance of system builders in developing specific VR applications by using some type of programming language—say, the C++ language—a VR-systems–development methodology (which is distinct from the end-user methodology) for computer professionals will be given later in the chapter. Fundamentally, this VR methodology gives system builders the capability of developing computer-generated environments that simulate real-world experiences. As such, the users of these VR applications can discover new relationships that previously lay buried in numbers. In many cases, these new relationships can be presented to a live audience rather than to just one person.[1]

GETTING STARTED ON A VR-SYSTEM PROJECT

Getting a VR-system project underway is not too different from that found in a typical management information system (MIS) project that focuses on newer directions in MISs, such as executive information systems and group decision support systems. Essentially, there are four areas that need to be addressed, namely, (1) identifying the management sponsoring the VR project, (2) establishing a VR-project team, (3) determining the scope of the VR project, and (4) justifying the time and cost of the VR project. Each of these areas are explored below after a brief introduction to creativity needed in the typical VR-system project.

Essentially, *creativity* assists systems analysts (i.e., systems designers) in designing new virtual worlds that have no counterparts in present systems. Their creative minds can trigger better methods and operating modes that should be incorporated into the new VR system. In essence, creativity is a starting point in the entire VR-systems-development methodology, such that, in the final analysis, the best virtual world is created for the business application under study.

A most important approach to creativity is *brainstorming*, which is a method of generating as many solutions as possible in a relatively short time. During the session, any idea is recorded no matter how ridiculous it may appear; no criticism is allowed. Generally, one idea is useful in suggesting others. The session continues until the group has examined a number of possibilities. Once the session has adjourned, those whose problem areas were discussed evaluate the ideas presented. Most of the ideas will be rejected; perhaps none will be a potential solution. However, the creative faculty of systems analysts may provide necessary impetus to modify one or more ideas as workable solutions to the VR system under study. Uninhibited and unrestricted free association can help solve VR-system problems where the proposed solutions are quite different from the existing ones.

Identifying the Management Sponsoring the VR Project

The first step in getting started on implementing a successful virtual world is to identify the corporate sponsor of the VR project. Generally, no VR system will succeed without a strong advocate at a high level. Ideally, it should be the number one or two executive in the organization. If top executive support is not there, the VR system is not going to go very far. This is like trying to undertake a VR project from a grass-roots effort. Overall, getting started involves obtaining the support of the president and CEO of a company or, at least, the support of the company's executive vice-president.

Additionally, it is most important that sponsorship goes beyond a corporate executive sponsor and includes an operating sponsor. As indicated, the corporate sponsor will be the most senior executive who makes the initial request for the VR system and oversees its development. But sponsorship means more than sitting back and saying, ''I'm for this project'' and then delegating all of the work. A successful VR implementation requires a commitment from a corporate sponsor who will personally spend some time on the project. Because the corporate sponsor delegates the work, the operating sponsor comes into play. The operating sponsor (or sponsors) is an executive below the corporate sponsor who knows both the business and something about VR technology. The person is capable of operating comfortably in either the business or technological areas of an organization.

Establishing a VR-Project Team

After the appropriate operating sponsor has been recruited, there is a need to establish a VR-project team to carry out the development and implementation of the VR project. Because the operating sponsor may be the individual for whom the virtual world is being developed, it helps if the executive is knowledgeable about and accepting of developing the VR technology. Ideally, the operating sponsor's representative should be available at least two days per week, have an excellent understanding of both the organization's and users' needs, and have priority access to the VR-project team.

To get a better idea of the composition of the VR-project team, a balanced mix of technology specialists and business/financial analysis is needed. The technical specialists from the MIS department are responsible for developing and programming the VR system, database aspects, networking management, and the like. The business analysts, on the other hand, are responsible for identifying, locating, and formatting the output from the VR system that will be helpful to personnel located throughout the organization.

Determining the Scope of the VR Project

Once the VR-project team has been established, the next item related to the development and implementation of a virtual world is to determine the scope of the system. There are two ways to approach this important factor. The less desirable way is to ask the corporate and operating sponsors what they want out of the VR system. A better approach is to use the opening line that a good psychologist uses: ''Now, what seems to be the problem?'' This approach centers on going in with a number of prototype simulations developed with the aid of individuals who generally supply the executives with answers. In effect, getting to kick the tires and take a test drive works well to get him or her to define the scope of the new system.

For the most part, the scope of a VR system does not cut across the entire organization. That is, the functional areas of corporate planning, marketing, R&D, manufacturing, engineering, purchasing, accounting, finance, and human resources are not integrated into one comprehensive and cohesive system. Rather, the focus is one selected area of the organization that may not have an impact on its component parts located throughout the organization. Typical areas and outputs found in a VR environment for a manufacturing company along with typical computer inputs are found in Figure 6.1.

Important questions that can be raised concerning the scope of the VR system center on the following. How real must the virtual environment be to be effective for the application under study? What factors determine how real a VR environment seems to be versus what it should be for the application? What are the technical problems in a VR environment and how can they be solved for the application? These typical questions must be answered by the VR analyst during this phase so that the development phase will be successful. Failure to address these types of questions now may result in less than desirable results for the application.

Justifying the Time and Cost of the VR Project

An important item for a VR project is the preparation of a time schedule. A time frame, say several months, may be necessary. Experience has shown that there is a tendency to underestimate the time element of the VR-system project. The time factor is a function of the objectives to be met and the resources to be committed. For a successful project, depth and thoroughness are important; the time factor becomes secondary.

Another question to consider is, "What is the potential payoff?" If the potential payoff is small, it is unwise to spend a considerable amount of time and cost on the VR project. When developing a time schedule, the VR-project team determines the amount of work and what personnel and skills will be needed. Consideration must also be given to the following steps: training, programming, program testing, delivery of equipment, physical requirements and installation of the equipment, files development, and conversion activities. The foregoing include the major items that must be included in a realistic schedule.

Regarding cost, it is necessary to determine what hardware and software is needed. Though a PC is the least costly approach to a VR system, it still is not inexpensive. A complete PC-based system that includes the required software can be assembled for less than $20,000. Because several different hardware and software combinations can be put together, an accepted method is to make a list of the essential elements of the VR simulation. That is, the user needs to match each requirement of the simulation with the appropriate hardware and software. Having determined these requirements, a cost/benefit analysis can be undertaken to determine what type of return can be expected from investing in a specific VR-system project.

Typically, payoffs are different from other types of information systems in

Figure 6.1
Typical Computer Inputs and Outputs Found in a VR Environment for a Manufacturing Company

Functional Area	Computer Inputs	VR Outputs
Marketing	Sales quotations, sales reps' reports, sales forecasts, sales invoices, listing of customers, advertising budget, customer credit data	Marketing sales analyses, sales by products and product lines, comparisons of company to industry sales, monthly actual versus budgets, salesperson commission analyses
Manufacturing	Production orders, receiving reports, shipping reports, purchase orders, time records, stock records, stock requisitions, personnel records, time standards	Production planning and control, production shipping schedules, changes in inventories, quality-control reporting, spoilage and scrap analyses, departmental amounts versus budgets, factory-turnover analyses
Accounting and Finance	Cash receipts, vendor invoices, fixed-asset records, tax returns, financial analyses and ratios, stockholder listings	Cash-flow analyses, projected sources and applications of funds, projected short- to long-range financial statements, sales registers, customer invoices and vendor payments, aging of accounts
Human Resources	New and present personnel data, skill inventories, wage and salary data, personnel search	Wage and salary analyses, salary curves by job classifications, salary surveys, skill-inventory analyses, and seniority analysis

that VR systems are often less tangible, less quantifiable. In implementing a new accounting system, for example, it is relatively easy to estimate specific savings from tracking accounts receivable more closely. With VR systems, the focus is more on providing company personnel with improved information. The real payoff is in giving company personnel access to visualizing information in new ways and making better decisions. Hence, company personnel can do a more effective job in performing their duties in the company. On the other hand, there can be instances in which savings or gains can be tied directly to the VR system. For example, doing a better job of buying and selling stocks can reap very tangible rewards for a stock broker. Typical VR intangible benefits are found in Figure 6.2.

Because of the difficulty in justifying the cost of a VR system, many functional departments keep from proposing such systems in the first place. If a manager who is pushing for the new VR system has enough clout, the cost-justification issue usually fades into the background. Usually, the cost of a large and expensive VR project is justified by one or more executives high up in the organization who say, "Give me virtual worlds to do this or I quit." Overall, justifying the cost of a VR system tends to be evasive as opposed to justifying the cost found in a typical information system.

UTILIZING DESIGN PRINCIPLES THAT ARE APPROPRIATE TO THE VR APPLICATION

There are a number of general design principles that can be applied to typical VR applications. As a starting point, there is a need for the *Principle of End-User Involvement* for effective systems development. Because end users need to be involved in a VR project, they can assist in defining what the new VR system will do and what end users will have to do to get the desired results. Failure to involve end users can be fatal to the success of the entire VR project. Typically, three commonly stated reasons for any project failure are that (1) the system does not work the way the end user wants, (2) the system does not do all that the end user wants, and (3) the end user is unclear about what the system will do and what it will not do.

Related to the above, the *Principle of Acceptability* is of utmost importance to end users. If end users are convinced that the new VR system will not benefit them, is a poor one, or has some other legitimate shortcoming, the new VR system can be in trouble. To overcome this resistance, participation by end users, particularly during the design phases, is necessary.

Essentially, the development of a well-designed VR system ensures that the right *information* (which is of an interactive nature) will go to the right *person* (user) at the right *time* (in real time), in the right *format* (3-D or otherwise), and at the right *cost* (low). If any element is faulty, it is doubtful that the VR system will be accepted by an end user who is to experience its results. In the process of doing so, VR designers must consider the fact that the human factor comes first and the equipment comes second. Systems designers must consider the capabilities and limitations of organization personnel first, especially their threshold of becoming sick or nauseous from a VR encounter. Comparable factors for the equipment itself can then be considered. Hence, there is a need for the *Principle of Placing the Human Element, or the End User, First.*

An important trademark of any effective VR system centers on the *Principle of Simplicity.* Another name is the *KISS Principle*, that is, "Keep it Simple, Stupid." Simplicity can be effected by providing a straight-line flow of an in-

Figure 6.2
Intangible Benefits That Come into Play When Trying to Justify the Cost of a VR Project

- Providing company personnel access to visualizing information in new ways not found in previous computerized systems
- Giving company personnel the capability of flying over specific information and looking at it from a new perspective
- Providing company personnel with new VR techniques to improve customer service such that customer requirements are anticipated better
- Giving company personnel better support of decision-making capability in the areas of marketing, manufacturing, engineering, R&D, purchasing, and human resources through more interactive simulations
- Giving company personnel—in particular, company managers—new types of information for planning, organizing, directing, and controlling everyday operations
- Providing finance personnel with closer control over capital investments and expenses
- Allowing manufacturing personnel to improve production and schedule planning and control through more efficient employment of personnel and machines
- Allowing company personnel to improve accuracy, speed, and reliability in information handling and computer operations
- Providing finance and accounting personnel with better control of credit through more frequent aging of accounts receivable and analyses of credit data
- Improving the stature of the company in the business community as a progressive organization utilizing the latest computer technology

teractive simulation from one step to the next, avoiding needless backtracking. Data should be utilized at the source, or as close to the source as possible, to reduce the need for coordination and communication. The simplicity of the end user's experience will help gain the allegiance of the end user.

Tied in with the above principles is the *Principle of Training and Educating End Users in Utilizing VR Technology*. End users cannot be expected to know about leading-edge information technology. Hence, it is up to the company's functional-information centers to disseminate such information to end users through formal or informal VR training and education. In turn, end users are expected to make requests to the information centers for implementing the latest information technology that affects their functional areas. Essentially, there is a joint effort between the functional end-user information centers and end users to leverage VR technology for the benefit of the functional units as well as the entire company.

In addition to these general design principles, there are specific ones that need to be addressed for typical VR applications—for example, the *Principle of a Friendly User Interface*. This is necessary to insure that users find their way to the right information in a way they are accustomed to. The mouse-and-windows interface, developed at Xerox and popularized via the Apple Macintosh, took over one hundred person-years of experimental development. Even with the fairly simple virtual-world business systems of today, it is clear that the 2-D window-based interface is inappropriate for the interactive 3-D world of VR.

Related to the above principle is that of *Consistency between Applications*. There is a necessity to maintain consistency between applications so that users feel they are in the same VR world they were in when they started their learning process. Moreover, everyday relationships, like up and down or left to right, and symbols that resemble ordinary objects, like a cassette tape or trash can, need to be used.

Another important principle is that of *Utilizing Lists from Which to Choose*. The designer should do as much as possible at the highest level. That is, the user should be offered lists from which to choose rather than be required to remember the name of a thing. Additionally, a simple, unambiguous, and narrow command structure should be built so that it is difficult for the user to get lost.

PHYSICAL CONSIDERATIONS FOR THE HUMAN ELEMENT

Related to the above principle—in particular, the *Principle of Placing the Human Element, or End User, First*, is the need to consider the physical aspects of VR and its effect on the typical person. All humans have a complex feedback mechanism that involves vision, touch, vestibular sensation, bodily position, and pressure on skin. These integrated mechanisms enable humans to walk, run, and perform other bodily functions. Although this integrated system is not completely understood at this time, there are a number of generally accepted facts that should be taken into account when developing VR systems for business or otherwise.

First, some people do not experience sickness problems up to a certain point, whereas others do—that is, some people adapt easily and some do not. Younger people generally have a higher tolerance level than older people. *Second*, visual simulators (e.g., flight simulators), both with and without motion bases, often cause symptoms indistinguishable from motion sickness and space sickness. *Third*, this sickness can cause not only nausea and vomiting but also fatigue and headaches, thereby resulting in lowered performance levels. The individual may not be aware that his or her performance has been degraded. *Fourth*, adding weight to a person's head can induce motion sickness because of the altered feedback loops involving muscle action and head motion. *Fifth*, delays in visual feedback, which can be caused by a number of factors, are a well-known source of sickness.

It should be noted that many of these phenomena are well known in the U.S. military, which has long operated extended-duration flight simulators. Navy guidelines report that symptoms can occur instantly or be delayed by as much as eighteen hours and caution that individuals who have experienced simulator sickness in the past have a greater probability of recurrence and should not be scheduled to fly for twenty-four hours following simulator sickness. At this time, there is no general theory that exists to predict what combinations of inputs and outputs will be easy or hard to adapt to or who will be most likely to feel the effects. However, designers of VR systems need to take these factors into consideration throughout the design process. Hopefully, with improved hardware and software, some of the problems can be minimized in the future. Failure to include these factors may cause the best-designed VR system to be unused or abused.

MODELING CONSIDERATIONS FOR THE VR APPLICATION

One of the most difficult tasks when developing VR applications is the design of the database (refer to Chapter 5). Generally, this is one of the most important of all the system-design factors. When a VR system is loaded with detail and textures, the graphics systems must work harder for every frame. The ideal database shows just enough detail to convey the idea but is sparse enough so that the graphics system runs well. For example, an appliance may not look accurate when examined closely, but in most situations, the relative complexity of individual objects is not important to the overall appeal of the room. Software-modeling packages, such as Autodesk's AutoCAD and 3D Studio, can be used efficiently to build 3-D databases. These two packages can feed geometry and models to programs written with the CDK (VR programming library of the C++ class). To the VR designer, this represents a good connection between the modeling and simulation environments.

Another aspect of database design that will affect the rendering speed and overall scene appearance is lighting. The most efficient lighting models are distant, directional, and ambient. The shading calculations in this mode usually do not affect rendering speed, but directional lights do not necessarily provide optimal illumination. For many desktop applications, simple lighting models are sufficient and will not reduce performance. Additionally, the ability to apply textures to a model is a must for any virtual world, but there are some problems in using textures. Too many textures will slow rendering to a point that will make the space unusable. This is the case with both hardware and software rendering.

The use of sensors (refer to Chapter 2) in a walk-through program is significant. Movement and interaction with the environment are important aspects of the VR application. The ability to move the viewpoint and manipulate objects is one of the unique features of working in a virtual world. Many kinds of sensors are available for the desktop, and most of them can be used in a visualization application. One common use of sensors is in the navigation of 3-D databases, which are very important in a walk-through application, for example.

Having a natural and convenient way to move through space allows the user to focus on the environment.[2]

VR-SYSTEMS-DEVELOPMENT METHODOLOGY FOR END USERS

If an end user undertakes the development of a VR-system project on his or her own whereby some type of VR-software package, such as an authoring system, is used, the recommended systems-development methodology consists generally of five steps:

1. training end users in VR software
2. defining VR-system requirements
3. designing the VR system
4. virtual prototyping to finalize the system
5. documenting

Each of these steps is explained below. Essentially, these steps are useful in developing somewhat straightforward applications. They are somewhat like those that are set forth in the next section of the chapter for more complex applications. No matter what VR methodology is used in the systems-development process, creativity (as discussed previously in the chapter) is essential for initiating new VR directions for business.

Training End Users in VR Software

To get end users started in virtual worlds, it is very helpful that they undergo training so that the off-the-shelf software will be easy to apply. More specifically, they need to spend at least one day going through the basics of the software package and its special features. They also need to go through examples so that they better understand what the VR software can do for them when they apply it to their specific applications. For example, the VREAM VR development system (as set forth in Chapter 4) lets users define, enter, and interact with a 3-D world in real time, and VREAM's 386-based DOS software includes a run-time system for executing VR applications written with the included Environment Editor. This software allows the user to define light-source position, force of gravity, movement, and other parameters. Hence, at least one-half day could be devoted to the basics and some examples. In turn, at least one-half day could be spent on developing simplistic examples of future projects for the end users.

Regardless of the software used in training, there is a need to discuss the effects that exposure to virtual worlds could have on human physiology. As VR-software products continue to mature and become realistic, end users may require a recovery period following exposure so as to regain their physical balance.

From another perspective, consideration should be given to including TQM requirements in the VR system. That is, trainers should stress the need for incorporating quality throughout the entire system-development process. Quality starts at the VR-system–requirements stage and continues through the design and prototyping stages. This area will be treated under "VR-Systems-Development Methodology for Computer Professionals" below for more complex VR applications.

Defining VR-System Requirements

This second step of a typical VR project from an end-user-development viewpoint is normally performed by the end user. Assisted by a VR-system-development guide (developed by the computer department), the end user describes the scope and objectives of the VR system along with the known requirements or specifications of the system. The tangible and intangible benefits expected from the proposed system are also included. Generally, the end user needs the approval of his or her functional departmental manager for undertaking the development work. At this point, the end user generally has a good idea of how much effort this project will take and its costs. After reviewing these data and approving the VR system, the functional departmental manager allocates the proper time so that the individual can develop the VR system. In addition, there may be an agreement with the department's information-center consultant about the level of support that the end user will need to develop the VR system. Overall, it is necessary that the end user define the VR-system requirements such that an available VR-software package can be used in its development.

Designing the VR System

In this third step, designing the new system centers on utilizing the software in which the end user was trained according to the first step above. Generally, the end user has some design process already in mind and can proceed on this basis. For example, if the end user was trained in the use of Virtus WalkThrough (a Macintosh modeling and visualization package tailored for architects and interior designers), the individual could create conceptual designs of buildings and interiors, then move through and around them on screen. With Walk-Through, the end user moves about freely, viewing the design from many different perspectives. Because the program renders scenes quickly, one can move through several rooms in a few seconds. The program's completely interactive spatial presentation even offers authentic touches such as shading. In fact, the end user could walk up to a wall, cut a hole in it, and instantly see trees outside.

As the number of VR software packages expands for designing the VR system, there will be need to identify the data to be included in the system. For example, the vrTrader requires data from the daily trading activity of the New York Stock Exchange. However, newer VR packages will require the utilization of data generated by the internal operations of a company. In fact, it may well be necessary for the end user to collect data from the documents used in his or her department along with the various attributes to be defined for each data item and the different kinds of relationships between data elements. End users may have to use the company's on-line data dictionary to locate and organize the data for their application.

Virtual Prototyping to Finalize the System

The largest portion of the total systems-development effort occurs in this fourth step of virtual prototyping to finalize the system. In the world of VR the end user creates an initial virtual prototype and then enters that prototype's virtual world and experiences its operation. Because virtual prototyping is basically iterative, a first attempt at the VR design leads from a more general design to a series of more specific designs and then finally to the final VR design. This step ends when the end user has a complete system that performs all the necessary functions that were originally set forth in the scope and objectives of the VR system as set forth in the second step above.

During the process of finalizing the new VR system, the end user could draw heavily on the computer department's advice via the functional department's information center. The end user might draw upon the department's advice and experience in how to develop 3-D models and how to develop and use data in the VR system. Since 3-D modeling and data usage are typically new to end users, for example, it takes some handholding from the company's computer personnel to help end users correctly utilize the VR technology. With the proper guidance and help, most end users can pick up on this new technology and become proficient in a short time period.

Documenting

Documentation is the end user's responsibility where the focus is on getting the details to those who need it today or some time in the future. Documentation is generally kept on-line although paper-based documentation can be utilized. An on-line approach is faster for those trying to get a full picture of what constitutes the VR system. It is suggested that there be a *feedback mechanism* that provides a means for maintaining and possibly improving the VR system. Although the end-user developer can possibly see room for improvement, a larger audience provides a better vehicle for system maintenance and possible improvements.

VR-SYSTEMS-DEVELOPMENT METHODOLOGY FOR COMPUTER PROFESSIONALS

For most VR systems that require the services of computer professionals, there is a need to take a slightly different approach. That is, for more complex and sophisticated VR systems, computer professionals are typically employed to undertake such projects since end users generally lack the appropriate skills. In addition, the participation and cooperation of the appropriate functional areas, represented by end-user departmental personnel, is very helpful to successful development. It is much easier to design the system to accommodate the constructive suggestions of personnel than to redevelop it at a later date. Too many installations have faced this embarrassing situation, only because appropriate personnel were not given an opportunity to evaluate the system's design as it progressed.

The six steps that can be utilized by computer professionals are as follows:

1. training computer professionals in VR-software tools
2. determining TQM requirements
3. defining VR-system requirements
4. designing the VR system
5. virtual prototyping to finalize the system
6. documenting

These steps are essentially the same as those set forth above for the end-user VR-systems–development methodology. However, total quality management is stressed so that the final VR system is a quality one.

Training Computer Professionals in VR-Software Tools

Because VR-software tools are relatively new to most computer professionals, these persons need to undergo training to bring their information-technology and programming skills up to date. Additionally, there is a need to undergo training regarding the physical considerations mentioned previously for a VR operating mode. The time needed to train computer professionals varies and depends on the software being taught and the VR environment in which typical business applications will operate on a day-to-day basis. Usually, at least one week of training is needed to learn a software package, such as a VR "toolkit," and a series of examples. In addition, the time would include the opportunity to develop a few simple examples. If a computer professional were to undertake training in Sense8 Corporation's WorldToolKit, much more time would be necessary to study and undertake VR-sample–development application than with a VR-software package aimed at end users, such as an authoring system.

Currently, Version 2.0 of WorldToolKit (WTK) allows for more functionality and greater flexibility for the development of visual simulation and VR applications than other basic VR-development packages. The WTK gives full twenty-four–bit color and real-time texture mapping of Targa images at more than three times the previous performance levels, with screen resolutions of up to 800 × 600. With variable-resolution textures and storage of over four-hundred different source textures, the WTK provides the real-time texture mapping required by demanding visual-simulation applications. Version 2.0 has additional capabilities such as Gouraud-shading, antialiasing, object constructors, viewpoint pathing, support for two Fire boards on one PC, the capability to read and write many popular data-file formats. For higher performance, this software is also available in a GL version on a Silicon Graphics workstation. It is an open architecture—one can imbed GL routines directly in the WTK source code and take full advantage of GL drawing capabilities. This software package supports Performer 1.0 for even faster rendering of textured objects. As can be seen from this brief description, this software takes a while to learn and become proficient in its use. If a programming language, like C++, has to be learned, the total training time would be considerably more.

Determining Total-Quality-Management Requirements

Just as computer managers have insisted on a TQM program for the development of all types of information systems—starting with preventing defects in system requirements or specifications—the same must be undertaken for VR systems. Previously, quality-improvement programs used techniques employing metrics for quality assurance (QA) during the design and prototyping stages of the development process. Unfortunately, these QA techniques were applied too late in the process to affect the overall quality of the system when viewed from an organization-wide perspective. To design and implement TQM programs for all types of systems, computer management must ensure that system requirements or specifications include organization-wide business rules that are communicated to both systems analysts and programmers. Most system requirements are too narrowly focused on the specifics of a system to reflect adequately concerns for sharing data or otherwise. This is a primary reason why systems are inflexible and unacceptably expensive to maintain in the face of changing business systems and conditions. As will be seen in Part 4 of this text, many business-oriented VR systems make great use of some data and new concepts not used previously.

Studies of information systems for business have shown that many of the errors reported during system testing and production can be traced to the initial stages of development. The most common cause of these errors are system specifications that are missing, erroneous, ambiguous, or conflicting. Only a small percentage of errors have to do with codes not meeting specifications. Even computer-aided software engineering (CASE) provides only limited help in identifying defects in the initial stages. Hence, computer managers, working with project managers and end users, need to establish TQM requirements for information-system projects.

In a similar manner, computer managers need to determine TQM requirements for business-oriented VR systems. As a way of ensuring that the TQM requirements are met, the organization's internal auditors can carry out this function at periodic intervals during systems development as needed. In this way, an objective third party can determine whether the resulting VR system is a quality one. Although an objective review is found currently in the development of typical business-oriented information systems by internal auditors, the same cannot be said for VR systems. Thus, internal auditors need to undergo training to ensure quality in the implemented VR systems.

Defining VR-System Requirements

Before the initial design of the new VR system can be started, it is necessary that systems analysts who are expert in VR systems or who have undergone training in VR systems define the scope and objectives of the VR system. In turn, the known requirements or specifications are developed in conjunction with end users. The result of this investigation is that a cost/benefit analysis is undertaken to determine the feasibility of a new VR system. (Reference can be made to a prior section of the chapter on justifying the time and cost of the VR project.) Assuming that the VR project is a viable one that has been approved by the appropriate level of management, there is a need for the systems analysts to develop a VR system that reflects the scope and objectives desired along with the appropriate requirements or specifications. In some cases, the development of the VR-system requirements is somewhat straightforward. For example, in a financial VR system, data contained in the company's database is essentially analyzed in an interactive way for the user. In other cases, defining VR-system requirements is not so straightforward. For example, a new market-research VR system needs to start collecting data not found in the company's database. This may simplify the whole VR project since only selected data are captured and used as output from the new system. However, the introduction of this requirement requires going one step further than was probably envisioned initially in the VR project. The time to collect this information may take several months or longer. Hence, defining VR-system requirements or specifications initially in the project can take unexpected twists and turns that must be addressed head-on.

Designing the VR System

An essential part of the total VR project is designing a system that best meets the needs of its users. To develop such a system, the appropriate VR software tools, a programming language, or a combination of the two are employed. When designing a virtual world, the visuals, the sounds, and the sensations should allow the user to undergo an actual experience. At the same time, the user should be given the capability of exploring the environment, gather information, and solve problems in an effective manner. Advances in computer technology are allowing VR designers to make possible the development of 3-D graphical and VR simulations of ever-increasing realism and ever-increasing affordability. The result is that users are getting better systems faster with advancing VR technology. Reference can be made again to Sense8 Corporation's WorldToolKit.

Fundamentally, this VR-software package is a complete one, which means there are no restrictions on the functionality that can be built into an application. From this view, the WorldToolKit 2.0 is not just power driven but is solutions driven. This software not only provides the means for high-level calls but also provides low-level access. This software is essentially not limited by the system, no matter what level of task is involved. The WorldToolKit 2.0 is also extremely flexible, which means there is often more than one way to develop a particular feature in an application. The software's product design is customer driven since each and every new function call put in was based on customer feedback. From another perspective, the WorldToolKit 2.0 provides very intuitive function calls to make application development as easy as possible. After using this software for a short while, it is often possible to guess a function call without having to look it up.

In a typical VR system, there may be a need for internal and external data for an interactive, real-time mode of operation. In many cases, the data would be available from the company's database. However, where the data is not available, it may be necessary to spend some time in getting the data from internal or external sources. However, if the VR-systems designers have taken appropriate action during the system-requirements stage (as discussed in the third step above), the data should be available currently or in the foreseeable future. With the newer VR software, if the data is available when needed, applications can be developed in a much shorter time period. For example, with the WorldToolKit 2.0, high-level function calls make application development much faster. Applications that used to take months or years to develop only take a matter of weeks. Overall, the design of a new VR system is expedited by utilizing the latest software packages that incorporate the newest VR technology.

Virtual Prototyping to Finalize the System

To finalize the new system, virtual prototyping is employed. Through an interactive process of virtual prototyping, systems designers working with end users discover new refinements that can be incorporated into the next version. Fundamentally, virtual prototyping is a trial-and-error process in which a version of the VR system is built, used, evaluated, and revised. Each new virtual prototype performs more of the required functions in an increasingly efficient manner. The last virtual prototype is the desired VR system that meets the objectives originally set forth in a VR project.

As an example, the U.S. Army's Tank Automotive Command (TACOM) laboratory (Warren, Michigan) is using virtual prototyping to allow designers to visualize a tank in action before it is actually built. This virtual prototyping process involves developing computer models and graphic displays realistic enough to substitute for the actual prototype. Information traditionally found on blueprints is input into the computer so that the designers can test the concept vehicle, thereby allowing the operator to actually interact with it. The process starts by creating a 2-D drawing of a concept vehicle. This is followed by a 3-D engineering model in which analytical models are applied, such as mobility, vehicle dynamics, track and suspension, survivability, and vulnerability. Analytical results are reflected in changes to the 3-D model to optimize the design through an interactive process. The concept then moves to a detailed design phase in which the 3-D model is refined to incorporate actual components, concurrent engineering, feedback from the user, and logistics-support factors in the design. The Army's TACOM notes that in addition to saving money in the design process, training costs are reduced by using virtual prototyping to simulate combat situations without human injury or vehicle damage. Currently, the Big Three automakers and their suppliers are applying VR and its prototyping process to automotive design.

Overall, virtual prototyping allows system designers to produce and test complex designs. Virtual worlds can usually be constructed for less cost and in less time than is required for physical models. In addition, virtual worlds can be very helpful in assisting designers in meeting TQM requirements. At the end of virtual prototyping, TQM requirements (according to the second step above) need to be examined to determine whether the final VR system is a quality one. The essential focus of establishing TQM requirements and fulfilling them is a positive one of preventing errors rather than a negative one of finding errors. To determine quality, appropriate measurements must be established and documented. That is, quality metrics can be kept on those measures that determine the degree of quality for the entire VR-systems-development effort. In the end, the real benefit of a TQM program is that the system implemented requires less maintenance. An additional benefit of this approach is improved credibility of VR-systems designers and programmers as well as of the TQM group.

Documenting

An integral part of VR-systems development is documentation throughout the design process. Accuracy, simplicity, and ease of understanding are the essential components since nontechnical personnel may have need to utilize the documentation. All data compiled on the new VR system can be stored on-line. In some cases, it may be necessary to keep a manual of all documentation as backup to on-line documentation. There is also a need for a *feedback mechanism* that provides a means for maintaining and possibly improving the VR system. Such a mechanism may indicate that the current VR system needs to be scrapped and replaced with an updated system or with a new direction in VR that has just been marketed.

PERIODIC REVIEW OF VR SYSTEMS

After the new VR system is installed and operating as originally intended, computer professionals and end users should review the tangible and intangible benefits to verify that these benefits are, in fact, being achieved. Discussions with managers of functional end-user departments will determine how well the new VR system is performing. Tangible benefits, such as higher sales and lower inventory costs, and intangible benefits, such as an upgrade in customer service and more meaningful information, are open to constructive criticism. Typical comments will be that certain benefits have been realized or that some are about the same. The task of computer professionals and end users, then, is to make the appropriate adjustments to realize the quantitative and qualitative benefits of the VR system as originally envisioned.

Over time, factors that were not previously problems in the VR system can become significant. Can the equipment be upgraded to expand its virtual-world capabilities? Should newer VR equipment be obtained? Can modification to the VR software be made to reduce time and cost? Or should new VR software be purchased? Answers to these questions must be evaluated by the computer department and the end-user functional departments through a periodic review of the system. The ultimate aim of such an investigation is improvements in the current VR system. In essence, it may be necessary to devise a new system for changed operating conditions.

SUMMARY

The focus of this chapter has been on starting a VR-system project and on a VR-systems-development methodology from an end-user perspective as well as from a computer-professional perspective. Underlying this exposition is the fact that the cost of developing a virtual world does not approach the outlay for the real thing—say, for an actual building or rebuilding a present store. Currently, virtual modeling that requires very powerful PCs, disk drives, video displays, and the like to present picture-quality images in real time is declining in cost such that widespread development and usage is now possible. This will be apparent in the final part of the text (Chapters 7 through 10) where VR technology is being put to good use in the fields of marketing, manufacturing, finance, and education, to name a few. Many new applications are right around the corner. As the technology matures, VR will become one of the most important computer-generated tools for companies of all sizes.

NOTES

1. Michael Moshell and Charles E. Hughes, "Shared Virtual Worlds for Education," *Virtual Reality World*, January–February 1994, pp. 71–73.

2. Brian Blau and Kevin Yurica, "Designing VR Applications for the Desktop," *Virtual Reality World*, September–October 1994, pp. 17–21.

Bibliography for Part III

Asch, T. "Designing Virtual Worlds." *AI Expert*, August 1992.

Bajura, M., H. Fuchs, and R. Ohbuchi. "Merging Virtual Objects with the Real World." *Computer Graphics*, July 1992.

Bandrowski, P. "Try Before You Buy: Virtually Real Merchandising." *Corporate Computing*, December 1992.

Banks, M. "What's New Online." *Computer Shopper*, March 1992.

Bishop, D. S., and P. G. Bishop. "Object-Oriented Enterprise Modeling." *Data Management Review*, July 1993.

Blau, B., and K. Yurica. "Designing VR Applications for the Desktop." *Virtual Reality World*, September–October 1994.

Brill, L. M. "Virtual Reality: Designing, Authoring, and Toolkit Cyber Software." *Virtual Reality World*, May–June 1994.

Bylinsky, G. "The Payoff from 3-D Computing." *Special Report, Fortune*, Autumn 1993.

Carlson, W. M., and B. C. McNurlin. "Do You Measure Up?" *Computerworld*, December 7, 1992.

Coyne, J. P. "Virtual Reality and Relational Databases." *Virtual Reality World*, November–December 1993.

Creecy, R. H., B. M. Masand, S. J. Smith, and D. L. Waltz. "Trading Maps and Memory for Knowledge Engineering." *Communications of the ACM*, August 1992.

Damore, K. "A Virtual Reality Developers' Kit Is Coming from Autodesk." *InfoWorld*, February 8, 1993.

Denne, P. "Virtual Motion." *Virtual Reality World*, May–June 1994.

Earnshaw, R. A., M. A. Gigante, and H. Jones, eds. *Virtual Reality Systems*. Boston: Academic Press, 1993.

Eliot, L. B. "Reality into Virtual Reality." *AI Expert*, December 1993.

Erickson, J. D. "Beyond Systems: Better Understanding the User's World." *Computer Language*, March 1993.

Feiner, S., B. Macintyre, and D. Seligmann. "Knowledge-based Augmented Reality." *Communications of the ACM*, July 1993.

Fitzsimmons, J. "Autodesk Releases Virtual-Reality Development Kit." *Computer Shopper*, May 1993.

Foss, W. B. "Fast, Faster, Fastest Development." *Computerworld*, May 31, 1993.

Freichs, D. "Bringing Real Applications to the Virtual Environment." *Virtual Reality World*, July–August 1994.

Furness, T. A. "Exploring Virtual Worlds with Tom Furness." *Communications of the ACM*, July 1991.

Glitman, R. "Bringing the Cyber Office to Corporate America." *PC Week*, January 14, 1991.

Green, D., and D. Green. "Virtus Excels at Prototyping on the Mac." *InfoWorld*, April 20, 1992.

Hamit, F. *Virtual Reality and the Exploration of Cyberspace*. Carmel, Ind.: Sams Publishing, 1993.

Hanna, M. A. "Move Is On to Tie Vision to Information Systems." *Software Magazine*, January 1990.

Isdale, J. "Cyberspace Development." *Software Development*, December 1993.

Jacobson, R. "Virtual Worlds: A New Type of Design Environment." *Virtual Reality World*, May–June 1994.

Jones, M. R. "Unveiling Repository Technology." *Database Processing & Design*, April 1992.

Karnow, C. E. A. "The Electronic Persona: A New Legal Entity." *Virtual Reality World*, January–February 1994.

Krueger, M. W. *Artificial Reality II*. Reading, Mass.: Addison-Wesley, 1991.

———. "The Emperor's New Realities." *Virtual Reality World*, November–December 1993.

Leibs, S. "Virtual Reality 101." *Information Week*, August 1993.

Martinez, C. D. "Depth-Defying Design." *Macworld*, August 1993.

Moshell, J. M., and R. Dunn-Roberts. "A Survey of Virtual Environments: Research in North America, Part One." *Virtual Reality World*, November–December 1993.

Moshell, J. M., and C. E. Hughes. "Shared Virtual Worlds for Education." *Virtual Reality World*, January–February 1994.

Mulqueen, J. T. "Certain Extinction?" *Communications Week*, July 12, 1993.

Palmer, R. J., M. W. Tucker, and J. B. King, Jr. "A Diagnostic Approach to Information Management Problems in the Organization." *Journal of Systems Management*, May 1991.

Pimentel, K., and K. Teixeira. *Virtual Reality, Through the New Looking Glass*. New York: McGraw-Hill, 1993.

Pinella, P. "Power Building Enterprise Applications." *Datamation*, July 15, 1993.

Puttre, M. "Virtual Prototypes Move Alongside Their Physical Counterparts." *Mechanical Engineering*, August 1992.

Ray, G. "CASE Tools Ups Productivity 50%." *Computerworld*, February 1, 1993.

Rheingold, H. *Virtual Reality*. New York: Touchstone, 1991.

Saffo, P. "Virtual Reality Is Almost Real." *Personal Computing*, June 29, 1990.

Schaffer, R. H., and H. A. Thomson. "Successful Change Programs Begin with Results." *Harvard Business Review*, January–Feburary 1992.

Semich, J. W. "Multimedia Tools Are Enterprise Ready." *Datamation*, October 15, 1993.

———. "Here's How to Quantify IT Investment Benefits." *Datamation*, January 7, 1994.

Spring, M. B. "The Virtual Library." *Virtual Reality World*, November–December 1993.

Stokell, I. "Autodesk Intros Cyberspace Developer Kit." *Newsbytes*, March 8, 1993.

Thierauf, R. J. *Creative Computer Software for Strategic Thinking and Decision Making: A Guide for Senior Management and MIS Professionals*. Westport, Conn.: Quorum Books, 1993.

Wilder, C. "Virtual Reality Seeks Practicality." *Computerworld*, April 27, 1992.

PART IV

Applications of Virtual-Reality Systems for Business

7

Retailing and Marketing in a Business-Oriented Virtual-Reality Environment

ISSUES EXPLORED

- To rethink the marketing function so that companies can reap the benefits of VR
- To explore why market leaders know what the customers want versus nonmarket leaders
- To demonstrate the utilization of creative computer software to assist in the development of innovative products and services
- To show how VR can benefit the typical customer in the buying of goods and services
- To demonstrate how VR can assist retailing and marketing management in a variety of customer applications

OUTLINE

INTRODUCTION TO RETAILING AND MARKETING IN A VR ENVIRONMENT

As noted previously in the text (especially in Chapter 1), more information will not solve today's marketing problems. The limiting factor today is new ways and fresh ideas. Information, analysis, and problem solving will not yield new marketing approaches because they are all focused on "what is." There is a need to refocus on "what can be" such that marketing managers can generate creative and constructive new products and services for customers. But even that change of mind-set apparently may not be enough. For example, Raytheon, which developed the Patriot missile but which also invented the microwave oven years ago, did nothing with the oven. Japanese firms turned the microwave oven into a huge market success. United States corporations continue to spend millions and millions on R&D projects in hopes of inventing creative new products and services. But if these corporations are run by stodgy chief executives who are "uncomfortable" with unproven new concepts, creative products and services will not go anywhere. Besides, new ideas should be a company-wide effort. In light of these current problems in the United States, the whole marketing function needs to be rethought within a VR environment.

Initially, the discussion in the chapter centers on new ways of rethinking and viewing the marketing function. In turn, this background serves as a means of exploring VR applications from an enlarged marketing perspective. As an example, the traditional solution is to design and build a prototype store. If it does not meet the customers' needs, the cycle may be repeated several times until the company arrives at a successful solution. Each time, designers, architects, and builders make money while the company does not. In contrast, a designer in a virtual world can walk through a prototype store and determine that the colors are all wrong, the new logo looks like an international warning symbol, and the like. In essence, the designer needs to go back to the electronic drawing board and make appropriate revisions before the store is built. Using 3-D modeling, visualization, and computer-aided design (CAD), marketing and design departments can sit down at a computer and virtually build an entire store with everything from walls to electronic cash registers.

NEW DIRECTIONS IN RETAILING AND MARKETING THAT ARE NEEDED FOR VR

For companies in the United States to have global success today and tomorrow, they need to go beyond the "me-too" product attitude. The focus should be on corporate visioning, which is a starting point for corporate strategic thinking. *Visioning* of the marketing function is envisioning markets for products and services that do not exist today. In other words, a typical U.S. company should generate new products and services such that the company is out there ahead, as Raytheon could have been with the microwave oven. In this century as well as into the twenty-first century, marketing battles will be won by companies that can build and dominate fundamentally new markets.

Creative new products, such as microrobots, speech-activated appliances, and self-parking cars, not only make the inconceivable conceivable, but also allow a company to influence the direction of the market. In the years to come, more and more companies will close the gap with their rivals on costs, quality, and delivery. But without the capacity to stake out new territories with products and services, many U.S. companies will find themselves faced with traditional and shrinking markets for products and services. Hence, there is a need for a new direction that is tied in with VR. This new marketing direction not only relates to new VR applications (as presented in the second half of this chapter), but also can be related to the concept of the "virtual corporation" (as discussed in Chapter 1).

By way of review, a virtual corporation is a situation that occurs when two or more companies get together for a single project. They do not create a formal company, joint venture, or partnership; they just work together on a specific project. Since the ultimate goal of the virtual corporation is to serve customers, companies will have to share customer databases. They will have to create joint business plans, thereby linking planning and financial systems. Eventually, all lines between partnering companies' stores of information will blur. Overall, the virtual corporation will be capable of doing things for customers that were not possible before.

Rethinking the Marketing Mix

Before exploring those items that can affect VR in marketing, it would be advisable to take a look at the marketing mix today and tomorrow. That is, the focus is on rethinking how the typical marketing manager views the marketing mix, that is, product, price, place, and promotion. For a company to be successful in the future, it is necessary that it offer the *right products* at the *right price* in the *right place*, along with the *right promotion*. Needless to say, a successful company must change with the times. There are fundamental changes in demographics and consumer preferences ahead for the end of this decade that will force companies to rethink their marketing mix. In addition, there are dramatic changes to take place in the twenty-first century.

Demographic projections indicate that the current population will increase 7.1 percent by the year 2000. But unlike previous population rises, this one will come more from increased longevity. The sixteen to twenty-four age group will continue to shrink as a percentage of the population and the twenty-five to thirty-four age group also will continue to decline. This decline may be more significant than the decline in the younger group because the twenty-five-to thirty-four-year-olds create new households and therefore purchase home furnishings, appliances, housewares, and similar items. The population in the thirty-five to forty-four age group has reached its peak and will continue at that level.

The group between forty-five and fifty-four, clearly on the rise since the early 1980s, is projected to increase 31 percent from 1990 to 2000. This age group is at the peak of its earning ability, while its largest expense—the mortgage—generally is low and close to disappearing. To win loyalty from this group (and capture some of its discretionary income), companies will have to cater to its new needs and preferences. Fueled by the aging of the baby boomers, this group will continue to grow and spend in the 1990s. The fifty-five to sixty-four age group also will rise from the mid-1990s as the immediately younger group gets older. In addition, the increased longevity owing to medical advances will increase the numbers in this age group. Many in this group will go into retirement, which means a necessary slowing of spending. But it also means more time available for shopping. Therefore, companies will succeed by offering these customers merchandise for travel and other leisure activities.[1]

In the retailing field, marketing executives must be responsive to the changing demographics and preferences (as mentioned above) in order to succeed. Altering *product offerings* is one way in which retailers can respond. Traditionally, retailers selected their merchandise assortments for breadth and depth. To meet ever-changing consumer preferences, however, retailers need to change their thinking. For example, retailers such as the Limited Stores and The Gap have stuck with their original formulas of offering a small focused assortment in great depth. A stroll through any of the regional malls reveals many similar specialty merchants—stores that exclusively sell sunglasses, nuts, brushes, bathing suits, and so forth. These specialty stores represent the traditional sections in a department store.

From another perspective, there are nationally prominent specialty merchants that dominate their categories. These merchants have successfully developed a following of their own and can make decisions about assortment, pricing, and location, independent of competitors. They will continue to wield huge market power, influencing everything from product development to pricing structures.

Regarding *pricing strategy* and *promotion*, retailers have a method to carve out a niche for themselves. The meteoric rise of discounters in the 1970s and the early 1980s has reached its peak, primarily because of heavy competition in that market. Currently, growth appears greatest among those firms that dominate their categories. The reason is that they are specialists that are able to create their own customers and that become market leaders within a chosen segment. The ability of these super specialists to offer both broader and deeper assortments within a limited category ensures them steady traffic without promotional price cutting.

In the 1990s, pricing trends will focus on everyday low prices and high/low promotional pricing. Although promotions encourage comparison shopping to obtain the best price, many people with demands on their time refuse to do that and instead will trade potential savings for time. This partially explains the success of WalMart. From a management perspective, everyday low pricing means labor savings because of reduced marking and remarking of price tags and fewer stock shortages on the promotional items. In addition, rather than ticketing an item at an expected selling price, the retailer sets an artificially high ticket price. Markdowns or promotions then bring the item down to the expected selling price. Retailers that choose this pricing and promotion strategy will have to be good merchants, combining fresh merchandising with crisper visual presentations and perhaps adding store attractions to keep the traffic flowing. The promotions of the department stores will most likely continue since they depend more heavily than others on selling quickly changing fashions.

The changing demographics are best illustrated in the emergence of *new channels of distribution* and the resurgence of some old channels of distribution. The demand for convenience, not just price, has allowed nonstore retailers to flourish. Since the technology is changing so rapidly, it is impossible to guess what the end of the next decade will bring, but here are some of the important trends: electronic shopping, mail-order catalog/direct mail, manufacturers' outlets, and hypermarkets.

Enlarged View of Core Competence to Develop New Opportunities

In order to create new markets for products and services, early and consistent investment in what is called "core competencies" is one important factor. In turn, corporate imagination and expeditionary marketing are the keys that unlock these new markets. A company that underinvests in its core competencies, or inadvertently surrenders them through alliances and outsourcing, generally robs its own future. But to realize the potential that core competencies create, a company must also have the imagination to envision markets that do not yet exist and the ability to stake them out ahead of the competition. In a few words, a company must anticipate what the customers·want before they are aware of what they want.[2]

A company will strive to create new competitive space only if it possesses an opportunity perspective that goes far beyond the boundaries of its present businesses. This perspective identifies, in broad terms, the marketing territory that top management hopes to stake out over the coming years, a terrain that is unlikely to be captured in anything as precise as a five-year marketing plan. The initial enthusiasm that several Japanese companies brought to developing high-definition TV (HDTV) grew out of just such a vision. Creative considerations of the many new opportunities that might emerge if HDTV could be made a reality led the Japanese companies beyond the traditional boundaries of color TV business to the identification of potential markets in cinema production, video photography, video magazines, electronic museums, product demonstrations, and training simulations, among others.

As this example demonstrates, a company's opportunity perspective represents its collective imagination of the ways in which an important new benefit might be harnessed to create new competitive space or reshape existing space. Commitment to an opportunity perspective does not rest on return-on-investment (ROI) calculations but on an almost visceral sense of the benefits that customers will finally derive should pioneering work prove successful. The more fundamental the envisioned benefits and the more widely shared the enthusiasm for the opportunity, the greater a company's perseverance will be.[3]

Although there is a need for core competencies to create new markets, there is also a need for an enlarged view of these competencies. Conceiving a company as a group of core competencies rather than as a group of products and services is one way to extend the opportunity perspective considerably. Because Motorola sees itself as a leader in wireless communications, it is not just a producer of paging devices and mobile telephones. Rather, the company's charter permits it to explore markets as diverse as wireless local-area computer networks and global-positioning satellite receivers. Ajinomoto, a giant grocery-products company, not only is in the food business but also applies the skills it has mastered in fermentation technology to the production of an elastic paper for Sony's top-end headphones. The point to be made from these examples is that if company managers are not able to think outside current business boundaries, they will miss important new opportunities that depend on the combination of skills from several divisions.[4]

Need to Go Beyond Traditional Approach to Market Research

In light of the above discussion wherein a company leads its customers where they want to go before customers know it themselves, NEC pursues a telephone that can interpret between callers speaking in different languages. Similarly, Motorola envisions a world where telephone numbers are attached to people rather than places and where a PC allows millions of out-of-touch business travelers to be reached anywhere. Market research and segmentation analysts are unlikely to reveal such opportunities because deep insight into the customers' needs, lifestyles, and aspirations are required.

There are many ways in which such insights may be garnered, all of which go beyond methods of market research. For example, Toshiba has a Lifestyle Research Institute and Sony explores human science as vigorously as it pursues the leading edge of audiovisual technology. Yamaha gains insights into unarticulated needs and potentionally new functionalities through a "listening post" that it established some years ago in London. Stocked with leading-edge electronic hardware, the facility offers some of Europe's most talented musicians a chance to experiment with the future of music making. The feedback helps Yamaha continually extend competitive boundaries that it has staked out in the music business. In effect, Yamaha's approach illustrates a basic point. To gain the most profound insights into its customers, the company must observe up close the coming needs of its most demanding customers.

Companies that succeed in leading customers to what is possible develop both marketers with technological imagination and technologists with marketing imagination. As an example, in one Japanese company, senior technical officers spend as many as thirty days a year outside Japan talking to customers. The aim is not to solve technical problems nor to close a sale but to listen and observe customers and absorb their thinking. In another example, a Japanese chief engineer of a major new business-development program lived for a time with an American family that was thought to be representative of the customers that his company hoped to win. In each case, the goal was not to improve the flow of information between marketers and engineers nor to manage the balance of power between the two groups but rather to blur organizational and career boundaries by ensuring that both communities had a large base of shared experiences. The net result was a good mixture of market and technical imagination.[5]

Utilization of Creative Computer Software to Assist Marketing Management

Generally, the development of innovative products and services takes one of the following three forms: (1) adding an important new function to a well-known product (Yamaha's digital recording piano), (2) developing a novel form in which to deliver a well-known functionality (automated teller machines), and (3) delivering a new functionality through an entirely new product concept (fax machines). Standard approaches to market analysis are not likely to lead to innovations like these. They are created when people substitute a matrix of needs and functionalities for the more conventional matrix of customers and products. The end result is a new, reworked view of the market.

To help marketing managers to conceive markets in relation to their needs and functionalities, creative computer software can be very helpful. Idea generators, for example, can be useful in developing new products and services along with market opportunities for marketing managers. Two such packages are IdeaFisher and Mindlink. IdeaFisher uses two tools. The QBank (first tool) guides the user through a series of stock questions (which can be modified or added to by the user), and it copies the user's response to a note pad for further filtering (this process also allows for interactive word searches while the user is answering the questions). The IdeaBank (second tool) lets the user compare two words and phrases and responds with every word or phrase cross-referenced to the two that the user entered. From a different perspective, MindLink leads the user through a series of questions and answers including a non sequitur here and there. After this, the program will ask the user to ponder the similarities and differences between the user's topic and some object that is determined. Included with the program are a number of different objects that the program may ask the user to ponder. This may be considered a wild approach to generating ideas, but that is just the point. The program makes the user shift gears in the hope of triggering a solution to the problem. Overall, IdeaFisher is better suited to marketing problems that require the use of words and phrases. In contrast, MindLink is more useful if the solution to the marketing problem is likely to be a plan of action.[6]

In addition to helping marketing managers to conceive markets in relation to their needs and functionalities, creative computer software can go a step further by helping marketing managers establish market leadership for their companies. The creation of new ideas for products and services by using creative computer software can assist in determining what customers want before they themselves know of a particular need. In order to reach this market-leadership goal, marketing managers must change their mind-set when viewing current and future products and services for their customers. But more importantly, marketing managers need to have the capability of utilizing creative computer software when deemed appropriate. Hence, creative computer software should become an integral part of rethinking the marketing function, that is, operating on a proactive or forward-thinking basis.

Utilization of Principles from Profit Impact of Marketing Strategies

Profit Impact of Marketing Strategies (PIMS) is a computerized approach for planning market strategy and is run by the Strategic Planning Institute. It is a data pool of information on the marketing experiences of its members.[7] Several hundred corporations submit data annually on a total of about three thousand of their business units, each of which is a distinct product-market unit. Each member provides PIMS with the most intimate details on such matters as its market share, investment intensity, product quality, and total marketing and R&D expenditures. Through computer simulation, the company can then test its own market strategies against the real experiences of hundreds of comparable companies, including competitors. What it receives are answers to questions such as these: What is the normal profit rate for a business or a product line given its combination of circumstances, and why? If the business continues on its current track, what will its future operating results be? What will happen to short- and long-term performance if certain strategic moves are made? What changes will create the best profits or cash returns?

Typically, what a member company wants from PIMS is to find out what it will cost to make a particular strategic move and how much better off the business will be afterward. For example, consider return on investment, which PIMS considers one of the best measures of how a business is doing. The PIMS models can forecast how much ROI for a business line will change because of a strategic move involving more marketing, R&D, capital-equipment buildup, or whatever—both what the ROI will be immediately following the move and what it will be several years in the future. Figure 7.1 sets forth some new as well as traditional principles that have emerged from PIMS computer models of the real-life experiences of its corporate members.

When extrapolating from the PIMS database, it is recommended that companies should not automatically compare themselves to competitors in the same industry or business category to find out how well they are doing. According to PIMS, industry breakdowns are not all-important. A better yardstick may be the performance of companies in other industries whose total situation is comparable. A tire company, for example, may have even more in common and more to learn from the market strategies of a small appliance manufacturer than from those of another tire company.

THE NECESSITY OF A CREATIVE APPROACH TO VR RETAILING AND MARKETING APPLICATIONS

In the preceding sections on rethinking the marketing function within a VR world, the focus was on being *proactive* to the needs of customers versus being *reactive*, as so often is the case today. For example, I have experienced the following situation that, in turn, can be multiplied by thousands of customers. I had phoned to reserve a room at a hotel for an eagerly awaited out-of-town vacation. After the dates and rates were agreed upon, the reservations operator began to ask the usual questions. I responded that I was a member of his frequent-hotel-guest program and gave him my number. After a brief delay, the operator came back and informed me that my frequent-hotel-guest number had been terminated because of inactivity. Although I had an urgent impulse to tell the operator that I had suddenly decided to stay inactive, my good judgment prevailed. However, in retrospect, I am appalled at the chain's lack of marketing savvy in regard to collecting information on my preferences that could have been used to lure me back relatively easily with targeted marketing. Instead, the hotel chain felt that it was better to ignore people like myself who have the time and money to take advantage of special offers. In essence, the lack of creative thinking caused this hotel chain to focus its sales attention on serving and expanding their relationships with active customers, thereby bypassing a huge potential market of inactive customers.

Figure 7.1
Principles That Have Emerged from PIMS Computer Models

- There is a set of operating rules that govern all businesses. Some 37 factors—including market share, capital intensity, and vertical integration—jointly explain 80 percent of the success or failure of any business; only 20 percent of a business's return on investment can be attributed to factors that are unique or special, such as the quality of working relations.
- Anything more than a minimal R&D program does not make sense for a company with a weak market position. Copying competitors' products rather than inventing them is probably a company's best bet. This can be a very profitable strategy.
- High marketing expenditures for low-quality products can have a devastating effect on profits.
- High product quality can offset a weak market position.
- Weak companies should not become vertically integrated, whereas strong ones should.
- High costs in more than one area—such as capital investment, R&D, or marketing—can ruin any business.

Currently, it is common for companies to purge their databases of inactive customers so that they do not waste magnetic storage. But reducing costs in this way is not a creative way to expand a customer base. In effect, these companies are throwing away customer names while their advertising and marketing departments are spending many thousands, even millions, of dollars to identify and entice prospective customers. The cost of storing the data describing an inactive customer is generally much less than a penny, while the cost of identifying a new prospect can range from tens to hundreds of dollars. Moreover, every company knows more about the preferences and buying habits of the inactive customer than of the prospective customer. Why not, then, design a marketing program to induce inactive customers to do business again? A company that undertakes a creative and proactive approach to inactive customers can utilize VR to help get a better handle on this past customer base.

RETAILING AND MARKETING APPLICATIONS THAT CAN BENEFIT FROM VR

Applications that can benefit from VR in the areas of retailing and marketing are varied, as will be seen in the second half of this chapter. The capability of retailing and marketing personnel to zoom under, through, and over landscapes that are 3-D depictions of marketplaces in real time will be apparent in the following discussion. For the most part, the skill with which a company's systems designers and programmers can portray key aspects of the changing retailing and marketing landscapes and the capability of marketing managers to make key decisions about the present and future directions of markets will make a very important difference between being somewhat successful to being extremely successful. From this perspective, marketing managers will be trying new and novel ways to spark fresh ideas for new products and services and to conduct their business throughout the entire marketing, manufacturing, and financial chain.

VR CUSTOMER-ORDER FLOW

Even though customer-order flows (COFs) vary from industry to industry and are different for products and services, almost every company has similar organization activities. Fundamentally, these activities define a company's business-information structure since they offer a company's managers an opportunity to look at its operations not only from its own viewpoint but also through the customer's eyes, that is, to see and experience transactions in the way in which customers do. From this dual perspective, every time the order is handled, the customer is handled. If the order sits unattended, the customer also sits unattended.

For effective and efficient operations, it is necessary to go beyond customers and products and examine customer-order activities. In the final analysis, it is the order that connects the customer to the company. Moreover, focusing on the COF offers managers an opportunity to improve overall operations and possibly create new competitive advantages. In effect, managers can examine the entire COF cycle in order to discover how various changes affect customers. When the COF centers solely on departmental interaction, the focus becomes narrow. On the other hand, the integration of the customer into the COF should become the overriding goal of the entire company, and department conflicts must give way to solutions, so that the customer benefits.

An excellent way for managers to learn about the ins and outs of the COF is to track an order as it moves through the entire cycle. This process starts with order planning, that is, sales forecasting and capacity planning of the company's factories. There is also a need to take a look at how the products are costed and priced before they are marketed. Next, there is a need to examine how orders are generated outside as well as inside the company. Essentially, the focus is on order receipt and entry, followed by order selection and prioritization of these orders. These activities are followed by scheduling of the orders along with how the orders are actually filled. Finally, there is a series of activities that are related to billing the customer. After the orders are shipped, there can be returns and allowances for these returns along with claims for nonreceipt of the goods. In addition, the company may need to provide some type of postsales service. Figure 7.2 illustrates these company activities that center on the typical customer's order. Overall, there are a whole host of COF activities that are related to the actual order. Similarly, the same approach can be applied to manufacturing

Figure 7.2
Customer-Order Flow for a Typical Company

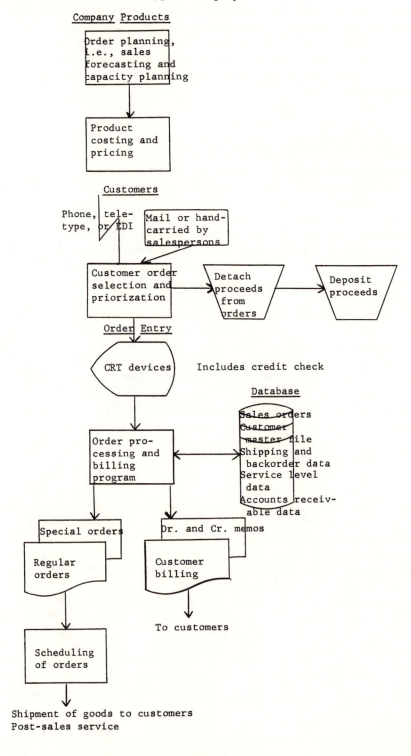

activities so as to determine what improvements can be made to make manufacturing operations more efficient and effective.

A thorough examination of the detailed COF activities for a typical company reveals a number of important factors. First, managers at the top do not understand the specific details of their customer-order–processing activities, while those at the lower levels see only their own individual details. Second, when an order moves across departmental boundaries, that is, from one function to another, generally no one is responsible or held accountable for it or the customer. Third, there is a need for order selection and priorization because not all orders offer the same profits. Typically, no one undertakes order selection and priorization since the sales force chooses the customers, and customer service representatives or production schedulers establish the priorities.

Modeling the Customer-Order Flow

There are several approaches to improving a company's customer-order flow so that the whole cycle from start to finish is clearly understood. It should be noted that the activities in Figure 7.2 are presented from an overview standpoint. In actuality, there may be several hundred detailed activities found in COF on a day-to-day basis. One approach to the COF cycle is to duplicate the detailed operations on paper and place the completed flowcharts on one or more walls for evaluation. Another approach is to use knitting yarn that charts the order flow from the first step to the last. In both cases, the focus is on highlighting problems and opportunities for improvement. Disagreements over improvements would allow reviewers to focus on *facts* rather than on *opinions* about how the COF really works. In effect, when managers walk through the entire COF cycle, they have the capability of asking whether each step can be improved with a computer or, perhaps, eliminated altogether with new technology and processes.

An integral part of either analysis requires that the company look at the COF from the customer's point of view. Although a typical company finds that 95 percent of all orders went out on time, a survey of the company's customers might reveal that only 50 percent were satisified with deliveries. To reconcile the difference, it is necessary for managers to look at the issue from the customer's angle and compare it with their own point of view. For example, a customer survey measured the date when the customer actually received the order, but the company's own system was based on the date when it shipped the order. In addition, if an order consisted of fifty items and the company correctly shipped forty-nine of the items, the internal system recorded a 98-percent perfect shipment. On the other hand, the customer who needed all fifty items before work could begin recorded the order as incomplete.

A preferred approach to analyzing a COF cycle is to develop a VR program that enables sales and marketing managers the capability of flying over sales and marketing data, thereby allowing them to observe 3-D bar graphs as they move over the regions examined. In each sales or customer location, 3-D bars show totals and breakdowns of information that would otherwise take hundreds of pages of number crunching. Next, another VR program is developed that allows functional departmental managers to navigate through the many, detailed COF activities on an interactive basis in real time and to visualize objectively in 3-D for improvements. In turn, these improvements can be the subject matter of meetings with functional departmental managers and their support personnel. Gaps will be found in the COF cycle not only from the company's perspective but also from the customer's perspective—which is most important in today's and tomorrow's business world. Overall, the modeling of the COF within a VR environment will go a long way toward creating an ideal COF that will more than pay for itself in a very short time.

The benefits of utilizing a well-run COF are many. Companies will fill orders faster and will be more accurate when doing so. Interdepartmental problems will tend to be minimzed compared to previously. In addition, the level of politicking will be at a manageable level. The net result of these benefits is that the company's financial performance should improve. Typically, companies have thrown money at their problems, building excess capacity, adding inventory, or increasing the number of employees, all of which are expensive and none of which solve the important problems. When an COF cycle is properly managed, a company can achieve its goals a lot more easily.

Although these benefits are oriented toward *efficiency* of operations in a manual approach to the COF cycle, a VR solution goes a step further by centering on the *effectiveness* of operations. More to the point, the capability of tying together the activities of the COF cycle in a comprehensive manner provides systems analysts with a new approach to improving a company's effectiveness among its numerous operations. Functional departmental managers can be shown that what they do at the various stages of the COF affects other departments down the line such that effective operations are interdependent and not islands unto themselves. Thus, a VR approach to the COF cycle can be quite beneficial to a typical company.

VR CUSTOMER DESIGN

Currently, architects and designers are learning to apply VR to the area of customer design. Some are testing a system designed by Prairie Virtual Systems (Chicago, Illinois) that lets a person don a special helmet and sensor-lined glove for a "walk through a room" existing only in a computer. Without a costly mock-up, the person can try the architecture and furniture to check placement, height, and other details. The system's cost ranges from $20,000 to $30,000. Because of its high cost, Prairie plans to open service centers where firms and other users can try VR on an hourly basis.

The system has some ardent supporters. One such is Herman Miller's Milcare, which furnishes health-care facilities. This VR system is better than 3-D computing because it allows the user to move things around and contemplate the consequences. In Illinois, Deerfield architects OWP&P have designed the new Coppley Memorial Hospital in Aurora. Hospital administrators insisted on building a traditional mock-up of a patient room for $25,000. But it was Prairie's VR that discovered a displaced sink bowl, which would have cost $8,000 to correct.[8]

Evaluation of a New Kitchen Layout

Working with VPL Research, the Japanese have come up with one of the first VR marketplace applications. In Tokyo, Matsushita Electric Works opened a showroom called "virtual kitchen" that is equipped with U.S.-developed headsets and DataGloves. Prospective buyers of the company's custom-built kitchens can experience what the kitchens would look and even feel like. For example, the customer's virtual hand has the capability of opening drawers or turning on the hot or cold water. A customer gives the dimensions of his or her kitchen to a salesperson and tells what appliances and cabinets are wanted. In turn, the salesperson enters this information into a computer. Next, the customer puts on the headgear and the DataGlove—and the new kitchen appears in the air before the customer. The individual can then move around the room, getting a feel for what working in it would be like. The customer can open the doors of the virtual appliances and cabinets to make sure that they are unobstructed (Figure 7.3).

Customers not only can lay out their dream kitchens but also can turn on faucets, pick up dishes—and even break them, if they happen to drop them while setting the table. When the company opened its virtual kitchen, the first entranced customer spent an hour in the make-believe room. However, the customer had to pay real money, that is, buying many thousands worth of appliances. In effect, this VR approach gives a customer the ability to create a virtual kitchen in about thirty minutes, about the time it takes a customer to have a cup of coffee. The customer's order is sent to the factory, and, typically, a customer has the custom-built kitchen within two weeks.[9]

VR MERCHANDISING

The VR showroom mentioned above is more than just a display center. It has become more of a design center where the customer comes into contact with Matsushita products. Matsushita has over thirty thousand different products, all of which it could never display at one place for the customer's inspection. The Matsushita kitchen is the first test case of a new approach to Japanese manufacturing being developed through the New Industrialization House Production Technology and System Development Project, sponsored by the Ministry of International Trade and Industry. Although the goal is to make a living environment more responsive to customers' needs, the project has also resulted in creating a new type of just-in-time, customer-driven production process. Hence,

Figure 7.3
Interior View of a New Kitchen Layout

Source: Reprinted courtesy of Worldesign Inc., 5348½ Ballard Avenue, Seattle, Washington, 98107–4009.

it is possible to envision a total production system that translates a customer's experience into a manufactured product.

The VR showroom can be extended beyond the kitchen to include the design of the customer's new house. In a virtual-building walk-through, the architect can add features and colors desired by the customer such that the customer has a real feel for what the final building will be like. By working with the customer, the architect can develop a floor layout, move walls around, and even change the landscaping. In effect, the customer can visit the interior of the house by walking around before making a commitment to the actual building. Both Intel and the Sense8 Corporation have developed a prototype of this application where it was tried out on several hundred people at the Computer Museum in Boston. A wand device is used to select, and objects move around in the virtual house. The wand can select from many architectural building blocks (walls with doors, windows, and the like) to construct a single or multistory house. The basic look of rooms can be changed with texture mapping, that is, each wall can be individually selected and its color changed. It is expected that in the future, VR design will be standard fare for developing a house so that the chance of errors or misunderstanding between the architect and the customer are minimized.[10]

Modeling of a New Store

This VR-modeling process can be extended to the modeling of a new store before it is constructed. The ways in which products are displayed within a department store or a supermarket are crucial to the business's ultimate success. To get a feel for the store's layout, a cross-section of customers can be invited to try out the new store in a virtual world, and their responses can be observed. Although this approach is somewhat subjective, it can point out important problems before the actual store is built. Too often in the past, stores have had to be redesigned after the store is built because some important considerations were ignored or not contemplated originally. This VR modeling of a store before the fact can save a typical company many millions over the long run because shoppers like to shop in "your store" versus the "competition's."

Just as new stores can be designed by using virtual worlds, the same can be done for remodeling a store. Layouts, including aisle displays, can be tested by customers to get their responses to redesigned stores. As with a new store, there is no need to undergo the changes until there is sufficient testing from the customer's viewpoint to justify the changes as far as cost is concerned. There is no need to make changes for the sake of change when there will be little or no impact on the store's profits. The modeling of a new store will be covered in more detail in Chapter 8.

Going beyond the modeling of a new store by using VR, the same can be done on a larger scale, as for a proposed new city or town, shown in Figure 7.4. From this perspective, VR allows city planners to develop from scratch a whole new world where people can live, work, and play. Or city planners can redo present cities or towns that are noted for specific products and/or services and can marry the best of the old with proposed new facilities, highways, and waterways. Hence, VR worlds can be beneficial to city planners since they allow the planners to interact with the ever-changing landscape.

VR ADVERTISING EFFECTIVENESS

Typically, traditional methods of measuring advertising's effectiveness are flawed by several assumptions. For one, advertisers assume that if a potential customer remembers a radio or television commercial, the individual is more likely to buy the product or service. This leads to overreliance on advertising that may be unique but may not influence buyers in a positive way. Or the same commercial may be repeated continually such that the potential customer is turned off by the repetition. Such approaches miss the point because the influence of an advertising campaign is revealed in many different and subtle ways. To come reasonably close to understanding the effectiveness of advertising, an advertiser must collect and analyze as much information about as many different variables as possible, from as many different sources. In turn, the advertiser

Figure 7.4
Desktop Monitor Projecting a Navigable Virtual World onto a Screen

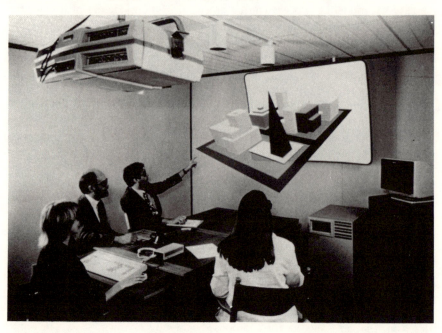

Source: Reprinted courtesy of StereoGraphics Corp., 2171 E. Francisco Boulevard, San Rafael, California 94901.

considers this information in light of the complete advertising program, and not simply as it relates to a specific advertisement.

Newer technologies in use can be found at the Arbitron Ratings Company, Nielsen, Information Resources, and other research companies. Nielsen, for example, installs universal-product-code (UPC) scanners, cousins of the holographic scanners used in supermarket checkout counters, in the same homes where its "people meters" track the TV programs each family member watches. After a shopping trip, family members scan the UPC codes on products they have purchased so that Nielsen can correlate what its surveyed families buy with the TV programming they watch. Analyzed along with records of total purchases (Nielsen and others buy from the supermarkets records collected by the checkout scanners), this information can reveal key correlations between an advertiser's share of the "ad space" and the advertiser's market share, even at a very local level. In the latest technology upgrade, Nielsen is using a new kind of "people meter" that knows who is in the room. The meter compares this information to the database of images it has stored on the system so that it can say exactly who was in the room watching TV. The ultimate goal of this technology is to provide advertisers with more information that is less influenced by biases. In effect, what is now available is better information about what is actually going on.[11]

Experiential Advertising

Without computerized tools, however, advertising managers cannot accurately assess all the information. Emerging are computerized software systems intended to help advertisers analyze research data from various sources along with their own data. Systems to analyze market data have been around for some time, but the new ones stress ease of use, broad access to multisource data, and graphical modeling tools. For example, Metaphor Computer Systems (Mountain View, California) markets what it calls its data-interpretation system, consisting of a workstation that features a Macintosh-style interface and software that accesses and combines data from many different sources, including Nielsen and corporate mainframe databases. Another example is the New York-based Interactive Market Systems (IMS), which sells a range of marketing-analysis software products that summarize and combine data from more than four hundred databases, including Nielsen, Gallup, Simmons, and others. The MixMastr is an intermedia planning system that evaluates total campaign reach and frequency based on all the media used—print, broadcast, or whatever. Another IMS product, Link, combines information from an advertising-expenditure database with audience information from several different databases to help advertisers assess audience delivery per dollar for print advertising.

Although these current computerized systems have made great strides in assisting advertising managers, there is a need to reassess the direction currently undertaken. More specifically, this centers around VR. Cyberevent Group (Brooklyn, New York) is offering a VR-software package called Experiential Advertising. It has the potential to be one of the most innovative applications of VR technology. Consumers will be able to enter and, more important, interact with marketing messages of all types. Consumers will be able to experience almost any marketing world, as shown in Figure 7.5. Virtual reality offers advertisers an excellent sampling opportunity that will draw attention to any product as well as provide important information about a company's products and services. In addition, information could be given about discounts along with the actual issuance of the discount coupons. Hence, advertising within a VR environment is an unusual opportunity for a company to influence the buying decisions of today's consumers where buying possibilities are varied and numerous.

OTHER RETAILING AND MARKETING AREAS THAT CAN BENEFIT FROM VR

In addition to the foregoing VR applications, several other areas of retailing and marketing can benefit from a VR world. Market researchers, for example,

Figure 7.5
Interactive Experiential Advertising Allowing Consumers to Experience Almost any Marketing World

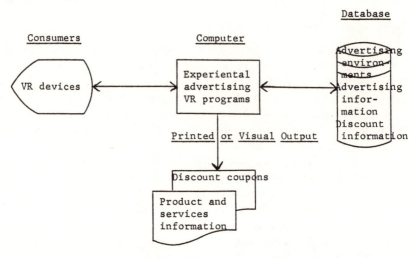

could simulate in real time a topographic map of the United States that includes detailed demographic data of the major and minor metropolitan areas. Maps of these areas show the same data at different intervals in the past. There could be a simulated comparison of the past versus the future. These data could represent gross statistical information about representative population samples, their total income, for example, being scaled to their medium age. There could be a further elaboration that could become much richer in exploring the demographics. Different variations could represent educational differences or the breakdown of data by sex.

In such a simulated environment where the past is compared to the future, market researchers could fly over this synthesized landscape and could look down and notice certain patterns of growth or decline. One particular area might show tremendous growth potential. Given the information available in this "cyberspace" system, the market researcher could note both prevailing patterns of change and new growth areas. The market researcher might see new patterns not evident in the traditional method of analysis. The individual could then zoom in for a closer look and might, while walking among the major and minor metropolitan areas, see that the higher levels of income are related to certain age groups, educational backgrounds, and residential patterns. These variables, then, would all be taken into account in further statistical-analysis models on metropolitan areas.

The focus of this VR exploratory process is that this investigation proceeds by actions that market researchers do most frequently and most intuitively. Market researchers view things and when curious move in a bit closer to see more of the detail. On the other hand, to gain a broader perspective, they move back a few steps. In this VR market-research application, the created VR distills multiple layers of what are typically varied and dissociated data. Because the VR variable is no longer mere abstraction or tabular representation, the data have become immediately more accessible and more alive to those in market research who have need of such data.

An important VR-marketing application is its use at trade-show exhibits. Millions of dollars are spent on trade shows for the purpose of putting a company's products in the best possible light, emphasizing whatever advantages a company's products may have over those of competitors. Virtual reality is ideal for this use since it can double both as a "flypaper" for trade-show exhibits and as an educational tool. Since companies pay hundreds of thousands of dollars for video creation and rental of video walls and custom fabrication of exhibits for the trade-show floor, the resultant attractiveness of these exhibits is sometimes questionable and is difficult to quantify. However, a company that uses VR in the trade-show environment can ride on the wave of enthusiasm for VR and benefit from the resulting free publicity. Virtual reality offers a proven means of attracting attendees to a booth as well as providing a unique educational experience. Typically, attendees will wait a long time to try VR versus video walls or traditional interactive computer programs and videodisks.[12]

Sales and marketing departments can benefit greatly from the utilization of interactive VR presentations rather than prerecorded audiovisual material or brochures. Products that are in the preliminary-design stage can be visualized in three dimensions, thereby highlighting quite effectively their benefits. Concepts and features, including motion, can be easily portrayed. For example, a company in the distribution and warehousing sector uses a desktop VR system to win new business via an interactive sales presentation that focuses on the visualization of the latest techniques in warehousing systems. The company is in the rapidly developing area of computerized warehousing wherein space optimization is the key criterion. Currently in use by the presentation department, the Virtual Reality Toolkit (VRT) is used in conjunction with other design packages to provide the company with a complete range of presentation media. Because interaction and movement are the most important elements, VR is used to show how an automated warehouse will operate in real life.

In this example, VR provides a sales medium for showing customers how their goods will be stored and transported. Using the VRT, objects are endowed with characteristics of friction, gravity, and movement, such that the complete workings of the warehouse can be displayed realistically. In the early stages of development, the company's designers used the VRT to create sections of a warehouse and to show pallet arrival, identification, and subsequent transportation to a user-defined destination. Stored pallets can also be retrieved from the system and transported to loading bays. In essence, a VR approach provides the needed assistance to the sales department to close a sale for a new warehouse.[13]

Other examples include salesmanship that conjures up the VR of the customer's dream. A company could pit itself against different market situations to see how it would come out. Or from another perspective, a company could take its sales history and apply it to future problems.

In all of the preceding retailing and marketing applications, a reader should have come away with a very important message concerning VR worlds. This will also be true of the remaining chapters of the text. If a person reads, he or she tends to forget. If a person sees, he or she tends to remember. In contrast, if a person experiences VR, he or she is undergoing a learning experience that is far superior to a reading or seeing experience. The ability to travel to places that most people regard as too remote, too complex, or simply too costly allows retailing and marketing personnel to visualize the results of incorrect decisions in ways not possible previously. This capability alone may justify the utilization of simulated virtual worlds.

SUMMARY

In this chapter, I emphasized the need to rethink the marketing function in order to make the most effective usage of VR. Marketing areas that need to be rethought include the changing marketing mix, the need for core competence to create new markets, market leaders who know what customers want, a closer look at competition, and the development of innovative products and services. Essentially, revamped marketing thinking stresses the fact that the company knows what its customers want before they know themselves and influences the direction that the market will take today and tomorrow. For many companies, profound changes in marketing policy must be undertaken, and the mind-set of marketing managers must be changed before implementing VR worlds. For the most part, creating a new way of thinking about marketing and VR-marketing directions must come initially from top management. In the second half of the chapter, I presented applications that showed the relationship of VR to rethinking the marketing function.

NOTES

1. Richard V. Sarkissian, "Retailing Trends in the 1990s," *Journal of Accountancy*, December 1989, pp. 44–55.

2. Gary Hamel and C. K. Prahalad, "The Core Competence of the Corporation," *Harvard Business Review*, May–June 1990, p. 79.

3. Gary Hamel and C. K. Prahalad, "Corporate Imagination and Expeditionary Marketing," *Harvard Business Review,* July–August 1991, pp. 81–82.

4. Ibid., p. 83.

5. Ibid., pp. 85–86.

6. Robert J. Thierauf, *Creative Computer Software for Strategic Thinking and De-*

cision Making: A Guide for Senior Management and MIS Professionals (Westport, Conn.: Quorum Books, 1993), pp. 159–73.

7. Paula Smith, "Unique Tool for Marketers: PIMS," *Management Review*, January 1977, pp. 32–34.

8. John Pierson, "Virtual Reality Offers a View with a Room," *Wall Street Journal*, December 3, 1993, p. B1.

9. Gene Bylinsky, "The Marvels of 'Virtual Reality,' " *Fortune*, June 3, 1991, p. 142.

10. Ken Pimentel and Kevin Teixeira, *Virtual Reality: Through the New Looking Glass*, New York: McGraw-Hill, 1993, pp. 187–90.

11. Ned Snell, "How Hard Is Our Advertising Working?" *EDGE*, January–February 1990, pp. 44–46.

12. Jonathan R. Merril, "VR for Medical Training and Trade Show 'Fly-Paper,' " *Virtual Reality World*, May–June 1994, pp. 56–57.

13. Andy Tait, "Authoring Virtual Worlds on the Desktop," *Virtual Reality Special Report*, published by *AI Expert* (San Francisco: Miller Freeman, 1993), p. 12.

8

Design and Manufacturing in a Business-Oriented Virtual-Reality Environment

ISSUES EXPLORED

- To set forth a starting point for VR design and manufacturing for a typical company
- To examine newer directions in design and manufacturing that can be related to VR
- To explore new design environments that can be improved by utilizing virtual walk-throughs
- To demonstrate the varied benefits that can be derived from 3-D simulation
- To show how a factory and its maintenance function can be carried out better by using VR

OUTLINE

Introduction to Design and Manufacturing in a VR Environment

New Directions in Design and Manufacturing That Are Needed for VR

    Reengineering to Improve Productivity

    Focus on Total Quality Management

    Value Analysis to Reduce Product Costs

    Computer-Aided Simulation of Manufacturing and Nonmanufacturing Activities

    A Practical View of Just-in-Time Inventories

Necessity of an Interactive 3-D Computer-Aided-Design Approach to VR Design and Manufacturing

Design and Manufacturing Applications That can Benefit from VR

VR Design of New Products and Environments

    Evaluation of Alternative Designs by Using Walk-throughs

INTRODUCTION TO DESIGN AND MANUFACTURING IN A VR ENVIRONMENT

As highlighted in the prior chapter, the marketplace is rapidly changing in the new ways that are different from the past. Worldwide competition demands a renewed emphasis on product and service quality. Typically, in a Japanese company, a product is examined in great detail before it is made, that is, in the design stage. In turn, the manufacturing process is engineered to be stable and reliable. If the design as well as the process is good, quality is inherent. In the United States, companies have now realized that quality improvement is essential. It is not just good business but is essential to a company's success. It is necessary not only to build a product faster and cheaper, but also to make that product better. This approach to quality emphasizes the cost effectiveness of *productivity* in all areas of a company—from design to the assembly line. It is easy to forget that improvement in the office is as important as improvement in manufacturing or elsewhere in a company.

It is from this perspective that there is a need to rethink the manufacturing function from a VR perspective—the subject matter of the first part of this chapter. Next, appropriate VR applications in design and manufacturing are presented wherein total quality management is assumed. The concept of total quality control centers on applying quality principles not only in the factory but also to every operation, including dealings with suppliers. The end result has blossomed into the "just-in-time" movement whereby parts are delivered to an assembly line at just the moment they are needed. This holds down costs, but it requires consistently high quality up and down the supply chain.

NEW DIRECTIONS IN DESIGN AND MANUFACTURING THAT ARE NEEDED FOR VR

Virtual reality offers an entirely new way to interface with the computer, a way that takes the user through the screen and into an entirely virtual world. As noted in earlier chapters, the first VR system was developed at the NASA

Ames Research Center and is useful for exploring space environments. The origins of VR can also be traced to the flight simulators that airlines and the U.S. Air Force use for training their pilots. Similarly, architects were among the first to embrace VR for designing, exploring, and modifying whole buildings without a single physical model ever being constructed. In many cases, the most important element of VR hardware is a lightweight headset containing two small liquid-crystal screens (one for each eye) and a sensor to track the position of the user's head. Stereo vision is of key importance for making wearers feel that they are actually within a simulated scene where the user can operate in an interactive, real-time mode.

During the next several years, designers and engineers, aided by gloves fitted with sensors, will be able to interact with computer-generated images appearing on tiny goggle-mounted binocular displays in order to participate in seemingly 3-D computer-aided design (CAD) sessions, aircraft flight tests, or even reengineering. Although existing VR systems require the power of a large computer and typically render their images as blocky polygons with jerky motion, newer and more powerful computer hardware will allow users to build smoother running systems, eventually transferring them to desktop or even portable computers.

In the area of design and manufacturing, there may be a need to extend VR to distant places. Within this context, the term used is *telepresence*, which refers to the ability to interact with a distant environment through robotic technology. Telepresence technology allows remotely situated operators to receive sensory feedback that lets them perform tasks in a remote place. Current work in telepresence, much of it occurring at NASA/Ames Research Center, involves using VR to control robots working in space.

In light of these present and future directions in VR, it is helpful to look at the total framework that underlies all considerations for a typical manufacturing company. Such a framework today and in the future centers on computer-integrated manufacturing (CIM). Generally, CIM means blending manufacturing with marketing, finance, accounting, personnel and other functional areas where deemed necessary. Computer-integrated manufacturing is currently crucial to the survival of manufacturers because it provides the levels of planning and control for manufacturing along with the flexibility to change with the times. The basic objective of CIM is to change management's thinking by establishing a framework within which manufacturing operations are defined, funded, managed, and coordinated. This framework requires specific mechanisms for production planning, cost control, projection selection and justification, project management, and project-performance monitoring. The role of the enterprise view of CIM is to ensure that the appropriate levels and types of integration are appropriate.

Today, when rethinking the design and manufacturing activities of a company, the CIM concept needs to be expanded to include virtual worlds. More to the point, expanded CIM virtual worlds have the potential to assist management in reengineering their operations to improve the productivity of the company. As discussed in the next sections, reengineering focuses on doing more with less such that the productivity of personnel and equipment are improved. As an example, an experimental assembly-modeling system at the Northrop Corporation has been tested that radically changes the way in which aircraft are produced. The prototype system makes use of 3-D stereo display and input devices to simulate the assembly process. The system could save money in development costs by eliminating the need for full-scale mock-ups. Thus, Northrop's assembly modeler is a good example of the benefits of stereo viewing and desktop VR in manufacturing. With the Northrop installation, the viewer is provided with a screen that acts as a window on the virtual world. Typically, stereo viewing systems have three major benefits in manufacturing. First, as a productivity tool, the systems can lead to shortened design cycles and improved accuracy. Second, they can make presentations more effective by providing lifelike imagery and simulations. And third, they can make communicating information more intuitive. As can be seen from this example, virtual worlds in design and manufacturing can have a very positive impact on the expanded world of CIM.[1]

From another perspective of the CIM concept, there is an emerging trend that centers on "agile manufacturing." The "agile" concept emphasizes ultraflexible production facilities; constantly shifting alliances among suppliers, producers, and customers; and direct feedback of sales data into the factories. This new direction of manufacturing may take Detroit out of the business of auto production and into the realm of coordinating superproficient suppliers via what has become known as the "virtual factory." Essentially, the assembly plant is not where the game is, but rather in managing its integration. In the virtual factory, suppliers will be involved in the very earliest stages and will help plan and design new components. As the company that buys the most from outsiders, Chrysler is moving fastest toward the virtual factory. Already it is handing over some of its traditional responsibilities to suppliers. Instead of surveying consumers about seating preferences like firmness, width, and color, the company entrusts that task to its supplier Johnson Controls. Chrysler is working more closely with suppliers so that both become links in the chain from raw materials to finished products.[2]

Reengineering to Improve Productivity

Reengineering is one of the most important directions for business currently because the most successful and promising companies must develop new techniques that will allow them to survive in an increasingly competitive climate. To reengineer, that is, reinvent their companies, managers need to abandon past organizational and operational principles and procedures and create entirely new ones. No matter what industry companies are in or how technologically sophisticated their products or services are or what their national origin is, they basically trace their work styles and organizational roots back to the prototypical pin factory that economist Adam Smith described in *Wealth of Nations* (published in 1776). Smith's principle of the division of labor embodied his observation that some number of *specialists*, each performing a single step in the manufacture of a pin, could make far more pins in a day than the same number of *generalists*, each engaged in making whole pins. Today's airlines, car manufacturers, accounting firms, and computer manufacturers, to name a few, have all been built around Smith's central idea. Typically, the larger the organization, the more specialized the work and the more separate the steps into which work is divided, whether it be a manufacturing or nonmanufacturing firm.

Business reengineering means starting from scratch, that is, it centers on forgetting how work was done in the past and deciding how it can best be done now. Old job titles and old organizational arrangements—divisions, departments, groups, and so forth—cease to matter. What matters, however, is how work is organized given the demands of today's markets and the power of today's technologies. At the center of business reengineering is the concept of discontinuous thinking, that is, identifying and abandoning the outdated rules and fundamental assumptions that underlie current business operations. Every company is replete with implicit rules of the past—for example, local warehouses are necessary for good customer service or local marketing decisions are made at headquarters. These rules are based on assumptions about technology, people, and organizational goals that no longer hold.

To reengineer a company's business procedures, it is necessary to rethink these procedures and redesign the *business processes* to achieve improvements so that the company's employees change from specialists to generalists in order to improve productivity. A business process is a collection of activities that takes one or more kinds of input and creates an output that is of value to the customer. For example, in filling an order the delivery of finished products is the value that the process creates. However, Adam Smith's notion of breaking work into its simplest tasks and assigning each of these to a specialist tends to lose sight of the larger objective, which is to get the goods into the hands of the customer who ordered them.

As an example of reengineering whereby employees change from specialists to generalists, consider the accounts-payable department of the Ford Motor Company. Previously 500 accounts-payable clerks (specialists) spent the majority of their time straightening out the problems with purchase orders, invoices, and receiving documents that did not match. However, with the new system, the clerk at the receiving dock takes in the goods and depresses a button on the terminal keyboard that tells the company's database that the goods have arrived. Receipt of the goods is now recorded in the database, and the computer automatically issues and sends a check to the supplier at the appropriate time. On the other hand, if the goods do not correspond to an outstanding purchase order in the database, the clerk on the dock will refuse the shipment and send it back to the supplier. Thus, payment authorization, which used to be performed by the accounts-payable specialist, is now accomplished by the receiving-dock generalist. The old process fostered enough complexity to keep 500 clerks busy.

The new process comes close to eliminating the need for an accounts-payable department altogether. Ford now has just 125 people involved in supplier payment. In some parts of Ford, the head count in accounts payable is a small fraction of its former size.[3]

Focus on Total Quality Management

After being viewed as a manufacturing problem in the past, quality has become a service issue not only for service-sector businesses like communications, health care, and finance but also for the service side of manufacturing companies as well. The focus is on *total quality management* (TQM), that is, quality in the offering itself and in all the services that come with it. If product quality is essentially the same across the industry, service becomes the distinguishing factor. Overall, TQM has become a prerequisite for survival today and tomorrow.

With TQM, the postwar quality movement has moved into its third stage. When the growing popularity of Japanese automobiles, televisions, and radios forced U.S. manufacturers to take another look at themselves in the late 1970s, most companies were still in what quality experts call the first, or inspection, phase, relying on sampling techniques to get rid of defective items. Too often, however, they did not. In 1980—the year an NBC *White Paper* introduced audiences to W. Edwards Deming, the American statistician who had shown the Japanese how to use process controls to catch defects at the source—manufacturers who took the issue seriously started moving into the second, or quality-control, phase. Now, with TQM, quality is no longer solely in the quality-control department. It is sponsored by top management and diffused throughout the company.[4]

In a survey conducted for the American Society for Quality Control (Milwaukee, Wisconsin) by the Gallup Organization in June 1990, it was found that today's workforce does not fully use their talents, abilities, and energies for quality improvement. Today's workforce is saying to management: "Of course, we want to be paid more and we want more job security, but more than that, we want a better chance to put our ideas to work." Lack of employee involvement is a twofold problem: (1) unwillingness or lack of motivation to participate and (2) lack of opportunity to participate. The most frequently cited explanations given by employees for not participating were that (1) the position was not offered or was not available, (2) they were too busy, (3) their participation would have no effect, (4) there was no particular reason, or (5) they had not been asked.

Essentially, employees see a gap between what the company says is important in regard to quality and the company's follow-through. Needless to say, this is less than a rousing vote of confidence in the quality performance of American businesses. Employees want to see better results. Substantial proportions of survey respondents said the quality programs in their companies have had either no effect or a negative effect in specific areas (ranging from 22 percent negative on communications to 42 percent negative on their pay and benefits). Workers stated that the two most important ways in which companies can make it easier for workers to do high-quality work are, first, to provide more training in job skills and, second, to offer job security. Going beyond these two items in order of importance are the following: have a more supportive attitude from top management, train workers in interpersonal working skills, respond faster to employee ideas, offer more up-to-date tools and technology, have a more supportive attitude from middle management, and offer better access to available information.

As an example, take Federal Express, which handles 1.5 million packages per day. The reason that customers can rely on such a complex organization is that Federal Express has made a 100-percent service level and a 100-percent customer-satisfaction level its key goals. Every employee has the right, the authority, or backing to do whatever is necessary to satisfy the customer. Essentially, Federal Express has put a lot into mechanisms to feed information back to the employees, so that if the employees have a quality problem or make an error, they know it and can fix it. The company has spent a lot of time training its employees in quality methods. Company employees are taught that good quality is essential to the company's future viability. In each of the preceding points, monetary issues play a role, but they are consistently ranked below other concerns by the survey respondents. These points are a road map to quality for a company's customers.[5]

Value Analysis to Reduce Product Costs

Because expanded CIM includes virtual worlds and is a very broad approach to manufacturing, it also includes the final product design by engineering. To assist a manufacturer in designing products that are profitable, *value analysis*, or *value engineering*, is needed. This approach requires that the engineer adopt a broader point of view and consider whether the parts contained in the finished product perform their required functions as efficiently and as inexpensively as possible. The appraisal focuses on the function performed by the part—or by the larger assembly containing the part. In an inspection-oriented plant, for example, more than half of all workers are somehow involved in finding and reworking rejects. The total investment in this process can account for 20 percent to 40 percent of production costs, and in extreme cases, it can account for 50 percent. In contrast, the Japanese inspect a product before it is made, that is, in the design stage, and engineer the manufacturing process to be stable and reliable.

To illustrate a practical value-analysis approach within a TQM environment, the product is dismantled, and each part is mounted adjacent to its mating part on a table. The point is to demonstrate visually the functional relationships of the various parts. Each component is studied as it relates to the performance of the complete unit rather than as an isolated element. A value-analysis checklist contains literally hundreds of questions and key ideas for reducing overall costs as well as maintaining the same level of product performance. Typical questions that can be used are set forth in Figure 8.1.

When using value engineering to appraise overall costs, possibilities for making component-part design simplifications are frequently more apparent than is possible under the conventional design conditions. This in no way reflects unfavorably on the work done by the design engineer; the discovery of such potential improvements is the result of an analysis with a substantially broader orientation than that possessed by the original designer. A value-analysis study undertaken by a typical company utilizes the background and skills of several people, because it is not possible to find the multiplicity of skills and experiences of that group in the person of a single designer. Resulting design changes often permit the substitution of standardized production operations for more expensive operations requiring special setup work. In other cases, an entirely different material or production process turns out to be more efficient than the one originally specified. In the final analysis, value analysis, operating within a TQM environment, contributes to the profitability of new products for a typical manufacturing-oriented company.

Computer-Aided Simulation of Manufacturing and Nonmanufacturing Activities

Simulations in the area of manufacturing are hardly new, although the ability to watch the simulations run as animated images is. To illustrate the simulation's results by using this approach, a simulation programming language from Systems Modeling Corporation (Sewickley, Pennsylvania), called Siman, is currently available. Siman's animation feature shows how a company's products move through an assembly line. Typically, what one gets out of the simulation is just numbers with stacks of computer printouts. The utilization of Siman allows the user to see what is actually going on

For the most part, simulations provide more information than just the start-to-end response time. They can graph how much traffic is in various queues and how much delay and productive time there is in different places. For example, if it turned out that the biggest bottleneck occurred in the lathe department, the company could assign more people to that department. That move would be the most efficient way of evening out the production flow as opposed to adding personnel to other production departments, like small assembly or major assembly operations. Overall, computer-aided simulation takes advantage of all the information available; and by performing the simulation in a structured way, it ensures consistency and traceability of its output.

Running an assembly line is just one kind of business process that simulation software can help streamline. With emphasis today on business-process reengineering (BPR), the Continuum Company (an Austin, Texas-based supplier of software and services to the financial industry) uses simulation to help insurance

Figure 8.1
Typical Value-Analysis Questions That Are Helpful in Designing Products

- Can the part be eliminated?
- If the part is not standard, can a standard part be used?
- If it is a standard part, does it complement the finished product, or is it a misfit?
- Can the weight be reduced with lower-priced materials?
- Are closer tolerances specified than are necessary?
- Is unnecessary machining performed on the item?
- Are unnecessary finishes required?
- Can one produce the part less expensively in the plant, or should one buy from the outside?
- Is the product properly classified for shipping purposes to obtain lowest transportation costs?
- Can the cost of packaging be reduced?

companies reconfigure the flow of paperwork. Queuing problems turn out to be a most important issue in business work flows. Needless to say, it helps to have a simulation tool actually calculate queuing problems. As an example, by retraining employees to perform more than one function at a time, an insurance company reduced the time it took a document to pass through this business process from between seven and ten days to less than one day with the same skill set. Without the simulation, recommendations would have been based on the intuition born of experience. Simulating the renovated process reduced the risk that intuition might prove them wrong.

Where experience is lacking, simulation can often take its place. One such area is in the design of client/server applications wherein software engineers decide what part of the application should run on the client and what should be on the server. Typically, businesses are somewhat unsure about client/server technology because there are a tremendous number of unknowns. Although mainframe systems have comparably few variables and can be handled somewhat easily, the same cannot be said for nonmainframe environments. Continuum Company developers, for example, simulated the performance of Continuum's work flow–management product, Business Process Manager, which incorporates an object-oriented database and a rules-based knowledge system. It expected to find a bottleneck at the computer's central processor where reasoning was taking place. Instead, the simulation revealed that the real problem lay with the capacity of a small utility that was used to move data around in the system. Hence, more attention was paid to how the utility was used.[6]

Simulation has also been used to reduce the risk in cost-cutting measures and business restructuring, addressing such questions as, "How much cost should be cut to allow the company to be competitive?'' A company may assume that if it cuts costs far enough everything will turn out fine. Generally, after it undertakes a few years of this kind of change, it discovers that is not going to survive in any case unless it does other things or gets out of a certain market. Through simulations, such companies can discern the likelihood of success under a variety of options. Similarly, by positing marketing decisions such as product introductions or price changes, companies can gauge customers' and competitors' reactions before the fact. Essentially, simulations help explain why things happen as they do.

A Practical View of Just-in-Time Inventories

The concept of just-in-time (JIT) inventories is not an entirely new one. Although originally used extensively by the Japanese and now by many companies in the United States and Europe, its potential during expansionary times has been fully exploited. However, its potential during recessionary times or in declining industries is now just being realized. For example, Corning, which makes kiln-baked ceramic parts for catalytic converters in automobiles, has lost 25 percent of its business recently. But this time, no shutdown has been necessary. About 100 jobs have been gradually eliminated, mostly through attrition, leaving more than 800 ceramic workers employed. In effect, it has managed decline. Starting a few years ago, Corning installed JIT inventory management at Erwin, New York, a system that includes supplying its customers with products a few days after the order is received rather than weeks later. Corning is now better able to track swings in demand and avoid getting caught with stockpiles that can take months to work off. Not only does JIT mean less handling of inventories, but also profits hold up better when operations slow.

Skill in managing inventories in times of slack demand as well as in declining industries is important to the U.S. economy. Many manufacturers today are keeping inventories lean so that there is little risk that bulging inventories will force them to cut production abruptly and lay off large numbers of workers. The manufacturers include not just Corning but also the automakers and a wide range of companies like General Electric, Motorola, and Rubbermaid. The net effect of their efforts is that inventories are low not only during the onset of a recession but also during an expansion and a subsequent contraction in the economy.[7]

NECESSITY OF AN INTERACTIVE 3-D COMPUTER-AIDED-DESIGN APPROACH TO VR DESIGN AND MANUFACTURING

Today, design and engineering tools used for the creation of visual elements in virtual worlds are becoming increasingly mature. Not only does high demand exist for such tools, in particular CAD tools, but also, CAD excels in the creation of complex geometry. The output of a typical CAD system often consists of a description of the scene's geometry. Essentially, this is the framework within which virtual worlds are built. Assisting CAD designers are large libraries of "stock items," consisting of furniture, building materials, humans, animals, and other objects. These are the clip-art elements of the 3-D-design world.

Typically, CAD programs begin with 2-D shapes like polygons, circles, curves, and typographic elements. In turn, these shapes are extended into the third dimension. An important visual element in 3-D is appearance that describes the color, shading, texture, lighting, and shadows. Often, computer-graphics designers create surface appearance by "painting" a 2-D image and then wrapping it around a 3-D object for what is known as texture. At other times, designers use mathematical models that generate desired patterns. Different kinds of materials are simulated by using other mathematical models.

At this point, the world becomes a bit more convincing. Appearance-creating tools are also reaching a relative level of maturity because of the computer-animation industry. Often these tools provide for import of geometric data from CAD systems or contain a CAD system themselves. Designers can choose from a wide range of coloring and texturing schemes and can show off their designs in the best possible light by setting illumination and shadows within the design program. The result is still a static world or an animated one with no capability of interaction. However, virtual worlds are interactive, that is, one or more participants can affect some aspect of the virtual world and change its behavior. If a person chooses to pick up an object, it moves with the hand. However, if the person chooses not to pick up the object, it stays motionless. If a person throws an object, it flies across the room, possibly hitting another object, setting off a complex chain of events as objects crash into each other, thus setting off even more reactions. As additional human participants enter the virtual world, the level of behavioral modeling required increases exponentially.

Currently, VR systems require less concentration on the ordinary events of such realities, leaving virtual-world designers and engineers to focus on creative aspects. This is achieved by providing programming tools that embody the behavior of the commonplace. The most obvious ways in which to start are with mechanical laws and Newtonian physics, and the most likely embodiments are libraries of the object-oriented class. By making entities in a virtual world instances of object classes, designers and engineers benefit by inheriting and adding new behaviors, specific to a new virtual environment, as derived classes. Under the VR applications that follow, the importance of object-oriented technology will be elaborated on.[8]

DESIGN AND MANUFACTURING APPLICATIONS THAT CAN BENEFIT FROM VR

Virtual reality is coming of age as far as design and manufacturing applications are concerned, as companies (such as Bechtel, Boeing, and VPL) design systems for factory controls, construction equipment, and experimental aircraft, among other things. In addition, research and experimentation continues on tactile control—an area in which VR technology is deficient. A basic VR system manipulates abstract objects via a disembodied hand that floats in space. The movements are then translated into commands that can control the visual display. Virtual-reality researchers are working on various approaches to solve tactile problems. One approach uses tactors—or tiny switches created from a "shape-memory," nickel-titanium alloy—that are sensitive to touch. Moreover, a force-feedback joystick is being experimented on that can mimic an object's texture. In the second half of this chapter, I will set forth current design and manufacturing applications of VR.

VR DESIGN OF NEW PRODUCTS AND ENVIRONMENTS

For years, design and engineering departments have been utilizing CAD and computerized drawing tools. In fact, most design tools today are 2-D or 3-D. However, with VR capabilities, the designs are no longer just images since they have become real to the designer. New, interactive, VR-modeling packages allow the designer, via the computer, to enter the design and walk through the model. For example, using Virtus WalkThrough (available from the Virtus Corporation), an architectural walk-through of a family room/living room is illustrated in Figure 8.2. Participants can walk through the room via mouse control and pass on either side of the chair facing the TV set. The set shows animated pictures and is actually a placeholder for Quicktime movies. Off to the side is a clip-art menu showing furniture selections. Participants can work with a designer and determine what the final room will look like under different conditions. Going one step further, some newer products allow the designer to view the virtual environment through the eyes of a seven-year-old and ask such questions as, Are the shelves the appropriate height? and Are the products properly placed for preplanned or impulse buying?

In the area of product designing, some companies are using virtual modeling such that marketing works with the product-design team to create anything from a new toaster to a new automobile. The design process includes the use of *value analysis*. As such, new products can be designed from an even broader perspective than before. (Typical questions that are useful in value analysis were set forth previously in the chapter.) Once the new product has been designed within a VR-modeling system, a person can actually use the product. Hence, a person can depress the start button of a toaster, for example, and virtually watch the entire cycle of a toaster in producing toast.

Although the person is not actually using his or her hands to turn on or off the toaster, the use of input devices, such as a mouse or an electronic glove, gives the person a realistic simulation of that action. Once there is a working product, the marketing department not only can let customers test the toaster with new built-in features not found in conventional toasters but also can suggest

Figure 8.2
Architectural Walk-through of a Family Room/Living Room

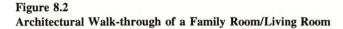
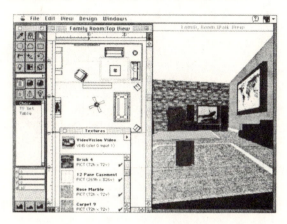

Source: Reprinted courtesy of Virtus Corporation, 117 Edinburgh Street, Suite 204, Cary, North Carolina 27511.

changes before it goes into production. In the automobile industry, consumers could, for example, take a virtual ride in a concept car and comment on the styling, placement of controls, color of fabrics, size of seats, and so forth. It should be noted that this approach to test marketing happens before the product is actually built. Although developing virtual product models is not low in cost, it is usually an order of magnitude less costly than building clay or plastic models or one-of-a-kind prototypes.

From the standpoint of designing new environments, the marketing vice-president of a retail-department-store chain could assess the company's situation and conclude that business is good but could be doing better. The vice-president might feel that a fresh image will attract new customers as well as retain current ones. For example, offering more self-service counters, moving toys down to a child's eye level, or even redesigning the storefront with a new logo could mean new business. Will it be worth the cost? How can the vice-president be sure about spending millions for the new image? The traditional solution is to design and build a prototype store. If this store is not successful, the experiment is generally repeated several times until a successful store operation is reached. Today, a logical approach for this marketing vice-president or any other one is to visualize walking around in a prototype store and commenting on the new environment. The vice-president can determine whether the colors are right, whether the new logo is appropriate for the times, and whether the self-service counters are sprinkled around the store where needed. After the walk-through the vice-president can let his or her own designers and marketers go back to the electronic drawing board, if necessary, to improve on the final design of the new marketing environment. Essentially, using 3-D modeling, visualization, and

CAD tools, design and marketing departments can sit down at a computer and virtually build an entire store with everything from walls to data-entry devices. A retail-department-store chain can go as far as placing products such as shirts and suits on store racks with their proper labels, packaging color, and product sizes.

Evaluation of Alternative Designs by Using Walk-throughs

Architects and designers are currently among the first and largest users of VR. Architectural walk-through programs that run on current PCs and workstations include a color version. The programs offer a highly realistic view of both the inside and outside of a building from different perspectives and allow changes to be made in the plans. As demonstrated previously, the Virtus Corporation has a low-cost program that runs on Macintoshes, IBM PCs, and others. Autodesk, which adapted CAD for PCs, has developed an operating system that it hopes will do for 3-D computing what Microsoft's Windows is doing for the conventional variety.

Researchers in corporate and university labs are developing a wide range of applications in the design area. Northrop, for example, now uses VR to design and test airframe assembly parts in a 3-D virtual world. The assembly-modeling application is directly linked to Northrop's CAD system and allows engineers to manipulate objects as if they were handling them on the shop floor. The VR system is designed to save millions in development costs by eliminating the need for full-scale mock-ups. In a similar manner, Boeing is using VR for use in designing and testing new commercial aircraft. Boeing is convinced that VR helps development teams address human-factor issues in preproduction designs. In the future, Boeing's Advanced Technology Center plans to extend the use of VR technology to the assembly and maintenance of aircraft.

As an example of VR design at Boeing, a designer can peer into the maintenance hatch of a virtual airplane and see that the pressure-gauge dial is obscured to view no matter how the person tries to get his head into the compartment. Typically, this type of problem happens in aircraft design. This sort of problem can be alleviated by rendering the design in virtual space when the aircraft is still in its infancy stage at the designer's workstation. Moreover, the interior of a virtual aircraft can be designed without the participation of customers. The designer may decide the aircraft needs a higher or a lower ceiling. At this stage, it is still fairly economical to make design changes.[9]

As another example of walk-throughs, a national women's-apparel retailer with several hundred stores found that it could save time and money by utilizing a 3-D VR drawing package for designing store layouts and storefronts. Prior to that time, it had used 2-D photographs and layouts in the final design of its stores, which meant actually going from New York to photograph the store. The company sped up the marketing-strategy process by not having to rely on time-consuming travel and multistep layouts. The VR package allows the store designers to change fixtures at will by using the program's library of stock architecture fixtures.

VR SIMULATION OF A NEW MANUFACTURING FACILITY

Computer-aided simulation, as discussed earlier in the text, has proved to be useful in manufacturing as well as nonmanufacturing activities. As early as the 1960s, languages such as GPSS (General-Purpose Systems Simulator), CSS (Continuous-System Simulator), and DYNAMO SIMSCRIPT proved that mainframe computers could be used to simulate real-world conditions. These provided powerful facilities for modeling new manufacturing facilities and proposed day-to-day operations. Because they were unfamiliar even to most computer professionals, the use of simulation was limited. Generally, this explains why mainframe, general-purpose, simulation languages have been all but invisible for PCs.

The current interest in VR along with object-oriented programming and systems opens the door to a renewed interest in simulation. In actuality, what is called VR is nothing more than the use of computers to create a simulated reality. It is, in effect, simulation by another name and viewed from a somewhat different perspective. Moreover, simulation is object oriented, at least in the sense that it involves re-creating objects existing in the real world within the representational world of the simulated system.

Modeling with a VR Local-Area-Network Simulator

Today, there is an important opportunity for PC-software developers to create a new generation of simulation tools that address a much broader range of real-world problems than do the limited and cumbersome mainframe simulation languages of the past. Personal computers make it possible to do so in a way that could be useful to a wide range of users. Going one step further, VR simulation on a local area network (LAN) would be of great value. One practical application would be a VR LAN simulator that allows LAN users to simulate a proposed manufacturing facility in an interactive way.

The simulation of a proposed new manufacturing facility using VR sometimes is referred to as a *pilot virtual factory* and is quite feasible within a LAN environment. In fact, a LAN operating mode allows multiple people from marketing and manufacturing to work on and interact with the same design while being separated by short distances. Similarly, a wide-area-network (WAN) operating mode could be used to interact with a virtual new factory so that a wider range of feedback (good and bad) could be obtained from personnel about the detailed aspects of the new factory. In either case, a virtual-design network for a new factory can result in a collaborative design although personnel are separated by distance. Moreover, this simulation approach is equally applicable to current manufacturing facilities.

To gain a better understanding of the simulation of a pilot virtual factory, a typical company needs a new information architecture, as shown in Figure 8.3. Essentially, there is a need to translate electronically higher-level sales transactions into lower-level material orders and production processes. As shown, electronic point-of-sale or sales data are passed via an electronic-data-interchange (EDI) system to a remote-order-entry system at the pilot virtual factory. This represents a virtual purchasing agent since it tracks sales and stock levels in the retail stores and automically replenishes fast-selling goods as needed while reducing stocks of slower-selling items. The data that is generated by the remote-order-entry system is passed to the master production-planning-and-control system at the factory. This is necessary so that the pilot virtual-factory's production-planning-and-control system can modify production requirements instantaneously and order new supplies or assign contract-manufacturing activities from outside suppliers. In addition, the remote-order-entry system provides input for the accounting function as far as receipts and payments are concerned. Because all of the foregoing activities are handled via EDI systems and services, such business transactions as orders, receiving notices, invoices, receipts, and payments are transferred automatically to the pilot virtual factory, the retailers, and the suppliers. Overall, EDI is used to communicate any changes in demand or supply across the factory-retailer-supplier chain. In a virtual world that is simulated for review, marketing and manufacturing personnel can experience this landscape and determine where there are problems and where improvements can be made throughout the entire factory-retailer-supplier chain. Needless to say, the activities represented in Figure 8.3 may number several hundred for a typical manufacturer.

An integral part of this simulation of a pilot virtual factory is the area of production planning and control. Basically, manufacturing operations are simulated interactively in real time. Included in this simulation can be the important manufacturing concepts set forth earlier in the chapter, such as value analysis and JIT inventories, which come under the umbrella of the CIM concept. Moreover, if reengineering is undertaken, this can be effected through the VR simulation. In turn, the interactive simulation in real time can take into account TQM such that the final products are of the highest quality. As I will point out in Chapter 10, VR can be helpful in training company personnel in the new manufacturing or process-control environments—in particular, on new equipment.

An important benefit from using a VR simulated approach to a new manufacturing facility is that the entire manufacturing process will be transparent to everyone on the design network. Those in manufacturing management will be able to monitor the development of products and anticipate new tooling needs as well as the kinds of human resources that will be needed in the future. At the same time, they will have control over the parts database from which designers and engineers draw. Similarly, product-marketing input on customer responses to products in development will be fed directly into the network.

Figure 8.3
Information Architecture for a Pilot Virtual Factory and Its Retailers and Suppliers

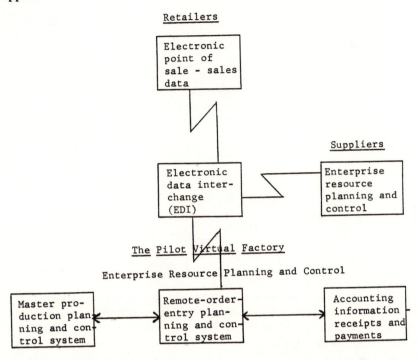

Overall, manufacturing management along with marketing personnel will have a better feel for the large expenditures required *before* the fact rather than *after* the fact. Appropriate changes can be made *now* to improve the new factory, thereby potentially saving a typical company millions of dollars.

In a similar manner, VR LAN simulators would be useful in simulating network configurations and patterns that would help determine if a proposed network configuration would provide adequate performance. Analysis of traffic flow, such as cars on a freeway or customers in a shopping mall, is another useful application. Essentially, the basic facilities of older simulation languages, combined with VR and modern object-oriented languages, have valuable practical applications in manufacturing or elsewhere.

VR SIMULATION OF CHANGES IN CURRENT MANUFACTURING OPERATIONS

Just as VR is helpful to companies engaged in the evaluation of alternative designs by using walk-throughs, the same can be said for changes in current

Figure 8.4
Interactive Assembly Modeler That Allows R&D Engineers to Design and Test Assembly Parts in a 3-D Virtual World

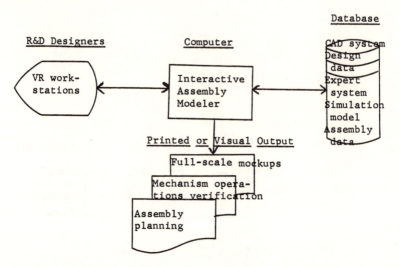

manufacturing operations. In effect, proposed changes in manufacturing operations can be evaluated to determine if they are balanced and are adequate in meeting the company's needs today and tomorrow. Such an approach to VR simulation is available from SimGraphics. In 1989, this company introduced the Assembly Modeler, a system that directly interfaces a corporate production, CAD system (belonging to Northrop Aircraft) with a VR system.

The interactive Assembly Modeler is part of the Automated Airframe Assembly Program, initiated by the U.S. Air Force to encourage technology development for cost reduction, quality improvement, and production readiness. The program is sponsored by the Wright R&D Center at Ohio's Wright Patterson Air Force Base (the birthplace of SuperCockpit, the grandparent of VR systems). Northrop is the prime contractor, and the "Northrop Team" includes Control Data, Hewlett Packard, Martin Marietta, Oracle, Price Waterhouse, and SimGraphics, among others. Their goal is to be up and running with Assembly Modeler and similar computer-integrated manufacturing technology by the mid-1990s.

Modeling with the VR Interactive Assembly Modeler

The recent implementation of the interactive Assembly Modeler lets Northrop's R&D engineers design and test airframe assembly parts in a 3-D virtual world. The assembly-modeling application, linked to Northrop's CAD system, incorporates an AI-based, rules-driven engineering system. This system provides basic tools for analysis functions, such as mechanism-operations verification and assembly planning. The VR system (Figure 8.4) lets engineers manipulate objects in the same way in which they would handle the real parts on the shop floor. The net result is that millions of dollars in development costs can be saved by eliminating the need to build full-scale mock-ups.

The motivating force behind the system was Northrop's desire for a custom system that would use their existing models and CAD system for manufacturing simulation in order to determine whether assemblies could be assembled manually or robotically on the shop floor. Northrop evaluated the DataGlove and torqueball devices and decided that Northrop needed something that was easier for its engineers to use. Northrop encouraged SimGraphics to build the flying mouse. At the same time, the U.S. Air Force wanted a system that would allow concurrent engineering—something that manufacturing teams and design teams could use at the same time and at the same points in the process. Essentially, this will be the next wave of systems design, with the computer more of an extension of the person using it and more suited to that person's abilities.[10]

VR MAINTENANCE OF EQUIPMENT

The utilization of VR need not end at the design phase. Virtual reality can be extended to the area of the maintenance of equipment. More to the point, VR can be useful in getting a better handle on the ability to maintain a company's equipment. For example, if a piece of equipment requires five hours to take the machinery apart, ten minutes to make the required repair, and then five more hours to reassemble the machinery, a virtual world should alert the designer to such a problem. Essentially, a virtual world changes the way in which designers work by not only placing them inside the piece of equipment but also providing them with the ability to give due consideration to the maintenance of the equipment.

As far as the actual maintenance of the equipment is concerned, see-through VR glasses, for example, can be employed by maintenance personnel in such a way that there is no need for the employees to take their hands off their work. Where the task is complex or where maintenance personnel do not have sufficient training, VR is an effective approach since it places all the information needed by the worker at his or her retina. Such is the approach being taken at Boeing. Through what is called an "augmented," or "see-through," reality, workers wear clear goggles with 3-D images reflected onto the lenses. The goggles superimpose a virtual image of the desired result on a real object, so that workers will know what to do with the object without consulting manuals or blueprints. An assembler inside a fuselage, for example, will see the real openings for hydraulic ducts or communications cables with a virtual image of the installed ducts or cables superimposed on them. The goggles would also reflect schematic and wiring diagrams, location of drill holes, and other information. Not only is time saved, but the quality of work is typically better.

In essence, Boeing engineers have built a computer model of a fictitious aircraft that allows users (i.e., maintenance personnel), wearing VR headsets and gloves, to open a maintenance hatch to inspect mechanical components. Similarly, they can peer inside the cockpit and cargo bay to examine the position of controls and the arrangement of seats. Boeing is currently working on linking VR with CAD workstations. This tie-in will enable engineers to test the placement of new parts, thereby making sure that these parts are accessible for repair long before an aircraft is actually built. The tie-in of engineers and maintenance personnel is found in Figure 8.5.

Enlargement of Maintenance Operations

In the future, such transparent glasses may even provide some kind of x-ray vision. In a jet-engine repair situation, the worker cannot see his or her hands because they are inside the engine. By having the capability of tracking the positions of the worker's hands in relation to the location of parts inside the engine, the individual can, in effect, ''see through'' the equipment to where his or her hands are working. This was referred to above as ''augmented'' reality.

Going one step further, VR will be put to work in a variety of ways, including telerobotic systems for removing hazardous wastes, toxic chemicals, bombs, and the like or fixing equipment in a hazardous environment. Or from this perspective, it may even be possible to utilize a robot under the control of a computer simulator to mimic (as in training) or actually repair a piece of machinery. By utilizing the robot, the worker can undertake the repair of machinery in a difficult environment. As such, the worker can track the position of his or her hands by using x-ray vision while the robot makes the repairs.

OTHER DESIGN AND MANUFACTURING AREAS THAT CAN BENEFIT FROM VR

Going beyond the areas set forth above, other VR applications in design and manufacturing are given here. For example, the virtual wind tunnel provides scientists with the same types of information they can obtain from a traditional wind tunnel at substantially less cost. The virtual tunnel entails a heavy commitment of hardware and software resources including a fast processor, high-resolution-graphics capabilities, and very large data-storage and -retrieval capacities, as well as a boom-mounted display and a DataGlove. The unit designed by Steve Bryson and Creon Levit uses simulated tufts to follow the flow of air around objects by injecting virtual massless-point particles into the flow and then integrating their trajectories.[11]

A most important VR application in the airline industry is the use of flight simulators. Delta's virtual training tool is a Hughes Rediffusion Simulation Boeing 737-332 Concept 2000 Full-Flight Simulator. The Rediffusion Simulation 737-332, the newest and most advanced of twenty five simulators at Delta's

Figure 8.5
Interactive Computer Model to Test the Placement of New Parts for Ease of Maintenance before an Aircraft Is Built

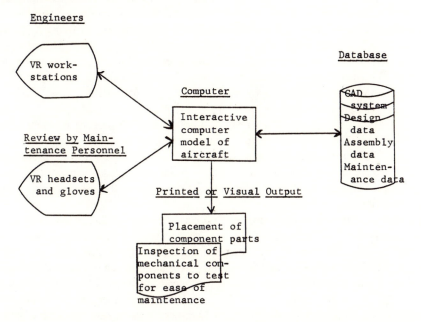

vast Flight Training Center at Hartsfield Atlanta International Airport, is the closest thing in commercial aviation to an airplane without wings. Classified by the Federal Aeronautics Association as a Level-D simulator (the current state of the art), the Rediffusion 737 is so sophisticated and so uncannily realistic that Delta's pilots can not only practice all manner of normal and abnormal procedures within its cockpit but can also do all of their training and even take their flight tests without ever setting foot in the real airplane. At Delta, simulators are lined up like rows of Lunar Modules, their chunky bodies supported by skinny hydraulic legs that move to create the sensations of flight. From each simulator, thick cables run to banks of refrigerator-sized computers on the balconies overhead. The air is filled with the hum of countless cooling fans, for if the temperature varies even a few degrees, the simulators will soon begin feasting on microchips.

Inside the simulator is an exact replica of a 737 cockpit. At the rear of the simulator there are two touch-sensitive video screens that have many functions. For example, just by touching a particular screen menu, the airplane can be moved to any airport desired or to any point in the sky. In addition, day or night (daylight images are found in only the most advanced and costly simulators) can be selected as well as almost any type of weather condition—rain, snow, hail, thunderstorms, and even wind shear—which the simulator can re-create accurately. And, of course, anything on the airplane—instruments, engines, control surfaces, and so forth—can be made to fail.

There are several reasons for the popularity of these flight simulators. First, these simulators are economical when compared to an actual flight. An hour in the Rediffusion simulator is worth about $500, while the cost of flying a 737 is about $3,500 for one hour. More important, though, the simulators give the pilot the ability to practice abnormal situations over and over again in complete safety. Because modern airlines are so reliable, a simulator is about the only way for pilots to experience a lot of abnormal flying conditions.

Essentially, the simulators are Delta's prime method of flight training. There are 280 flight instructors who work constantly with Delta's staff of more than 9,300 pilots. The training schedule is never ending since each pilot comes in once a year for a refresher session that consists of two days in the classroom and two days in the simulator, including a proficiency check. Hence, the simulators are running morning to night—and even through the night—to keep up with the demand for training.[12]

From a more practical perspective on simulation, the Battletech Center in Chicago is as close as most people are likely to get to experiencing a military flight simulator. For $7.00 and up to ten minutes of play, as many as eight people can enter a compelling VR set in the year 3028. Once shut into individual pods, players find themselves on a 100-square-mile desert plain spotted with boulders and some leafless trees. Each cockpit is equipped with a Motorola 68020 CPU, a memory board with thirty two megabytes of random-access memory, a scaling board for geometric computations, a sound board featuring a number of processors for both synthesized and sampled sound, and a Commodore Business Machines Amiga 500 computer. Arcnet network, with a few 25-MHz Intel Corporation 80386-class computers attached, ties it all together for the participants.[13]

Virtual reality has found a home at NASA. As an example, Marvin L. LeBlanc, head of the NASA Johnson Space Center Flight Planning and Pointing Section, is responsible for a number of computer-automation projects and for planning half of NASA's space-shuttle flights. He is recognized for his work on the Distributed Earth Model and Orbiter Simulation System (DEMOS) that has saved the agency more than $10 million in the development of VR applications. According to LeBlanc, DEMOS is the Mission-Control Center's (MCC) first real-time application of VR technology. It gives flight controllers the ability to see what the spacecraft is doing via a 3-D, high-speed visual. An added benefit is that the system is broadcast on NASA's public-affairs satellite link, thereby allowing the public a view of the spacecraft in real time.[14]

Currently, the Department of Defense (DOD) is developing networked VR technology to fulfill its battle-training mission in the era of shrinking budgets. The DOD's Office of Director for Research and Engineering (ODR&E) made the development of Synthetic Environments (SE) one of its seven major Science and Technology Thrusts in a recent document. Synthetic Environments will provide complete participation with full visualization in virtual theaters of war. Both LANs and WANs of computers will create SE using precise models of human behavior and hyperrealistic effects. Civilian computer-assisted training is sure to benefit from SE R&D. It will improve simulation models of real-world environments, vehicles, and thinking human beings and will develop databases to support them. It will construct wideband networks capable of performing huge data transfers and will standardize their protocol. Finally, it will make super-realistic user-interface devices available at low cost.[15]

In the prior exposition on VR LAN simulators, the focus was on internal operations and not on tying in with the customers. Ross Operating Valve Company (Troy, Michigan), for example, typifies a new breed of manufacturer that specializes in rapid product prototyping. The company, which produces proto-types and valves, has connected its CAD workstations to those of its automotive-industry customers, thereby allowing on-line, interactive design. Essentially, there is an exchange of CAD data. When a company is networked with its customers, there is a fast exchange of CAD data that gives a company a real advantage. This type of on-line concurrent engineering could help break down barriers between a company and its suppliers, customers, and even competitors, and go beyond prototyping to the manufacturing of end products.[16]

Another use of VR is to demonstrate the safety of Volvo cars. The fully immersive VR crash simulator runs on a Provision system, designed and built by Division, which also developed the software that both re-creates the accident and models the interior of the Volvo 850 automobile. Living through the five-minute crash sequence, immersed in VR, each motorist will experience a twenty-five-miles-per-hour side impact and walk away unharmed. The simulation created by Division is based on Volvo's advertisement and realistically shows the benefits of Volvo's side-impact-protection system. Division created two complex sets of software for the simulation. First, life-size models of the car and its interior, the road, the countryside, and the collision vehicle were built as a VR environment. Then the animation sequence had to match that of the advertisement. The models are constructed in such a way that the impact and consequent car-body deformation realistically portray actual events while allow-ing the user to experience fully the VR environment.[17]

A final VR application is to make buildings safer. Colt Virtual Reality (CVRL) is part of the Colt group, a specialist manufacturer of smoke ventilation, environmental-control systems, and other building products. Virtual reality is currently being used in specialty niches by CVRL, which includes an innovative ''people-movement'' package called Virtual EGress Analysis System (VEGAS). This package mimics the way in which groups respond to emergency scenarios in a built environment. For example, a fire can be simulated and the responses of building occupants can be observed. Allowances can be made for the elderly or the very young, who move more slowly, and the curious, who try to find the source of the blaze.

At this time, Colt has modeled fire and smoke and has run practical tests and experiments that can now be presented in a real-time visual manner by VR and, coupled to appropriate "people" modeling, can be used to improve the built environment. The medium affords an experimental environment where "what-if" changes can be tried both quickly and at minimal cost. The architect or engineer can view the overall effect of changing a door width or location, for example, without recourse to formal calculation. With random elements incorporated, simulations can be run repeatedly to produce a clear picture of a structure's suitability.[18]

SUMMARY

An underlying theme of virtual worlds, in this chapter and the preceding one, is that fast-changing times are having a direct effect on companies. Manufacturers are finding that skilled labor is getting harder to attract and retain. Product cycles are accelerating at a breakneck pace. Applications and computer systems are becoming more complex and integral to the business. Manufacturing business processes are changing faster than the information systems upon which they depend can adapt. Hence, companies need to find new and creative manufacturing approaches to make them competitive in today's and tomorrow's changing environment. In this chapter, I presented newer VR applications that assist design personnel, and I described typical VR applications that give manufacturing personnel some help in directing their companies' efforts wherever improved productivity is the name of the game.

NOTES

1. Dave Holbrook, "Stereo Viewing: Looking 'into' Manufacturing," *Manufacturing Systems*, January 1991, pp. 30–31.

2. Alex Taylor, III, "The New Golden Age of Autos," *Fortune*, April 4, 1994, p. 61.

3. Michael Hammer and James Champy, "The Promise of Reengineering," *Fortune*, May 3, 1993, pp. 94–97.

4. Frank Rose, "Now Quality Means Service Too," *Fortune*, April 22, 1991, p. 100.

5. Lura K. Romei, "Quality Becomes Integral to American Business," *Modern Office Technology*, July 1991, p. 10.

6. Mickey Williamson, "Some Simulating Experiences," *CIO*, November 1, 1993, p. 34.

7. Thomas F. O'Boyle, "Last In, Right Out: Firms' Newfound Skill in Managing Inventory May Soften Downturn," *Wall Street Journal*, November 19, 1990, pp. A1 and A6.

8. Tony Asch, "Designing Virtual Worlds," *AI Expert*, August 1992, pp. 22–25.

9. Paul Bandrowski, "Try Before You Buy: Virtually Real Merchandising," *Corporate Computing*, December 1992, p. 210.

10. Linda Jacobson, "Virtual Reality: A Status Report," *AI Expert*, August 1991, p. 26.

11. Steve Bryson and Creon Levit, "The Virtual Wind Tunnel," *IEEE Computer Graphics and Applications*, July 1992, p. 25.

12. Arthur St. Antoine, "The World's Greatest Toy," *Car and Driver*, June 1993, pp. 92–99.

13. Ellis Booker, "Fighting Your Battles in a World of the Future," *Computerworld*, March 18, 1991, p. 20.

14. James M. Smith, "Space Center's Rising Star Says His Job Is a Real Blast," *Government Computer News*, October 26, 1992, p. 16.

15. Dee Howard Andrews, "Warfighting Training R & D in the Post Cold War Era— with a Special Emphasis on Synthetic Environments," *Educational Technology*, February 1993, pp. 36–40.

16. David H. Freedman, "Quick Change Artists," *CIO*, September 15, 1993, p. 34.

17. Products, "Volvo Demonstration Uses VR," *Virtual Reality World*, July–August 1994, p. 6.

18. Products, "Colt Virtual Reality Ltd. Using VR to Make Buildings Safer," *Virtual Reality World*, July–August 1994, p. 4.

9

Accounting and Finance in a Business-Oriented Virtual-Reality Environment

ISSUES EXPLORED

- To show how a typical small company can benefit from virtual accounting from the company's inception to the actual running of the business
- To set forth a number of new directions in accounting and finance that are tied in with VR applications
- To examine typical accounting areas that lend themselves to VR, that is, cost accounting in addition to financial statements and ratios
- To examine typical finance areas that can make use of VR, that is, capital investment decisions and stock market analysis
- To set forth other accounting-and-finance areas that can benefit from VR

OUTLINE

INTRODUCTION TO ACCOUNTING AND FINANCE IN A VR ENVIRONMENT

An important part of a VR environment in the areas of accounting and finance is a *vision of the future*. For a typical company, top-level managers must want their companies to be the leaders in their industries, say, in five years, or their companies must do this to better service their customers. Vision is not merely financial long-range planning intended to realize more sales but a perception that the company must change to become competitive or achieve a leadership role. Examples include Fred Smith's vision when he launched Federal Express. Max Hopper's vision, along with that of several others, created American Airlines's Sabre flight-reservation system. Emil Martini's vision helped put a terminal in every drugstore for ordering inventory directly from Bergen-Brunswig. Each of these ideas—radical changes in business operations—were answers to items that solved business needs and achieved phenomenal success. In turn, visioning is linked directly to a company's critical success factors (CSFs) and key performance indicators (KPIs). Essentially, CSFs and KPIs are tied in with a company's financial performance, which is generally captured by the accounting system.

I will first give an example of a typical small company that illustrates the use of virtual accounting in helping to get a new business off the ground and in keeping the business running. Because of the importance of accounting and finance in a typical company, I will also look in the first part of this chapter at the beneficial consequences of VR for accounting and finance. Virtual-reality accounting-and-finance applications that can benefit a typical company are set forth later in the chapter. Because today's traders on Wall Street and financial analysts deal with an incredible amount of data about individual companies, economic forecasts, market movements, and other news events, VR can help financial professionals make better sense of all that data by visual, spatial, and aural immersion. As will be seen, some brokerages are using VR applications that let their staff surf over a landscape of stock futures, with color, hue, and intensity indicating deviation from current share price. In addition, sound can be used to convey other information, such as current trends or the debt/equity ratio. At the touch of a finger, single industries, regions, or volatility levels can be highlighted.

NEW DIRECTIONS IN ACCOUNTING AND FINANCE THAT ARE NEEDED FOR VR

To better understand a typical company's financial operations, it is necessary for treasurers, financial executives, controllers, and their staffs to enlarge the scope of their thinking. Essentially, this means allowing them to "get the big picture" when reviewing the company's total activities so that there is optimization of resources for the entire company versus one or just a few parts of it. The success that the typical company has in attaining its mission as well as its short- to long-range goals and objectives depends on the degree of integration of its operations. Enlargements of the scope of organization activities as well as the rethinking of traditional accounting and finance activities from a newer view are set forth in this chapter. This background is helpful to place VR applications in their proper perspective.

To illustrate the need to rethink concepts about accounting and finance, take the typical small company. Starting with the Internet (as discussed in Chapter 5), the small company can reap some of the advantages of large-scale operations by creating virtual planning, accounting, legal, personnel, and administrative departments. These departments would be privately managed companies that are available to all small companies under a certain size. For example, if one wanted to start a hardware store, the individual could sign on to the new-business start-up service. Guided by an expert system, this service would ask a person for the information needed to set up the business records and apply for a business license. In addition, it could perform any other service needed to start a business.

Initially, a person could be tied in to a planning service that would help create the business plan. Like a human advisor, this service would ask penetrating questions about the type of hardware store a person wanted to open, the local market for the hardware store, competition, and the like. Questions that could not be answered would be forwarded to a research service that would automatically find a set of best answers. Once the plan was complete, the Internet facilitator could even help raise money by forwarding the plan to the appropriate private financial institutions.

After the hardware store is in operation, there could be a virtual accounting department that would manage accounts receivable, accounts payable, payroll, and the like. Properly set up, it could be automated so that receipts would be fed into the system upon transaction and bills would be automatically sent to an on-line address and paid by wire transfers from the bank account. Reports could be received whenever requested.

In summary, these intelligent services would help one finance, set up, and manage a business every step of the way. And the role of the government would simply be to facilitate, through regulations and some investment, the availability of such virtual services. As the business grew, the owner might reach the point where a human accountant would be added, but the person would be aided by the Internet virtual systems. A business that grossed $10 million or more a year might only need one person to handle accounting instead of half a dozen. Hence, until the business reached a certain size, one could do it all without the expense of an employee or outside service.[1]

Rethinking of Cost Accounting to Reflect a Company's Real Costs

To compete in the global markets, U.S. companies must get control of their production costs. The good news is that U.S. manufacturers began meeting that challenge recently with computer-integrated manufacturing, automation, robotics, and just-in-time (JIT) methods (referred to in the previous chapter). The bad news is that even with these manufacturing advances, costing systems still cannot compete in high-volume markets. If U.S. companies are doing the right things in manufacturing, then why can't they compete? The answer is that U.S. companies have fixed just about everything except their costing systems. Generally, today's product-costing data are wrong, often by extremely large margins. Without more accurate costing methods, the bottom line is a continued competitive crisis. Hence, there is a need to rethink cost-accounting methods for the 1990s and beyond. More specifically, there is a need to take a hard look at activity-based costing as well as technology accounting and life-cycle accounting.

Activity-based costing (ABC) directly relates costs to the resources used to manufacture a product. A starting point is analyzing a company in order to determine all its production and support activities. All costs are then assigned to activities. Next, activities are measured and linked with the products that consume the activities. The total cost of the finished product is an accumulation of the activities required to make the product. In addition to assigning the costs to the products that actually absorb the activities, ABC identifies cost drivers and isolates non-value-added activities. Figure 9.1 shows how product-cost reports that show non-value-added activities can reveal cost-reduction opportunities. With this information, a company can establish priorities that focus on eliminating or reducing non-value-added activities.

Technology accounting is based on the concept that the costs of technology—such as plant, equipment, and information systems—should be treated as direct costs, equivalent to direct labor and materials. Today's technology costs, for the most part, are accounted for by amortization (or depreciation) and are included in overhead. The problem with this method of accounting is that conventional amortization methods are time based, not production based. A time-based

Figure 9.1
Separation of Value-Added Costs from Non-Value-Added Costs for Activity-Based Costing

Product Costs	Value-Added	Non-Value-Added	Total
Direct labor	$160,000		$160,000
Rework		$25,000	25,000
Setup time		70,000	70,000
Direct materials	100,000		100,000
Scrap		10,000	10,000
Direct technology	80,000		80,000
Underutilized capacity		45,000	45,000
Material controls		40,000	40,000
Quality testing		240,000	240,000
Engineering	40,000		40,000
Productivity support	45,000		45,000
Expediting		30,000	30,000
Distribution	20,000		20,000
	$445,000	$460,000	$905,000

method equates time with cost and often causes amortization of idle machinery to increase overhead costs when there is little or no production. This encourages constant and ineffective production to maintain a desired cost per unit.

Product costs are further affected by the inclusion of the time-based amortization in overhead, which must then be allocated to production. By adopting a direct production-based amortization method such as units of production, costs are matched more accurately with products manufactured. When determining the number of units over which to amortize an asset, only the planned production of the asset should be considered. Simply using the asset's total lifetime production capacity does not solve the problems associated with a time-based method. Total units used for amortizing an asset should be limited by planned production, product demand, and obsolescence of the asset's technology or the manufacturing process. As with activity-based costing, the choice of an overhead allocation method can significantly alter product costing. As technology costs increase as a percentage of total product costs, any misallocation will improperly influence managment decisions and possibly the financial results of the company.

Life-cycle accounting accumulates the costs of activities that occur over the entire life cycle of a product, from inception to abandonment by the manufacturer and the consumer. A primary objective of life-cycle accounting is a better match of revenues and expenses. All costs are capitalized as incurred. These costs are charged to earnings as units are sold, based on the total planned number of units to be brought to market. The shortcomings of the traditional cost-accounting model, then, are largely due to the changing manufacturing environment. To remain competitive in today's global marketplace, the time has come for U.S. manufacturers to adopt new cost-accounting methodologies so that they know the true cost of their products and make informed cost-management and pricing decisions.[2]

Although the foregoing cost-accounting methodologies are quite useful to assist a company in telling the true story about costs, a more pragmatic way to get a handle on costs is to follow the Japanese. That is, it is necessary to take a look at costs before the fact rather than afterward. More specifically, a Japanese cost-management system guides and motivates planners to design products at the lowest possible cost and gives them considerable freedom in introducing new products as well as getting them to market quickly. Like its famed quality philosophy, Japan's cost-management system is ahead of its global counterparts.

American companies in developing a new product, for example, typically design the product first and then calculate the cost. If it is too high, the product goes back to the drawing board, or the company settles for a smaller profit. On the other hand, the Japanese start with a *target cost* based on the price that the market is most likely to accept. Then they direct designers and engineers to meet this target. The system also encourages managers to worry less about a product's cost than about the role it could play in gaining market share. This strategic thinking approach is a big reason why the Japanese so often come out with winning products.

The crucial feature of the Japanese cost-management system is its focus on getting costs out of the product during the planning and design stage. That is the point at which virtually all subsequent costs are determined, from manufacturing to what customers will have to spend on maintenance. This target-cost technique, which is used by such companies as NEC, Sharp, Nissan, and Toyota, comes in countless variations. The stripped-down version has several important features. The team in charge of bringing a new product idea to market determines the price at which the product is most likely to appeal to potential buyers. From this crucial judgment all else follows. After deducting the desired profit margin from the forecasted sales price, the planners develop estimates for each of the elements that make up a product's costs: design and engineering, manufacturing, as well as sales and marketing. Each of these is further subdivided in order to identify and estimate the cost of each component that goes into the finished product.

Overall, U.S. companies tend to build a model of the product, determine what it is going to cost, and then ask whether it can be sold at a certain price that is based on costs. In contrast, the Japanese turn it around; they say, ''It's got to sell for X dollars. Let's work backward to make sure we can achieve it.'' This is not currently being done with the same intensity by U.S. companies. Western-style cost management, by basing costs on given standards, tends to maintain the status quo. The Japanese approach is dynamic and constantly pushes for improvement.[3]

Analysis of a Company by Using Financial Measures

There are a number of ways to measure the financial performance of a typical company. They center on return on investment (ROI) and related financial ratios. Because ROI is a measure of good, average, or poor performance of an organization's resources, financial managers should consider various ways of improving its ROI. Divestment of business operations that have a low return, acquisition of investments that have a high return, pruning of low-return product lines, cost reduction and profit improvement, improving asset utilization, and changes in financial structure are constructive ways of increasing an organization's ROI. An optimum allocation of financial resources that considers these alternatives for increasing ROI is a necessity for reaping a higher return. However, a word of caution is appropriate. If this allocation means raising ROI, it also means balancing long-term commitments and noneconomic constraints such as social responsibility. Reduction of commitments seems preferable to taking on a whole series of marginal projects that will reduce the organization's ROI in the long run.

Because the calculation of a company's, a division's, or a product's ROI is an excellent way to measure performance, ROI analysis can be used to judge present performance and to evaluate future investment opportunities. Managers can also use ROI to rate managerial effectiveness and to compare potential profitability of divisions. While the technique of ROI analysis is uncomplicated, the potential applications are varied and valuable. Basically, the ROI equation is earnings divided by total assets.

A problem in calculating ROI arises in identifying what is meant by earnings or total assets. Although there is no single, correct way to figure ROI, it is customary to use earnings from operations before taxes; sales after returns and allowances for bad debts; and net, year-end book value of assets. It is important that there be consistency and that the same measure of earnings, sales, and assets be used when figuring ROIs for different periods. Moreover, managers should be prepared for apparent surprises when comparing the company's ROI to another company's, that is, the other company may have used different measures in calculating its ROI.

In addition to ROI, there are a number of financial ratios that can be applied to a typical company. The ones illustrated in Figure 9.2 focus on the overall aspects that assist in financial strategic thinking. They can be calculated as needed and thereby serve as the basis for management by exception where appropriate ranges are assigned to each ratio. For example, the ratio of current assets to current liabilities should be about 2 to 1. Typically, to calculate these financial ratios, there is a need for a management-information-system (MIS) operating mode whereby a corporate database is used in conjunction with a computer for determining these ratios. Hence, when a financial group requests a specific statistic or ratio, the calculations are automatically performed to obtain the desired results. Basically, these statistics and ratios provide an insightful look for measuring actual results against the corporate strategic plans (short range to long range). Management effectiveness can be measured by the capital-turnover ratio, asset profitability, and ROI. In addition, the corporation's performance can be gauged through the return on sales, days of sales in backlog, inventory utilization, and receivable collections.

From a slightly different perspective, these financial ratios can be viewed from the standpoint of a typical manager. Managers know the problem of battling the daily, even hourly, barrage of operating data that assaults their minds. The realization that they cannot track every detail of business comes as their days get longer and their nights get shorter. Like most managers who were faced with this problem, they tried delegating. Yet they still monitored or second-guessed everything they delegated. The net result was that they did not save any time. The most effective way for them to monitor what is transpiring in their companies, then, is to look at the ROI and the financial ratios.

Analysis of Capital-Investment Decisions

Capital-investment questions from finance managers can benefit from a thorough analysis of financial alternatives or other factors by using appropriate fi-

Figure 9.2
Typical Financial Ratios That Are Useful for Financial Strategic Thinking

Measurement	Financial Ratio	Calculation
Management efficiency	Capital turnover	$\dfrac{\text{Sales}}{\text{Assets employed}}$
Liquidity status	Current ratio	$\dfrac{\text{Current assets}}{\text{Current liabilities}}$
Measure of solvency	Investment status	$\dfrac{\text{Investment}}{\text{Total assets}}$
Immediate liquidation	Acid test ratio	$\dfrac{\text{Cash + securities + net receivables}}{\text{Current liabilities}}$
Operation efficiency	Return on sales	$\dfrac{\text{Net income}}{\text{Sales}}$
Inventory utilization	Inventory turnover	$\dfrac{\text{Annualized sales}}{\text{Average inventory}}$
Days of sales in backlog	Undelivered commitments	$\dfrac{\text{Backlog}}{\text{Sales per day}}$
Credit strength	Net worth debt ratio	$\dfrac{\text{Shareholders equity}}{\text{Total debt}}$

nancial software. As an example, a simplistic model using Lotus 1-2-3 can be employed to evaluate the purchase of a new piece of equipment, say, costing $30,000. Expected savings are estimated to be $10,000 annually; the equipment has an expected useful life of five years and has a discount rate of 12.5 percent that represents what the company would have to pay on money borrowed to finance the purchase. Using the present-value method, this investment would bring future savings that have a present value of $35,606 more than the investment cost. Given this set of assumptions about savings, useful life, and discount rate, the equipment should be purchased. Estimates for interest rate, annual savings, and useful life, on the other hand, might deviate from these assumptions. To illustrate, assume that the interest rate has been projected accurately but that the useful life and annual savings estimates are more suspect. Lotus 1-2-3 allows the manager to perform either a one-way or two-way analysis to examine potential changes. The *one-way analysis* allows the present values to change in response to a variation in annual savings. In contrast, a *two-way analysis* allows the present values to change in response to two different variables, that is, cash savings and useful life in years. If the financial manager prepared another two-way analysis that examined discount rate and years of useful life, the results would be much more sensitive to changes in the useful life than in the discount rate, evidenced by larger changes in results as the useful-life projections changed. Thus, specific ''what-if'' questions can be answered for financial managers about present values when related to cash savings and years of useful life or discount rate and years of useful life.

Analysis of a Company's Performance versus Competition

A most important factor of reviewing corporate financial performance via financial ratios is to assist in giving direction to an organization's top-level managers and its corporate planning staff for furthering financial strategic thinking. By relating external environmental factors to internal ones for a typical company, the growth and profitability of comparable firms in an industry are compared to the company. This financial analysis indicates whether the company is increasing its market share and giving a fair return to its stockholders when considering the industry's current state. This overview of financial ratios needs to be supplemented by a more detailed analysis of competitors' financial statements, frequently referred to as *content analysis* of periodic financial statements and annual reports.

Basically, content analysis provides valuable clues about competitors' corporate strategic thinking. It is a source of both financial information and new directions by competition. Content analysis of competing companies can be of real usefulness in getting a handle on specific issues of corporate strategy and can serve as a primary or supplementary source of information. It can be used to analyze current changes and past correlates of performance and for more general investigations of questions of interest to top-level executives and their corporate planning staff.

As an example, content analysis may disclose that one of the company's competitors is showing improved cost performance, that is, its costs are declining. The appropriate corporate response is for a typical company to get involved in a cost-analysis technique called *benchmarking*, which focuses on what the competitor does and how much it costs to do it. In the company's lab, analysts tear apart the competitor's products and estimate the cost of designing and procuring each part. The analysis extends beyond product costs. To pin down distribution and handling costs, top-level managers need to order some of the competitor's products, then trace where they were shipped from and examine how they were packed. Typically, cost savings on a particular product start at the earliest stage, with engineering determining the product design. The challenge is to find ways to make engineering more cost effective without stifling creative efforts.

Concerning a thorough analysis of overall performance and variances that are tied in with financial ratios, there is a great need to employ graphics. Although financial ratios can be compared on a day-by-day, a week-by-week, a month-by-month, or some other time-period basis, the purpose of this analysis by finance executives is to determine whether the company is improving its financial stature. Of equal importance is the fact that financial-ratio analysis that uses graphics discloses whether or not financial managers are really managing the company effectively over the short term to the long term.

Generally, "at-a-glance" graphics presentations of information allow managers to start their thinking processes quickly. The usual method—and the slower method—involves a lot of reading. A "picture" may tell managers immediately what they want to know. Information in this visual aid might otherwise be buried in stacks of computer-generated reports. From another viewpoint, managers may view graphs on a display screen and also employ a paper printout of graphics data to ponder later, as in problem finding. Based on either perspective, computer-prepared graphics are very effective in supporting decision making and getting managers to think about new ways of running their operations.

Research studies have shown that graphics is a valuable tool for executives and people below them. The most often cited study justifying the use of business graphics was performed at the Wharton School at the University of Pennsylvania. It assessed the effects of overhead transparencies in business meetings. Among the findings were that (1) more executives decided to act on the recommendation of a presenter who used transparencies than on the recommendation of a presenter who did not; (2) presenters who used graphics were perceived as better prepared, more professional, more persuasive, more credible, and more interesting; (3) groups in which a presenter used graphics were more likely to reach consensus on a decision than groups in which no transparencies were used; (4) individuals reported making decisions earlier when graphics were used; and (5) meeting length was shorter when overhead transparencies were used. In addition, the study found that speakers supported by visuals won approval for their projects twice as often as speakers not supported by visuals. Graphics shortened meeting times by 28 percent and generated on-the-spot decisions 33 percent more often.[4]

A Client/Server Architecture for Accounting and Finance

With increasing frequency, accounting-and-finance software packages are being developed around client/server architecture. This type of software offers flexible configurations and simplifies implementation. Users can alter or choose the hardware or operating systems on which to run their applications, without having to change the application code. The client/server accounting- or finance-software scheme separates most of an application from the data on which it will be working. The data resides with the server, along with the data reconciliation and related software utilities, while most of an application resides with the client. In the basic client/server model, the bulk of actual data manipulation happens locally with the client.

Fundamentally, the driving force behind client/server is not technology but actually economics. With more and more companies downsizing today, users want the software to be easy to use as well as robust enough to handle sophisticated accounting and financial processing. Moreover, organizations are demanding client/server-based software to achieve fast delivery, that is, JIT information. Accountants and financial analysts want and need their information much quicker and cannot afford to wait until batch jobs or monthly reports are compiled.

Within a client/server framework, vendors are making accounting-and-finance software easier to use through flexible configurations and customization features. The trend is to concentrate the computing power where it is really needed. Some products, for example, are designed according to a relational or object-oriented database model, thereby allowing account structures to be redefined. Other offerings provide template screens that enable users to define their own business transactions and to set up configurations that they want. For example, users can create and change customized order-entry forms relevant to them. Overall, these products do not put the burden on users but are designed to make the user's job easier, not more complicated. A large MIS staff is unnecessary and no program changes have to be made to implement the software. Some accounting and finance software can be run in a distributed mode on any network that supports open systems.

It should be noted that a client/server architecture is not without its disadvantages. The advantages of client/server are more options and ways to do applications on different systems. The drawbacks, however, are that it becomes more complex to configure a system and more troublesome to support the management of the system. Currently, some vendors feel that they need to create a more elaborate client/server architecture based on their customers' needs.

NECESSITY OF AN INTEGRATED DATABASE APPROACH TO VR ACCOUNTING AND FINANCE

When VR is applied to the areas of accounting and finance, a starting point is an integrated database that ties together the diverse elements of a company. More specifically, marketing, engineering, manufacturing, and personnel data are tied together with accounting-and-finance data such that company personnel can access these data for use in their day-to-day activities. Essentially, a client/server architecture is employed in utilizing an integrated database for accounting-and-finance applications. The focal point is on knowing what to ask of the integrated database and where to find the information on it.

Today, databases are internal and external. *Internal databases* are compiled by users and usually consist of customer and client or of industry data that an organization collects for its own use. Because such information packages are generally fashioned by the users, they are custom designed. A most common internal database consists of name-and-address files for bulk mailings. An internal database that starts out as a customer mailing list can be combined with a commercial or a government database to provide more comprehensive information, including financial status, product, or services provided, and the like.

In contrast, *external databases* are packaged by information organizations— in particular, commercial publishing companies, industry or professional trade groups, and government agencies. Users can either purchase such databases outright or buy access rights for a specified time period. There are many external databases of interest to companies. Vendors serve a wide variety of company needs such that some databases are on-line, that is, the data are stored remotely and are accessible by modem. Others are packaged on CD-ROMs or on floppy diskettes and sent to users. Such databases require periodic updates to remain current.

The proper way to access a database is to follow a specific search format. Unfortunately, not all integrated databases use the same format, so there is a learning curve associated with the use of external databases. To minimize the search cost and to ensure a successful search, inexperienced users, even if they know a particular database's format, should conduct preliminary research to fine-tune search queries as precisely as possible. It is a good idea to turn to colleagues with extensive database experience to be sure the query is asked correctly.

Large and costly databases become more economical as more people gain access to them. One way to increase usage is to place a database on a network (LAN, MAN, or WAN). If the data originate on a CD-ROM, special drives can be installed on the network, or they can be part of a stand-alone PC configuration. Regardless of the database selected, users will face training costs. Some of the database services provide training programs and user manuals. Others have on-line tutorials and toll-free customer support lines. Additional information on the various types of databases that can be used in conjunction with VR worlds can be found in Chapter 5. It is sufficient to say that an integrated database approach facilitates VR accounting-and-finance applications as well as other applications found in this text.

ACCOUNTING-AND-FINANCE APPLICATIONS THAT CAN BENEFIT FROM VR

In accounting and finance, spreadsheets have been viewed more recently as replacements for general ledgers used by accountants and financial analysts. In reality, spreadsheets have been used to simulate the behavior of companies in a financial way given a change in certain variables. As such, spreadsheets can explore a number of ''what-if'' scenarios, such as an increase in sales prices or a reduction in production costs. They allow accountants and financial analysts to get a handle on company operations before actual changes are made. In contrast, VR computer simulations that are interactive and in real time work essentially the same way. Only this time, the focus is on taking the financial information and giving it life by creating large-scale *virtual flow sheets*. Bradford Smith, Director of Research for the Institute for Nonprofit Organization Management, has been working on the design of just such a flowchart program to monitor the operations and resulting health of a company. He likens the information compression in a business flowchart to that of complex weather patterns shown moving over the earth's surface on the nightly news. The weather display compresses about one day's worth of data into a period of a few seconds, thereby allowing the viewer to gain an understanding of the weather that no numerical presentation of data can possibly convey. Essentially, a virtual flowchart allows the viewer to watch several days in the life of a company go by in a few seconds, wherein each day is a compilation of complex variables contained or desired from profit-and-loss statements, balance sheets, and cash-flow analyses. A virtual flowchart actually shows the viewer a company's evolving nature and is helpful in making predictions about the company's future behavior, just as weather forecasters do. In this section of the chapter, this important VR approach will be an integral part of accounting-and-finance applications.[5]

VR COST-ACCOUNTING ANALYSIS

Traditional cost-accounting systems are criticized today on the grounds that they do not provide useful information for internal decision making. An important reason given for this lack of usefulness is that the systems were designed to provide cost data for inventory valuation in financial statements rather than for cost management. Other reasons were given in the prior discussion on cost accounting. However, with recent advances in computer technology—in particular, PC, spreadsheet, and database software—less costly analysis of cost data in different ways is available.

To provide information for cost management, newer cost-accounting systems need to be flexible enough to analyze costs in different ways. If a system is flexible, it can yield a variety of costs, including inventory valuation, product costing, life-cycle costing, quality cost evaluation, and productivity analysis. An accounting system for supporting cost management must include various types of data. At the most basic level, the data consist of the activities causing the costs, that is, the cost drivers and the costs incurred. As an example, receiving-department costs may be caused by the number and size of the deliveries, along with inspection and handling times of these deliveries. If the receiving department's costs are to be apportioned to the products causing the costs, the cost drivers must be identified and used for tracing costs to specific products. When this is done, the cost-accounting system becomes activity based (as discussed previously in the chapter) rather than volume based (as with most current cost systems).

One means of developing an activity-based system is to use a database approach, which means recording events, activities, and costs in a computer database in enough detail so that they can be retrieved, analyzed, and summarized in multiple ways as the need arises. Such an approach in reality involves recording some information not required for financial reporting, such as the numbers of deliveries and purchase orders and the numbers and times of inspections and handling. However, the database of costed activities not only supports the cost-attachment process for product costing but also provides a useful tool to support planning, coordination, and control across multiple dimensions. On the other hand, a second means to cost activities is one that makes use of VR and is discussed below.

Evaluation of Manufacturing Costs to Improve Productivity

Although a database approach to activity-based costing is helpful to cost accountants and their managers, a preferred approach for a more in-depth analysis of changing costs is the utilization of VR in conjunction with a company's integrated database. This approach not only assists cost personnel in really understanding costs but also helps to visualize how costs affect a company's financial operations. A VR environment gives cost personnel the look and feel of an alternative world. More to the point, costs can be analyzed by cost accountants for a number of products to determine what effect the elimination of certain costs—such as costly training of machine operators or assmmbly operators—would have on the company. Perhaps senior personnel could act as mentors to eliminate or reduce training costs. Similarly, inspection of assembly operations may be better left to assembly personnel where production-line personnel are permitted to shut down production if there are quality problems. Changes in production activities and their resulting costs, then, are related to the company's financial statements. The analysis need not end here. An interactive VR approach in real time could be extended to the concept of target costs set forth earlier in the chapter: changes in cost activities could be related to desired costs for comparison of one product against another. In effect, cost accountants and management have the ability to navigate through complex data in a 3-D graphical way (like that shown later in this chapter for a stock-market analyst).

The utilization of a VR environment can help cost accountants and management determine whether costs incurred in production or nonproduction activities really benefit the company. From this perspective, a *true cost-benefit analysis* can be undertaken not only for manufactured products, but also for costs related to the marketing and distribution of costs by products and product lines. Thorough analysis gives cost accountants the capability to uncover new relationships that were previously buried in cost figures. Thus, a VR approach can be used for obtaining different costs for different purposes, thereby highlighting problems and exceptions that were ignored or neglected in the past. In light of these comments, the question can be raised: How can a company in these fast-changing times not utilize the latest in computer technology to undertake a periodic cost-benefit analysis of its operations and products manufactured?

VR FINANCIAL STATEMENTS AND RATIO ANALYSIS

In today's fast-changing business environment, accountants and financial analysts must be able to access crucial data when there is need for it. If they cannot get vital information from any location in their company in real time, the company is at a competitive disadvantage. And no information is more crucial than core accounting data, that is, the numbers that tell corporate management how well the company is performing, how efficiently the company's employees work, and how the company interacts with suppliers, distributors, and customers. In essence, the better the accounting-and-financial systems are, the better management's strategic view of the bottom line, that is, profit or loss from everyday operations.

These comments, in turn, are linked to the fact that no company can grow profitably over the long run without an accurate accounting system that helps managers understand and forecast results. Unfortunately, growing companies often get blindsided by a common mistake, that is, they fail to invest enough in financial systems. Growing companies typically view this as an area in which to save money, so they hire too few people for the back office. They also keep the salaries of these staffers too low, so that they cannot hire the most qualified people. And they usually buy the cheapest computer systems, which means that they cannot keep up with their own growth. Accounting problems usually do not surface until there is a failure to predict a cash-flow crisis or until a bank rejects a badly needed loan.

Examination of Specific Decisions to Determine Possible Financial Results

Referring to the previous comments about Bradford Smith and virtual flow-charts, Smith wanted to create icons and metaphors that were isomorphic to a business's own environment. In effect, he wanted to condense data while preserving the structure. As such, there are three concepts underlying his flow sheet. First, there is a boundary between the system to be described (the company) and the environment (competitors, suppliers, government, and the like). Second, the flows of value are measured over time. Third, the reservoirs where value accumulates are measured at any instant in time. Openings in the boundary around the company represent the flow of value (represented in dollars) in and out of the system. The size of these flows can change depending on the amount of value entering or leaving the system. Icons are used for representing various product groups, services, or departments. In contrast, cash, fixed assets, debt, and the like are reservoirs that are depicted by a stepped icon that conveys a range of magnitude. For example, cash funds might increase in value from an increase in sales and then decrease as funds are directed to R&D or used for paying off debts.

The virtual flow sheet depicts, then, the flow of resources in and out of the organization and is used as a framework for the collection of information about the organization, that is, information about company personnel, the physical plant, and inventories. The flow sheet can be run at different rates, stopped, run backward, and changed to specific time periods—weekly, monthly, quarterly, and yearly. Additionally, accountants and financial analysts can use these virtual flows not only to examine the present performance of a company but also to examine possible future results stemming from specific financial decisions. It should be noted that these results can be expressed on a wide screen for review by many individuals who can view the data together and exchange their views on the display based on their own knowledge and experience. Overall, this virtual flow sheet is extremely useful since it is very flexible. Accountants and financial analysts can see and move within an extensive range of flows and reservoirs based on making specific financial decisions.

In the future, it is expected that the state of the art will have progressed to the point where voice commentaries will be heard as the viewers examine the details of particular flows along with extensive financial-ratio analyses. Windows will have the ability to open with video clips and appropriate data about assets, liabilities, capital, or assumptions about the future. The same graphical displays, or flows, will be used for representing divisions within the company and then departments within divisions, and so forth. The net result is that favorable and unfavorable patterns will be assessed and analyzed in some detail by using financial-ratio analysis. The viewers will get a total or holistic representation of the entire system as well as its detailed parts by using ratio analysis.[6]

Underlying these virtual flow sheets are the data they are based upon. As noted in a prior section of the chapter, integrated databases are a must in order for the virtual program that produces meaningful financial output to have the appropriate input from the company's database. Fragmented databases and disorganized databases are not viable for producing virtual flow sheets. Only integrated databases that are based upon the open-system concept are feasible candidates for serving the needs of accountants and financial analysts in interactions with virtual worlds. Thus, it may be necessary to reorganize a company's database before undertaking virtual flow sheets for assessing present and future financial results.

VR CAPITAL-INVESTMENT DECISIONS

For capital projects that require substantial sums of funds for implementation, a financial officer, typically, under the direction of the company's treasurer, decides on the optimal financing method. After reviewing an analysis of the capital project, the financial officer interrogates the company's database for financial-structure data that is primarily of a long-term nature. A financial-structure report is generated for review by the financial officer. That officer is now prepared to make a financing recommendation after considering the current debt-equity ratio, current borrowing rates, interest charges for which the company is currently committed, and current and projected sales as well as other factors pertinent to the decision.

Once a decision, such as bank borrowing, has been made about financing, the financial officer incorporates this information into the analysis of the capital project. The formal report is prepared and then forwarded to the top-level executives for a review and approval. Typically for these capital projects, the vice-president of the department that is initiating the project, the vice-president of finance, the treasurer, and the executive vice-president are consulted. When the project is finally approved, a copy of the approval is then forwarded to the financial officer, who takes the necessary steps to obtain the funds for implementation. If the project is rejected, the financial officer forwards the reasons for the rejection to the initiating department.

Although the above scenario is typical of what happens today in most companies, the same need not be said about tomorrow's operations. More specifically, the use of virtual flow sheets mentioned previously is applicable here for capital-investment decisions. Their use can be of great help to financial officers who are responsible for keeping a company's cost of capital low over time. Moreover, the use of virtual flow sheets can be helpful relative to changing financial conditions—in particular, the ups and downs of interest rates.

Evaluation of Future Revenues and Costs to Determine
Appropriate Capital Investments

In the above section on financial statements and ratio analysis within a VR framework, the focus was on the flows and icons that can be integrated into a display that fosters discussion about the performance of the company and the possible future results of specific decisions. From an overview standpoint, this is reflected in the upper part of Figure 9.3 that shows how funds move through a typical company. Related to this figure is the source and application of funds shown in the lower part of the figure. Essentially, this virtual flow can be run by using different interest rates from various financial institutions for the capital investments, can be stopped, can be run backward, and can be shifted to reflect specific time periods (say, quarterly and yearly). Just as with financial-statement ratio analyses, the financial officer can contemplate the cost of capital for the company today and tomorrow. In effect, the officer can see the possible future results of specific capital investment decisions on the company's total investments and its return on these investments.

VR STOCK-MARKET ANALYSIS

One of the most difficult undertakings in the financial world is predicting the movements of the stock market. Much has been written about the strategies employed by mutual funds, pension funds, insurance companies, and individual investors, whether large or small. The action of stock-fund investors in the 1987 crash fit the behavior of individuals in bear markets over the last thirty years. Typically, small investors do nothing in the face of a market fall. Once the market rises and investors recover their losses, they then redeem shares and only slowly return to stocks.

Just as individual investors are changing the stock market with their purchasing power, so too are the latest advances in computer technology changing the way in which stocks are picked. Today, money managers analyze information for thousands of companies and cut the figures by any number of criteria, such as low price-earnings ratio, to come up with undervalued stocks to buy. The problem is that too many investment institutions have the same ideas about the kinds of stocks they want to purchase and have the same computing ability to arrive at the stocks to buy. The net result is that these stocks are now overvalued because the institutions have bid up the prices.

To get around this problem, one of the stock analysts of Fidelity Investments has been using neural-network technology since 1989. Essentially, neural-network technology gives the stock analyst the ability to float in random space, thereby allowing the neural network to identify obscure patterns in data that tell when the time is right to buy or sell specific stocks. With conventional technology, patterns can go undiscovered if a manager does not know what to look for. For example, automobile stocks tend to rise just after the companies announce dividend cuts—a pattern at odds with conventional computer-screen wisdom that says stocks usually languish then. Thus, the neural network's ability to find new patterns that are not apparent to the average investment manager is its unique feature.[7]

Figure 9.3
Virtual Flow of Data Related to the Source and Application of Funds for a Typical Company

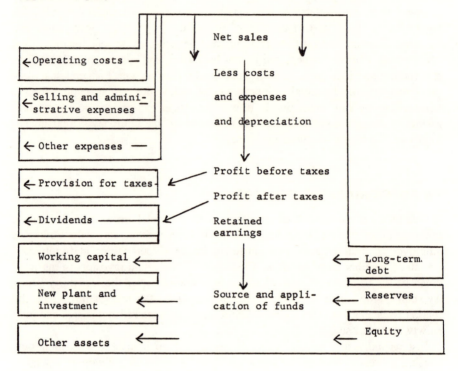

Evaluation of Stocks That Have the Potential to Outperform the Stock Market

Complementary to neural-network technology is VR technology that has the capability of representing vast amounts of stock-market data in an interactive, real-time mode. This capability allows stock-market analysts to organize information in new ways and find new relationships that were not apparent before. Typically, the major stocks in one specific industry can be evaluated by the analyst. Or several selected stocks in different industries can be evaluated against each other. Essentially, the analyst can fly over the stocks where the volume of the stock for the day is shown along with the price range of the day. The shape, position, and color of the stocks are dependent on conditions in the market. The stock analyst can assess the behavior of the stocks to help determine whether or not a specific stock would be a candidate for a buy or sell (see Figure 9.4). From this perspective, VR offers an effective way to condense and streamline financial information for stock-market analysts.

Figure 9.4
The Stock Market's Gyrations Brought to Life with vrTrader's 3-D World

Source: Reprinted courtesy of Avatar Partners, 13090 Central Avenue, Suite 3, Boulder Creek, California 95006.

In Chapter 4, information was given on vrTrader for Windows, a software package for PCs. There is another package, called vrTrader for stock-market professionals (see Figure 9.4). Essentially, this package consists of a world in which stock, option, and commodity data are represented by 3-D objects, real-time graphs, and text. Stocks are projected onto a matrix characterized by user-defined labels and stock-market exchanges. The behavior and color of each stock object, as well as the presence of user-specified "alerts" (spinning or blinking rings and auditory cues), are used to indicate buying or selling opportunities. Specific characteristics of each stock, such as the existence of recent news reports, are dynamically updated and displayed. The vrTrader system uses Data Broadcasting Corporation's Signal box that receives real-time quotes via FM radio and cable television. The stock-market analyst can view up to 300 stocks, market indices, or futures simultaneously from a choice of more than 55,000 issues. Both real-time and delayed (15 minutes) quotes are supported. The analyst can assign visible thresholds and auditory alerts to monitor each stock's volume and price. This package is offered by Avatar Partners (Boulder Creek, California). The vrTrader will run on an 80486- or Pentium-based system with

Figure 9.5
Operations of the vrTrader

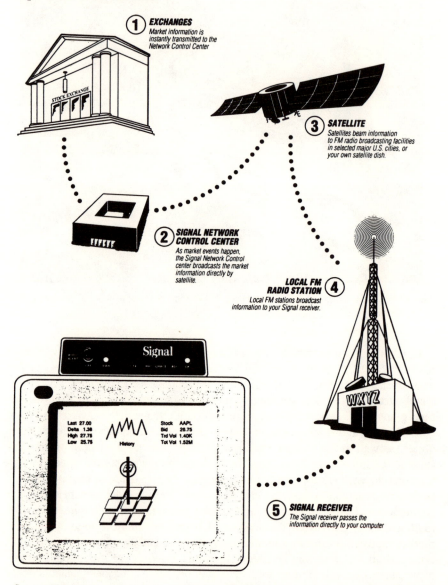

① **EXCHANGES**
Market information is
instantly transmitted to the
Network Control Center

③ **SATELLITE**
Satellites beam information
to FM radio broadcasting facilities
in selected major U.S. cities, or
your own satellite dish.

② **SIGNAL NETWORK CONTROL CENTER**
As market events happen,
the Signal Network Control
center broadcasts the market
information directly by
satellite.

④ **LOCAL FM RADIO STATION**
Local FM stations broadcast
information to your Signal receiver.

⑤ **SIGNAL RECEIVER**
The Signal receiver passes the
information directly to your computer

Source: Reprinted courtesy of Avatar Partners, 13090 Central Avenue, Suite 3, Boulder Creek, California 95006.

one SPEA FIRE graphics board for rendering. A minimum of 8 megabytes of memory are required. Data Broadcasting Corporation's Signal box and subscription service are also necessary.

To get an idea of how the software package operates, see Figure 9.5. Market information as it happens is transmitted instantly to the Signal Network Control Center. As the market events happen, the Signal Network Control Center broadcasts the market information by satellite. In turn, the satellite beams information to FM radio broadcasting facilities in selected major U.S. cities or to one's own satellite dish. Local FM stations broadcast information to one Signal receiver. And finally, the Signal receiver passes the information directly to one's computer. The cost of the vrTrader software is $1,995.00, and the SPEA Fire 860 Board costs $1,795.00. Prices for the Signal box vary from $295.00 for FM to $495.00 for Cable. The real-time–quote subscription service starts at about $250.00 per month for AMEX, NYSE, and OTC. The vrTrader can also be used in an exhibition or trading-room environment. It supports a variety of display options for projection TV and stereo viewing. In addition, sound and voice control are available.

Prior to the marketing of the above VR stock-market package was the software from Maxus Systems International (New York). Maxus developed a VR application that allows the managers of financial portfolios to fly into and around a virtual landscape made up of equities and bonds. The system, called Metaphor Mixer, has been on-line since June 1992 and was built with Sense8's World-TookKit software. The system runs on a 486-50 PC clone, equipped with an Intel DVS-2 card, space ball, and color monitor. It can display 5,000 to 10,000 stocks in one world and provides close to twenty frames per second update rate.

The design of the world is a grid, with the industrial categories (metals, electronics, banking, and so forth) in rows and the financial markets (such as Hong Kong and Tokyo) in columns. Each stock is represented by an icon; a polygon has its shape assigned by the user. The colors of the icons change to show current price trends, that is, blue means that the stock is headed up, red indicates that the stock is headed down, and gray reflects little or no change. In addition to different colors and shapes, each stock can be blinking or spinning, indicating that some predetermined condition has been met. The distance of the shape above or below the grid surface shows the relative price of the stock compared to others in the group. Inside, the user will find traditional stock charts and other textual data, thereby providing even more information.

The system gets its data from another Maxus application called Capri, which accepts and analyzes financial data coming off the wires and then feeds the data to the VR system in real time. Metaphor Mixer is used to manage the over $100 billion portfolio of TIAA-CREFF, a college and university teachers' pension fund, where it has proved to be valuable in helping managers spot trends and movements in Pacific-rim markets. The system is available only to Maxus's clients on a lease basis. Such a graphics system capitalizes on the fact that the brain is much better equipped to group data presented visually than data presented as numbers and text.[8]

OTHER ACCOUNTING AND FINANCE AREAS THAT CAN BENEFIT FROM VR

Accounting-and-finance applications, as discussed previously, can benefit greatly from the utilization of VR. Today, companies deal with an incredible amount of data about economic forecasts, market movements, and, in particular, their own operations. Virtual reality has the potential to turn a company's integrated database into a giant simulated structure that is much easier for people to understand. In fact, many of the important new VR accounting-and-finance applications will make great use of the company's database to get a grasp on a company's operations. Virtual reality, then, can help accounting-and-finance professionals make better use of all their data.

Another VR accounting application that can utilize an interactive, real-time, simulated mode is an analysis of a company's overhead. By virtually flying over the overhead structures of a company's various devices, departments, and the like, accounting-and-financial analysts can look for exceptions in one part of a company versus another part and can possibly highlight for review by management the reason that overhead rates are higher in one part of the company versus another. In effect, analysts can navigate through complex overhead data in a graphic way that results in their looking extensively into an alternative world. They can find new overhead relationships that were previously buried in a stack of manufacturing reports that focused on material, labor, and overhead together. In other words, a picture of what constitutes a company's total operations can be broken down for further analysis and for possible improvement based on a virtual-world analysis.

Related to the capability of a company's integrated databases and accounting-and-finance VR applications coming on-line is the *virtual office*. If a PC or a Macintosh is used, Windows or a Mac Desktop can serve as a "virtual desk." Systems are being developed that will make it possible to place data in this desk, first with a pen-based tablet system, then by pointing with a DataGlove, then via speech recognition. This approach, in turn, can be expanded into a virtual meeting environment not only for accounting-and-finance personnel but also for all company personnel. This area was explored in Chapter 5.

Although the VR applications in this chapter are designed to give the user a more realistic picture of a complex business environment, visualization techniques could also have been used for the most part. These techniques have been used for years in the science fields, but the advent of faster, more powerful CPUs, and real-time computer graphics programs along with VR technology encourages accounting and finance experts to try the same approach. Needless to say, a number of ideas have been bounced around. One way, for example, suggests representing a stock as a stalk of wheat. By having a whole field of wheat and having price fluctuations and market trends propagate like wind across the field, program securities would turn a bright orange when they reach a particular price. Stock-market analysts could then put on the HMD and goggles and walk up and down the fields and watch the way the market is moving. The net result is that traditional information is presented in a way that does not require a lot of conscious mental processing.

SUMMARY

The focus of this chapter (and the two previous ones) has been on applying virtual worlds to typical accounting-and-finance situations. However, this exposition was preceded by important new concepts and views on accounting and finance. The need for newer approaches is necessitated by the environment in which companies operate today. The environment in which financial decisions are made is highly dynamic, complicated, and information intense. Investment banks, commercial institutions, regulatory institutions, and brokerage houses find their staffs increasingly strained in financial times—good and bad. To help streamline operations and keep up with the times, it is necessary to provide the most intelligent, timely, and focused information by using VR capabilities. As a result, accountants and financial analysts can view data in virtual worlds as a whole or in detail, can see elements in association with each other or individually, and can link those elements. Judgments can be made faster than they could were that data viewed in numeric form. Thus, a creative approach to VR accounting-and-finance applications is the desired one today as well as in the future. To do otherwise is to place a company at a competitive disadvantage.

NOTES

1. David Bunnell, "Virtual Accounting," *NewMedia Magazine*, October 1993, p. 8.

2. Dennis Peavey and Jim DePalma, "Do You Know the Cost of Your Products?" *Coopers & Lybrand Executive Briefing*, May 1990, pp. 7–9.

3. Ford S. Worthy, "Japan's Smart Secret Weapon," *Fortune*, August 12, 1991, pp. 72–75.

4. John Desmond, "Window to MIS: Graphics Focuses Business Picture," *Software News*, April 1987, p. 54.

5. Ken Pimentel and Kevin Teixeira, *Virtual Reality, Through the New Looking Glass* (New York: McGraw-Hill, 1993), pp. 164–67.

6. Ibid., pp. 166–67.

7. Susan E. Kuhn, "The New Perilous Stock Market," *Fortune*, December 27, 1993, p. 58

8. Ben Delaney, "Where Virtual Rubber Meets the Road," *Virtual Reality Special Report*, published by the *AI Expert* (San Francisco: Miller Freeman, 1993), p. 17.

10

Training and Human Resources in a Business-Oriented Virtual-Reality Environment

ISSUES EXPLORED

- To explore changes that have occurred in American education that are conducive to help popularize VR
- To explore the importance of problem finding to help solve human-resource problems before they arise
- To show the need for a human-resource-management system that can serve as a background for VR applications
- To illustrate typical examples of training within a VR environment
- To demonstrate the application of VR to human-resources management as well as wage and salary administration

OUTLINE

Introduction to Training and Human Resources in a VR Environment
New Directions in Training and Human Resources That Are Needed for VR
    Training as a Prerequisite for a Company's Upsizing or Downsizing
    High-Tech Training Programs
    Solving Human-Resource Problems before They Arise
    Software for Human-Resource-Management Systems
Necessity of a Simulated Approach to VR Training and Human Resources
Training and Human-Resource Applications That Can Benefit from VR
VR Training
    Typical Training Programs in VR
VR Human-Resource Management

INTRODUCTION TO TRAINING AND HUMAN RESOURCES IN A VR ENVIRONMENT

Related to the three previous chapters on business applications of VR is the training and human-resource functions. Essentially, these areas are tied in with the need to design new learning environments so that the full potential of VR can be achieved. From this view, an important value of VR is that it can be a highly participative as well as motivating activity for structured, individualized learning. The technology enables the user to enter and participate in new realities that were not available in the past.

As a way of putting this subject matter in perspective, I refer the reader to a landmark publication entitled *A Nation at Risk*, released over ten years ago. This report from the U.S. Department of Education's National Commission on Excellence in Education prompted those in the teaching professions to establish closer ties with business so that industry's needs are better understood. At the same time, this publication coincided with the growth of the PC. Awareness of the need for fundamental change in learning and in the educational system along with the arrival of tools to facilitate that change proved highly fortuitous. It is from this union that training and human-resource functions are treated in this chapter.

NEW DIRECTIONS IN TRAINING AND HUMAN RESOURCES THAT ARE NEEDED FOR VR

Today, new directions are occurring in education that affect the workforce before its members begin employment. Education has gone from teaching children about computers to helping them learn with computers. Instead of only rotating children through computer labs, schools are bringing computers into classrooms and integrating them into daily learning activities. Similarly, libraries are being transformed into campus media centers to serve all students.

Research supports what educators have been observing in their classrooms about what motivates and empowers students to learn. That is, students learn best when put in control of their own learning and when enabled to solve problems that are relevant to their lives. In a similar manner, students need to be given opportunities to collaborate with others in this problem-solving process.

They must have access to the high-tech tools that are commonplace in the world of work and must have the ability to select from among these and other tools and to use a range of technologies to solve problems. Finally, they need the support, guidance, and encouragement of instructors who facilitate exploration rather than merely impart information. All of these factors parallel those that should be found in the workplace. The transition from student to employee is less traumatic for the average person from this enlightened perspective.

For decades, designing has been part of the worlds of education and industry. However, the advent of powerful graphics software running on desktop PCs is putting design tools within reach of large numbers of individuals not previously counted among those undertaking systems analysis and design. Schools that integrate design activities into the curriculum are already realizing major benefits for learners. More specifically, there is greater teamwork, improved interdisciplinary study, increased abilities in the areas of problem finding, and an important leap forward in hands-on learning. Colleges and universities are discovering that design is increasingly relevant to virtually every discipline. Moreover, companies that face increasingly competitive global-market pressures are seeking graduates who understand how to apply new design strategies, skills, and technologies. Hence, there is a realization that students require the same technology tools available to science and business.

In light of these comments, emerging technologies promise to change the current direction of education in a fundamental way. Already CD-ROMs, videodisks, on-line databases, and satellite links are making an impact on school classrooms, and in the near future will become a much more integral part of the teaching process. In addition to these information sources, various forms of computer graphics software are becoming standard school equipment. Students use these applications, such as computer-aided design (CAD), multimedia, and desktop-publishing programs as their basic tools. In like manner, hardware and software vendors are marketing VR environments that are wholly created by a computer. With specialized input and output devices, students experience artificial environments. Numerous VR applications have been given in prior chapters and more will be given in this chapter.

Training as a Prerequisite for a Company's Upsizing or Downsizing

Today, there are continuing headlines featuring the *Fortune 500* companies, most of which are downsizing, although several are upsizing their operations to meet their short- to long-term-growth goals. No matter the structuring approach taken, there are significant problems facing these companies. *First,* many new workers need training in a growth company, whereas the remaining workers in a downsized company are underskilled and need to be trained to take on new duties and responsibilities. *Second,* there is a need to improve a company's commitment to a total-quality-management (TQM) program such that continuing quality improvements can be made throughout the year. *Third*, the continuing sophistication of newer products and services requires expanded training for company workers at all levels. *Fourth*, whether a company is upsizing or downsizing, there needs to be a renewed emphasis on customers within or outside the organization. *Fifth*, in conjunction with the prior problem, there should be a team or group effort to meet customer needs as opposed to the individual trying to do the whole job alone. Not to mention others, these problems are reason enough for a typical company to undertake appropriate levels of training for its personnel.

In actuality, training is an obligation that a company owes to its employees and itself for continued existence. Without training, a company can be hobbled by the ''check-your-brains-at-the-door work'' methods that make no sense in today's business world. If a company wants to build a high-performance and flexible organization, then it has to train its workers. Whether it is large or small, a company that does not train does not gain in the short or long run for its employees or itself, which includes its stockholders.

Today, some of the best training in America takes place at Motorola, where factory workers study the fundamentals of CAD, robotics, and customized manufacturing. This is accomplished not only by reading manuals or attending lectures but also by inventing and building plastic knickknacks. The company runs its well-known training programs from Motorola University, a collection of computer-equipped classrooms and laboratories at corporate headquarters (Schaumburg, Illinois). Just recently, Motorola University, which includes regional campuses in Phoenix and Austin, delivered approximately 100,000 days of training to employees, suppliers, and customers. Because this school does not employ many professional educators, it relies on a cadre of outside consultants (including engineers, scientists, and former managers) to teach the bulk of its courses. Their role is to prod, guide, and orchestrate. In a class on reducing manufacturing-cycle time, for example, senior managers break quickly into teams to devise new ways to get a product to market faster.

Motorola calculates that every dollar it spends on training delivers $30 in productivity gains within three years. Since 1987, the company has cut costs by $3.3 billion—not by the normal expedient of firing workers, but by training them to simplify processes and reduce waste. Sales per employee have doubled in the past five years and profits have increased by about 50 percent.[1]

High-Tech Training Programs

The face of corporate training is changing with the times. Corporate America is offering its employees personalized, high-tech training programs that cover everything from the three Rs to the latest in information technology. The reason is quite simple. Only with an educated staff can a manager run the lean and flexible organization demanded by today's competitive corporate climate. And to the extent that modern training methods are designed to take workers to peak performance quickly, the company that invests both resources and commitment in training gains a competitive edge.

To assist in being competitive, training can take several directions. First, there are *self-paced materials* that include all forms of manuals, workbooks, programmed materials, audio- or videocassettes, and so forth. The distinguishing features of self-paced training are not the kinds of training materials used but the ways in which they are used without the presence of an instructor and often outside the classroom setting. Second, there can be great use of *on-the-job training*. The importance of on-the-job training is rising, in part because of a range of sophisticated workplace technologies that have up-skilled most job categories.

Today, the traditional approach to training, that is, *instructor-led classroom instruction*, remains one of the most popular since employees like the comfortable social environment of the classroom, and they like the personal interaction with the instructor. However, most corporate training departments do not have adequate staff to support all students on all topics. To solve this problem in the computer area, companies have contacted hardware and software stores, such as Business Land, to provide the curricula, equipment, and instructors.

A very viable solution is *computer-based training* (CBT) that provides an instantaneous feedback that seems to be its key benefit. With CBT, the computer takes the role of a tutor. Just as the tutor might say, "Okay, the first thing we're going to do is to log on," so does the computer communicate that to the student. As the student types the command, the computer screen changes, simulating the product being taught. Based on an analysis of the student's responses, CBT courses can branch to new topics or can drop back to remedial sessions when the student demonstrates a need for them. Computer-based training has the ability to train the student quickly as well as the ability to slow down and review material for the student. Because students are actively engaged in hands-on learning, they learn fast and effectively. Users are, in effect, using the technology to learn the latest technology of benefit to them. Moreover, CBT has proved cost effective. The training costs can be low when compared to sending a student to a vendor-provided class.

One of the limitations of CBT is that it is tied to the capabilities of the computer. On the other hand, *VR training* allows for an interactive, simulated mode such that students interface with the subject matter in a more meaningful and intensive way. According to a recent article in *Training and Development Journal*, "People retain about 25 percent of what they hear, 45 percent of what they see, and 70 percent of what they see, hear and do. The power of IVI [VR] is that it keeps the learner seeing, hearing, and doing."[2]

From the standpoint of newly hired employees, they could learn about their jobs by using computer simulation. This way of learning how their jobs are to be performed efficiently and effectively is faster and better than a videotape or traditional training methods. In addition, it adds more interest to the daily routine. In fact, to train a large number of production workers in government-required health and safety measures, some progressive companies have installed interactive video workstations in their plants. During lulls in production, employees can interact with 30 to 45 minutes of self-paced training. The net result is that many dollars are saved in training costs.

It should be noted that most training managers agree that no training-delivery system is a panacea for new and inexperienced company personnel. Although it is too early to tell, most companies will eventually find that the best solution is an *integrated* training program that combines self-paced materials, on-the-job training, classroom instruction, computer-based training, and VR training (as discussed later in this chapter). As such, the program must be designed to achieve both individualized and corporate goals. Any training program must fit the company's objectives, budget, and staff/user ratio. But whatever the method or methods selected, training is a key strategic investment for keeping a company competitive. In the final analysis, only by teaming up with today's advanced training technologies (which is shifting to virtual worlds) can corporate trainers meet the challenges of tomorrow's business environment.

Solving Human-Resource Problems before They Arise

The human-resource function in a typical organization is called upon to assist senior management and its corporate planning staff in ways that result in more effective use of both human resources and the capabilities of the personnel system. This enlarged perspective requires that the personnel decision process change from problem solving to problem finding. Hence, there is a need to expand on this approach to provide for the effect of human factors on organizational success and productivity. This realization leads to bringing human resource specialists into corporate planning. Once admitted, these specialists begin to shift administration's orientation from *reactive* administration to *proactive* management and planning. The organization and its human-resources department begin to think of projected labor needs, five-year hiring plans, anticipatory talent development, employee recycling, productive-task distribution, and cost accountability.

Since these issues have for the most part not been seriously contemplated before, the typical organization finds that it has neither the collected data nor the analytical capability to tackle them and has turned, in many cases, to outside consultants for assistance. The consultants, in turn, have developed tools to create the forecasts and models that clients are requesting. Only recently have some of these tools begun to appear as software for human-resource-management systems.

The message should be clear. The real value of a human-resource-planning system is not after-the-fact analysis but an anticipatory capability. The crucial need is to solve problems before they arise. The human-resources system, then, must be increasingly aware of the significance of the organization's human resources today and tomorrow. It must review the efficient use of existing personnel at its present and future levels of development, assess the level of present and anticipated performance of company employees, and concern itself with the enhancement of the individual's skills and talents currently and in the future in order to improve productivity and the overall contribution of the workforce.

Software for Human-Resource-Management Systems

Because an organization's most valuable resource is its employees, every employee represents an obligation to utilize that resource in the most beneficial way. Moreover, every employee represents a vast amount of record keeping, not only for the organization's internal needs but also for governmental (external) needs. In the past, a typical human-resource-management system (HRMS) was performed manually. Hours were spent searching files to locate specific information needed for a list or report. Today, however, performing these tasks manually can bury the human-resources department under an avalanche of details, increasing government and labor-union compliance demands, and a growing assortment of employee benefits.

Software for HRMSs is available to fit the needs of most organizations and operates on a wide variety of hardware and networking environments. This software is relatively inexpensive, relatively easy to install, and pays for itself in time saved and penalties avoided. These HRMS systems are staking a vital claim in the structure of strategic planning. Human-resource-management systems can be used in a variety of ways to meet internal and external needs. They can track such information as skills, prior employment, and training courses to aid in career-path planning. They can be used for recruiting, training, and educating employees. They can track and administer employee benefits and monitor absences.

A most important element related to HRMSs is the planning for human resources, commonly referred to as manpower planning. Human-resources planning is greatly needed because of the decreasing supply of high-talent personnel. The Research Institute of America has stated that management not only is the most urgent need of the future, but will be the most crucially short resource. As a result, planning must be aimed toward management development. Not only management but also personnel with high levels of technical knowledge will be in short supply. This latter shortage is due to rapid technological change. It is difficult for even a qualified professional to keep abreast of any field, a fact that may cause obsolescence of technical manpower. The increasing shortage of management and technical personnel, together with their high cost, has forced organizations to recognize that manpower itself must be considered a resource as important as other corporate resources. To assist in the forecasting process, personnel models are useful in manipulating available human-resource data by using mathematical and statistical models. They provide a simplified and logical view of the levels and flows of personnel throughout an organizational system. They focus on variables considered by managers to be significant and consider assumptions or parameters underlying system behavior.

The role of the HRMS has expanded to include the full range of human-resource functions. One way to justify the investment in HRMS software is to identify the benefits and costs in each of the areas set forth in Figure 10.1. Another way to justify the cost of this software is to focus on its role in performing key functions of greatest concern to top management, such as the planning and implementation of strategic changes as well as employee benefits administration. Typically, a cost-benefit analysis will indicate that investing in HRMS software is a wise move for a company.

NECESSITY OF A SIMULATED APPROACH TO VR
TRAINING AND HUMAN RESOURCES

Currently, many companies organize their personnel function independent of their other functional areas. However, the most successful ones focus their attention on integrating short- to long-range strategic planning in the areas of training and personnel directly with the activities of the human-resources department. As such, there is a great accent on human-resource planning and control whereby the decision-making process centers on three important human-resource activities (1) identifying and acquiring the right number of people with the proper skills and training, (2) motivating them to achieve high performance, and (3) creating interactive links between overall organization objectives and people-planning activities. Therefore, for training and human resources to be effective in the context of human-resources planning and control, it must be capable of providing a "good fit" among employee, task, and organizational unit. If there is a "poor fit," the employee will not be as productive as possible, not to mention the cost to motivate the individual to at least a satisfactory level of performance. The underlying thrust of the training and human-resources functions for a typical company, then, is to provide a good fit for personnel throughout the organization. This is the starting point for using a simulated approach to VR training of personnel and human resources.

As noted previously, there are various ways of training workers in a changing work environment. Very popular ways are on-the-job training and formal courses given by inside personnel or outside consultants. However, when it comes to teaching tasks, especially of manual dexterity and physical movement, most trainers agree that simulation is the ideal training method. This is particularly true in high-risk environments where simulation is the only acceptable method. Until recently, simulation systems were either simple software programs that did not portray the real experience or complex hardware systems that cost millions of dollars. Today, VR gives a computer-created sensory experience that so completely immerses the participant that the individual can barely distinguish a "virtual experience" from a "real one." Although the graphics-animated technology behind VR is still somewhat in its infancy, VR gives trainers a new approach to simulation. One of the most important facts about VR simulation is its ability to create an environment that can be shared by several people.

Figure 10.1
Areas Served by HRMS Software in a Typical Company

- Human-resources planning
- Salary planning
- Pension planning
- Benefits administration
- Career planning
- Career postings
- Management development
- Training
- Equal Employment Opportunities
- Applicant tracking
- Recruitment
- Skills inventories
- Testing
- Relocation
- Time and attendance
- Employee directory

- Strategic planning
- Succession planning
- Productivity programs
- Employee communications
- Job posting
- Labor relations
- Payroll
- Health claims
- Performance evaluation
- Potential evaluation
- Flexible benefits
- Employee access
- International human resources
- Position control
- Postemployment services
- Employee relations

Moreover, objects within a virtual environment can be made to behave according to whatever rules of physics the user writes into the system.

Just as VR is proving helpful to business firms, the same can be said about education. Typically, students are passive in the classroom. Applying VR techniques to learning can do wonders. Researcher William Bricken said that he enchanted a group of seventh-graders with a VR tour of Seattle in his University of Washington lab. Now he and his colleagues have devised a VR program for algebra in which students act as parts of the equations. An equal sign could be represented by a balance beam; in the equation $6x = 4y + 50$, students become blocks of different sizes representing $6x$ or $4y$ and try to bring the pieces into equilibrium. In a similar manner, difficult concepts like events in the world of quantum mechanics, where electrons act as both waves and particles, may become easier for students to understand if they are submerged in a virtual quantum world. Simpler visual presentations of such complex material have been shown to increase comprehension so much that even average students turn into good ones.

This important leap in comprehension of the subject matter is not confined to students. For example, Eastman Kodak engineers gained new insights much faster after they used a supercomputer to process in three dimensions the intricate interactions of such variables as heat, temperature, and pressure in the injection process that the company uses to make plastic items from film spools to camera cases. To visualize six or seven variables is a very powerful experience. A person can start to understand the dance that polymers do to untangle themselves and see things that were not evident from the equations. By making those polymer pirouettes visible, Kodak can design lighter, thinner parts that require less material and meet environmental standards.[3]

TRAINING AND HUMAN-RESOURCE APPLICATIONS THAT CAN BENEFIT FROM VR

Virtual worlds that have demonstrated the practicality of their application to business firms will be brought to a close in this final part on training and human resources. At this time, VR hardware and software are just getting into the mainstream of business organizations. In like manner, VR is just entering the classroom where a computer-based, interactive, multimedia environment allows the student to be a participant. The central value of VR in business or in the classroom is that it can be a highly participative, motivating activity for individualized learning. Overall, the technology enables participants to enter and get involved in realities that they would otherwise not have access to: creating and altering places and things that would otherwise not exist, interacting with people in remote locations or in nonrealistic ways, representing and manipulating abstractions, and even interacting with virtual beings.

As a way of contrasting prior systems to VR systems for company employees, see Figure 10.2. While each of these prior systems (see Chapter 1) performs an intended purpose for the typical company, VR systems for business go a step further by allowing employees to comprehend relations or abstractions more quickly than they could by examining columns of figures or lines of text. As such, VR systems allow company employees to experience what is essential to their everyday business activities and operations.

VR TRAINING

Formal training in VR is currently available as part of college or university programs in the physical sciences. In the early 1990s, the CAD Institute (Phoenix, Arizona) launched the nation's first accredited degree program in VR. The CAD Institute offers education, training, and services for CAD and computer-information-systems specialists. It is the world's largest authorized AutoCAD training center. The Institute teaches AutoCAD 2D and 3D, CAD-systems management, animation, desktop publishing, and AutoLISP and C programming courses, offering certificate and diploma programs. The diploma program encompasses majors in four areas: manufacturing, civil- and geographical-information systems, architecture, and VR.

Those who major in VR at the CAD Institute explore engineering sciences

Figure 10.2
Computer Systems Found in Business That Are Helpful to Company Employees
in Conducting Their Everyday Activities and Operations

Information-Processing Systems

High-volume sorts, lists, and merges
Straightforward calculations
Display of information
Ability to audit and spot discrepancies

Expert Systems

Codification of knowledge and experience
Distribution of expertise
Recommendation of action
Education

Decision Support Systems

Optimization of decision alternatives
Support for research
Speeded up discovery
Group decision making

VR Systems

High participation for individualized learning
Alteration of places and things
Interaction with people in distant places
Representation and manipulation of abstractions

(physics, calculus, trigonometry, creative thinking, logic, and so forth); CAD utilization, design, and integration; and applied sciences (ranging from public speaking and English composition to economics, algebra, psychology, and chemistry). In the VR-related courses, students learn about VR's history, evolution, implementation, and applications; C++ object orientation; advanced C programming; and human-computer interfacing. They experiment with VR gear in computer lab work and again when they engage in their research projects. The VR curriculum also includes a management course, providing a study of management techniques in project planning and implementation, human resources, and ethics.

In the environment-construction class, for example, students learn the ins and outs of the VREAM VR Development system (the leading, low-cost VR software for IBM-compatible PCs). They step into six space to deploy the 3D world editor, implement various interface devices, and build virtual worlds, linking multiple environments and worlds as well as optimizing objects and details. The program's strength lies in its diversity of approach. "Soft courses" provide the basics in VR's foundation, taxonomies, and theories. "Hard courses" let the students get virtual dirt under their fingernails. They delve into issues of environment construction, pondering texture use and polygon considerations, display clarity, lighting, mapping, auditory components, visual feedback, physical dynamics of virtual objects, and "intelligent" characters.[4]

As illustrated in Figure 10.3, students utilize a variety of VR devices that center on training in their usage and also employ some of these devices to develop VR programs and implement these programs for specific VR applications. Essentially, the students are subjected to a variety of VR experiences whereby they find themselves in "cyberspace," or virtual worlds. As noted throughout the text, VR is a completely spatialized visualization of information of global-information-processing systems along pathways provided by various types of communications networks, thereby enabling students to interact with virtual worlds. Additionally, students are involved in the simulation of virtual worlds by utilizing authoring systems and "toolkits." From this perspective, students are involved in taking several "soft" and "hard" VR courses that let them experience virtual worlds.

In another VR program at the Software Technology Branch (in Building 12 of the Johnson Space Center), a team is investigating the uses of VR for training both astronauts and high-school physics students. The National Aeronautics and Space Administration (NASA) has developed a pair of demonstrations using VPL's RB2 system that make it obvious that VR can provide important advantages for both groups.

To illustrate one of the NASA activities, there is a simulation of a repair mission. With this system, a basic problem is addressed in astronaut training. It is impossible on earth to replicate accurately the way in which objects in zero gravity react to being touched. This problem was made obvious on a recent repair mission. The orbiting satellite refused to behave as expected, resulting in the need for an ingenious but dangerous impromptu maneuver to snare it. Researchers at NASA hope to obviate this problem by using VR to train the astronauts. In the system being developed, the proper physics of orbiting objects are included. The operator of the system uses flight-certified controls that replicate those of a manned maneuvering unit (MMU), permitting flight around the model of the Hubble telescope. Further refinements will include texture-mapping photos of the real telescope on the model.

For physics students, a virtual lab has been developed where experiments in motion and gravity may be undertaken. The lab includes a pendulum of variable length and two balls with variable restitution (bounce). A control panel that floats in the lab space lets the student control gravity, friction, and time. In addition, the panel's readout displays either elapsed time or distance. In the lab, time may be stopped to take measurements, and the bouncing balls can leave trails that allow the student to see their paths. Another feature of the lab is the "gravity sphere," a wire-frame ball enclosing a smaller, solid ball. The relative height of the small ball in the sphere indicates the gravitational constant in effect at that time, which may be positive or negative.

Basically, this lab provides a first look at how VR may be used in teaching

Figure 10.3
Interactive VR Training and Students' Development of Virtual Worlds

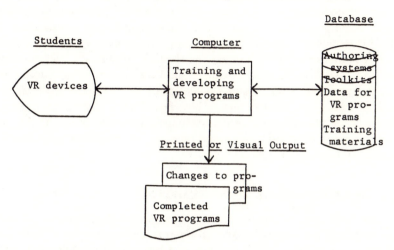

basic physics concepts. A student can learn about gravity and Newton's Laws not only by reading or watching a demonstration but also through experimentation and trial and error. Time can be stopped or slowed to observe what happens in a fast-moving experiment. The simple and intuitive interface does not impede learning, and to a large degree the teacher's attention is not required while the student is in the lab since there is nothing to break or blow up. Such a lab would be used in concert with classroom instruction, typically in a networked system where the instructor would enter the lab when needed, then move on to another student, all without leaving his or her desk.[5]

Typical Training Programs in VR

Typical training programs in VR employed by business firms center on lowering the costs of a company's operation. For example, the Electric Power Research Institute has teamed up with the MITRE Corporation to determine if an electronic mock-up of a power-plant control room using stereo projection displays can be effective in training plant operators. Training rooms for fossil-fuel plants currently cost up to $1 million. Utilizing VR, the cost might be around $100,000.

Virtual reality may also be helpful in training workers at Boeing. As noted in Chapter 8, Boeing is developing techniques to project job instructions onto see-through goggles worn by assembly workers or onto the work space in front of them. In this way, instructions can be used to replace hours of training in which workers learn jobs, then must be trained again when the task changes. A worker might assemble wing flaps with such displays, then switch to nose cones on the same day with little loss of productivity.

Developers of such systems must solve some novel problems. For example, why do some people become nauseated when navigating in virtual space. And if there is a trade-off between complex, realistic graphics or live-action motion, which is more important for maintaining the illusion of reality? The answers to these type questions lie in the cognitive and behavioral sciences. More specifically, there is a need for greater knowledge of the structure of the brain and how it processes information, that is, how people think and perceive. Such research already indicates why virtual worlds are quite effective in training since people reason or solve problems based on cases, examples, and experience, not so much by learning rules.[6]

VR HUMAN-RESOURCE MANAGEMENT

In the continuing battle to meet and beat competition, managers must control labor costs and motivate employees to improve customer-oriented performance and, at the same time, search out new and better ways of doing both. These strategic objectives must be met in the face of a shrinking head count and a global environment in which employees are more culturally diverse and located throughout the world. From this perspective, relatively routine tasks of human-resource record keeping and legal and regulatory compliance are intensified. Such complexity also demands more sophisticated applications of strategies that go beyond simply improving the management of routine tasks. Essentially, company managers have a stake in exploiting appropriate strategies to better manage their human resources.

More recently, these strategic objectives have centered on downsizing. All companies of any size have been involved in the restructuring process. Restructuring in most companies has left human resources with a smaller workforce and yet with equal or greater responsibilities and new demands. Time has become as crucial a resource as talent and money. Human resources, then, must review its own work to define strategic priorities. What work must continue to be done? Of that work, which can be done better by searching out efficiencies and economies of scale? Which can be done better by delegating and collaborating with line managers and employees or other functional staffs? Which would most benefit from creative time, talent, and resources? In essence, how can human resources best work harder, smarter, or with more vision?

In the area of searching out efficiencies and economies of scale, company managers, assisted by those in human-resource management, could advocate streamlining the processing of employee records, payroll, and benefits by standardizing and eliminating unnecessary paper handling and reporting. This can be accomplished by utilizing an HRMS. In this manner, an HRMS could allow the company to be a low-cost provider for crucial administrative work as well as a more accurate and timely provider of human-resource information. To improve delegating and collaborating with line managers and employees, human resources can collaborate with line managers or others to become more responsive to their needs. For example, human resources could replace a merit-pay process requiring product-line managers to follow an imposed standard set of guidelines with a system encouraging human-resource and line managers to customize pay-increase plans jointly for their units. While human resources contributes the incentive-design expertise, line managers contribute their hands-on understanding of customer demands and the rewards that would best motivate employees to achieve those demands. Under an innovation strategy, human resources could allocate 10 to 15 percent of staff time to exploratory, creative projects with uncertain short-term to long-term payoffs. Perhaps, human resources could reach new customers by providing expertise to other organizations, thereby making human resources a profit center.

Ability of Human-Resource Strategies to Effect Improvement in Productivity

The real purpose of utilizing an integrated HRMS is to reduce the costs of routine personnel tasks, especially when performed on a local area network. However, there is need to go a step further and include the three items discussed above as they relate to human-resource strategic objectives. Typically, these objectives can be somewhat opposed to one another. For example, the cost of processing human-resource records must be as low as possible, but employees must be offered the widest possible range of fringe-benefit options so that desired employees can be retained. From this enlarged view of HRMSs and human-resource strategic objectives, how to place all items in the proper perspective can be far from clear. In most cases, work division is not clear-cut. The proper assignment of human-resource work to cost leadership, quality/customer satisfaction, and innovation strategies must reveal to company managers how resources might best be allocated to support one specific strategy over another.

In order to undertake an evaluation of different strategies within an HRMS environment, it is helpful to take a VR approach. More specifically, a user could utilize a head-mounted display device that allows the individual to fly over the various alternatives that are changed interactively in order to find the best strategy that meets the needs of the company. If an evaluation is performed without the use of VR, the user would tend to miss new relationships that lie buried in mounds of detail. Thus, the individual can navigate through complex data in a graphical way that has not been possible in the past. A "good fit" among the user, the task, and the company can be realized by using a virtual world, so that new relationships not envisioned before can be seen to effect improvements in productivity throughout the company.

VR WAGE-AND-SALARY ADMINISTRATION

Typically, wage-and-salary administration can take several directions since it involves working with selected data and ratios. In many companies, it centers primarily on utilizing various types of wage-and-salary analyses to answer "what-if" questions. In other companies, it includes these analyses and delves into other human-resource issues by evaluating output on the effectiveness of human-resource management in controlling departmental budgets, the backup of key positions in the office and in the manufacturing plants, the amounts paid to factory production workers, the promotability of office and factory employees, the company's progress toward affirmative action, and, in general, the human-resource–department goals and progress toward realizing them. Although all of these areas can utilize some type of computer-generated environment that can simulate real-world experiences, the focus will be on wage-and-salary administration.

To place VR in perspective, consider a company that has five manufacturing plants with attached warehouses throughout the United States along with corporate headquarters located in a large midwestern city. An annual salary survey is a part of the wage-and-salary analysis. Many questions can be asked and answered in a graphical way. For example, management could evaluate how wages and salaries in each plant and warehouse compare to budget, how the cost of wages and salaries compares to sales, and how one plant or warehouse ranks against other plants or warehouses and against the company average. As another example, management might want to compare each plant and warehouse to the industry average and other industries and determine whether the company is overpaying or underpaying its employees. All of these analyses are easily produced in a graphical way by a typical management information system (MIS) today.

Similarly, management may want to undertake analyses that focus on present and future human-resource problems. The company may want to know if it has paid fair wages and salaries over the past several years; to determine the impact, if any, of wage imbalances because of different costs of living for each of the plants and warehouses; and to determine, given the economic conditions, the impact on employees of adjusting salaries. From another perspective, management might want to know whether or not its workforce will be paid equitable wages and salaries with appropriate fringe benefits next year and in the following one as well as five years hence. To facilitate these future evaluations, management needs reports, such as future wage-and-salary information, of comparable positions and skills for the plant's and warehouse's geographical area, the estimated future cost of living and consumer price indices for each plant and warehouse, and the optimal wage-and-salary packages that the company should offer to its workers for certain skills and positions. As noted above, an MIS operating mode can be quite helpful to management for understanding today what wage-and-salary administration problems they might face tomorrow.

Although such an operating mode is capable of answering these questions (which are normally posed as "what-if" questions), it does not allow the user to interact with the data such that new relationships are discerned by the user.

A Complete Evaluation of Wage-and-Salary Information

In reference to the material presented in the first part of this chapter, people learn best when put in control of their own environment and when enabled to solve their own problems. This is especially important since our global-knowledge base is doubling every three to five years. For those persons who have interest in their work, the ever-expanding knowledge base will be helpful. Of course, today, this knowledge expansion includes the use of virtual worlds to help analyze a company's problems, like those found in the wage and administration area. This means going beyond what has been represented to them in two dimensions or possibly three dimensions in an MIS graphical world. Virtual worlds center on giving the user computer-generated environments that simulate real-world wage-and-salary experiences. In effect, the user can navigate through complex wage-and-salary data in an alternative reality.

To better understand this alternative reality when comparing present and future wages and salaries, an analyst could convert the numbers to a 3-D schematic of colored squares that move up and down and symbolize each plant or warehouse as it moves from the current year on up to five years. The analyst may look at the squares that are flashing red and represent a particular plant or warehouse. Such situations indicate an increasing cost rate over the coming years—in particular, the later years. In a similar manner, the individual might look at the adjoining plant or warehouse and find that all of the squares are flashing green, which means that the costs appear to be within an acceptable range given the geographical region of the country. In the first case, the analyst can use a mouse to "fly" into the structure and, if outside a specific cost range, help determine what is causing it. This process takes seconds, thus allowing the analyst to recognize exceptions, identify potential cost problems, and make appropriate decisions quickly. In such a virtual world, the analyst discovers new relationships that were not evident previously.

OTHER TRAINING AND HUMAN-RESOURCE AREAS THAT CAN BENEFIT FROM VR

There are a number of other training and human-resource areas that can reap the benefits of a virtual world. In a typical training environment, instructors need no longer be constrained by the limitations of prerecorded video and film. Different training scenarios can be constructed and then altered by variety. Trainees can have complete freedom to move and interact with the training environment. For example, West Denton High School (Newcastle upon Tyne), as part of a project funded by the Department of Employment and a number of companies in the United Kingdom, is using desktop VR as a training aid. Students are undertaking projects related to health and safety, foreign-language education, and arts awareness.

In the area of health and safety, West Denton uses a VR program called "Dangerous Environment." Students use the VR training to author a dangerous environment in a manufacturing firm. As an example, the world includes a bank of lathes, all operated by push-button control. This allows the student to experience how such a piece of equipment would operate in the real world, but without any of the inherent dangers. The lathes faithfully reproduce the characteristics, such as rotation, of the real equipment. The lathes stop if the student carries out the wrong procedure. In effect, the VR program is designed to reinforce the health-and-safety-training message such that the virtual world is extended to show what happens when something is not done according to the correct procedure.

Another example of a virtual world at West Denton is that being used to help in the teaching of foreign languages. At the present time, a typical office virtual world is used. The student wanders at will around in this world, interacting with objects, which automically display their names both in English and in the chosen language.[7]

Going off in still another direction is a VR world designed to help disabled children. The pilot program at Meadowside School in Liverpool, England, and at Shepard School in Nottingham (the United Kingdom's largest school for children with severe learning difficulties) is directed toward helping students master vocabulary basics by associating hand signs and symbols with objects. Using the Dobbshire Assessment Scheme, the children's vocabulary skills are ranked incrementally; the children are then started on a program at the next step on the scale. The project gives students a greater degree of control over their environment through communication. Teachers at the schools have worked closely with the Virtual Reality Research Team (VIRART), which originally started at Nottingham University, to incorporate VR as a new learning tool. Dimension International (Berkshire, England) approached VIRART and asked if it would like to use their Superscape program to work on its projects. The VIRART programmers then went to work using Dimension International's beta equipment. The end result was this effort in the schools.

In this pilot program, the Makaton symbol and signing system, a technique used for many years to teach vocabulary skills to disabled students, was incorporated into a series of virtual worlds. Through this system, the children have access to interactive, 3-D environments that display images of words, together with the appropriate symbol and sign, rather than just static pages of information. Using the VR system, it is possible to create a 3-D car, which the child can get into and drive around the virtual world while the 2-D Makaton symbol remains constantly in view. The system helps the child to understand the generic image of a car, associating it with different colors and movements.[8]

Another interesting VR application in this area is one that assists high-school students before they start a job search. Specifically, a VR kiosk for junior-high-school students would allow them to investigate jobs and careers. The students could navigate through a "job city," and enter buildings and offices to find out more about a variety of jobs. In effect, they find out from an overall standpoint whether or not the jobs interest them. In turn, the students could take on one or more jobs and explore them in more depth through the VR kiosk as well as by the efforts of their high-school counselors and on their own.

Related to the whole area of training and human resources is an accent on the human factors. In the world of human-factors engineering, the user can be immersed in a virtual world and test the dynamic factors of certain designs. For example, if an airplane manufacturer wants to design a new aircraft, the designers can design the plane from a human-centered orientation. A specific illustration is an engineer who is trying to grab a lever and/or turn a release valve from the inside of a maintenance shaft. By allowing designers to test this ability inside VR, they can instantly know whether they have a good design or need to redesign from a human's viewpoint before expending time and money to build a physical prototype. Similarly, in a human-factors training program, a user can learn the procedural and kinematic knowledge of how to use or repair a sophisticated system, like a jet engine or a power-plant control system. Hence, human factors can play a significant role in virtual worlds that require the need to assess these factors before the actual product or service is developed.

In the area of the military, the U.S. Navy is centering its research laboratories on a handful of VR projects to examine the feasibility of maintaining or improving training and tactical operations. Basic training objectives are to compensate for the educational levels of recruits, fewer skilled instructors, and fewer locations for high-quality classroom facilities. Additionally, training should be more efficient and affordable, should accommodate varying geographic demands, and should increase the possibility of team training. The objectives for tactical operations, on the other hand, are to increase operator performance by reducing workload and, consequently, improving decision making.

The development and implementation of Navy VR applications require a team of experts with widely different backgrounds. There has been assembled diverse teams with elements of art, science, design, education, security, and creativity. For example, Navy special-operation missions are performed by SEALs (Sea-Air-Land units) under the direction of the Naval Special Warfare Command. Because these missions demand extensive planning and perfect execution, attention must be paid to the performance of the individual as well as the collective response of the unit throughout the training. A characteristic of special operations is the inability to provide real-world environments with the same fast-breaking action. However, VR systems supplied with body-function information bring these forces closer to a believable and natural simulation. The Artisan Group is developing several VR conceptual platforms for the special-operations community.

Essentially, VR simulations consist of the planning, rehearsal, and execution phases of a mission. Some simulations include Navy SEAL Mk-VIII swimmer-delivery vehicles and the future, Mk-V fast surface vehicle. Direct-action missions with high-altitude, low-opening– and high-altitude, high-opening–parachute insertion, demolition raids, and close-battle environments contain multiple variables that can be adjusted in real time. Body-function information, such as blood pressure, pulse rate, fatigue, temperature, and so forth, can be captured and automatically displayed in a virtual world. The coupling of this information can produce more precise fatigue and alertness indicators, as compared to present behavioral and body-function responses taken by overt methods.

Current Naval scenarios require the replacement of humans by machines for hazardous duties. The VR system makes teleoperated and robotic vehicles simpler to control, thereby reducing the operator's stress. By providing full-immersion audio and video and realistic manual-control movements at the control site, repair and maintenance of ground, air, and underwater vehicles becomes much more natural. Full immersion can be achieved with microphones and cameras that are positioned on the remote vehicle or site. Realistic manual control can be achieved by duplicating the physical vehicle that is remotely controlled or by interpreting hand, foot, head, and eye movement by tactile or optical sensors. A VR system provides a simulated war-gaming environment for multiunit tactics coordination. By providing full immersion helmet-mounted units, the need for the physical simulators is eliminated. By tracking hand and body movement, the physical actions required in today's simulators can be replicated without the need for the physical mock-up of the vehicle.

At this time, the Navy has made a commitment to develop and test new weapon-system concepts that could benefit from VR systems. This is a natural extension of eliminating the need for physical simulators and mock-ups since new weapons and new concepts for deploying those weapons in the battlefield can be simulated in a virtual world. New weapon-system concepts can be explored without the expense of developing prototypes. Onlookers can invisibly take a point of view from anywhere within the battlefield to evaluate tactics and strategies. Information that is invisible to human senses, then, can be evaluated visually or audibly in a virtual world.[9]

SUMMARY

The training and human-resource systems for a typical company are related directly to other systems because all functional areas depend on the human element to accomplish a company's objectives. Regarding the data used, human resources rely heavily on the payroll function of the accounting system. Similarly, information available from the manufacturing system, such as the technical skills required for specific jobs and the apprenticeship requirements for a certain job level, are of great help to the human-resource function. However, despite this important level of integration, many methods and procedures evolve from the human-resource function itself. As illustrated in the chapter, the development of an effective human-resource system centers on providing timely and in-depth management information for changing conditions. But more important, such a system includes training new and experienced personnel to enter virtual worlds where computer-generated environments simulate real-world experiences. Personnel have the capability of experiencing the reality of the situation.

NOTES

1. Ronald Henkoff, "Companies That Train Best," *Fortune*, March 22, 1993, pp. 62–75.

2. Beatrice Jordan Garcia, "Training the American Team," *EDGE*, July–August 1990, p. 53.

3. Gene Bylinsky, "The Marvels of 'Virtual Reality,'" *Fortune*, June 3, 1991, p. 150.

4. Linda Jacobson, "Reading, 'Riting, 'Rithmetic, and Reality," *Virtual Reality Special Report*, published by *AI Expert* (San Francisco: Miller Freeman, 1993), pp. 39–42.

5. Ben Delaney, "Where Virtual Rubber Meets the Road," *Virtual Reality Special Report*, published by *AI Expert* (San Francisco: Miller Freeman, 1993), pp. 16–17.

6. Joan O'C. Hamilton, Emily T. Smith, Gary McWilliams, Evan I. Schwartz, and John Carey, "Virtual Reality: How a Computer-Generated World Could Change the Real World," *Business Week*, October 5, 1992, p. 100.

7. Andy Tait, "Authoring Virtual Worlds on the Desktop," *Virtual Reality Special Report*, published by *AI Expert* (San Francisco: Miller Freeman, 1993), p. 13.

8. Julie Shaw, "Getting a Virtual Education," *AI Expert*, August 1993, p. 48.

9. Mark Gembicki and David Rousseau, "Naval Applications of Virtual Reality," *Virtual Reality Special Report*, published by *AI Expert* (San Francisco: Miller Freeman, 1993), pp. 67–72.

Bibliography for Part IV

Ames, B. C., and J. D. Hlavacek. "Virtual Truths About Managing Your Costs." *Harvard Business Review*, January–February 1990.

Andrews, D. H. "Warfighting Training R & D in the Post Cold War Era—With a Special Emphasis on Synthetic Environments." *Educational Technology*, February 1993.

Argyris, C. "Teaching Smart People How to Learn." *Harvard Business Review*, May–June 1991.

Asch, T. "Designing Virtual Worlds." *AI Expert*, August 1992.

Ashenhurst, J. "A Look at Technology to Come—What Will an Agent Be Able to Use?" *Rough Notes*, May 1991.

Badaracco, J. I., Jr. *The Knowledge Link: How Firms Compete Through Strategic Alliances*. Boston: Harvard Business School Press, 1991.

Bair, T. "Flexible Manufacturing, It's Gotten Easier to Change on Demand." *Computerworld*, February 11, 1991.

———. "Experts: Time to Put It Together." *Computerworld*, October 28, 1991.

Band, W. A. *Creating Value for Customers: Designing & Implementing a Total Corporate Strategy*. New York: John Wiley & Sons, 1991.

Bandrowski, P. "Try Before You Buy: Virtually Real Merchandising." *Corporate Computing*, December 1992.

Banks, M. "What's New Online." *Computer Shopper*, March 1992.

Barker, Q. "Virtual Reality Market Analysis." *Virtual Reality World*, March–April 1994.

Barlow, M. A. "Of Mice and 3D Input Devices." *Computer-Aided Engineering*, April 1993.

Barr, C. "Virtual Reality Goes Mainstream." *PC Magazine*, April 28, 1992.

Barr, D. S., and G. Mani. "Using Neural Nets to Manage Investments." *AI Expert*, February 1994.

Barrett, J. "Process Visualization." *Oracle Magazine*, Fall 1993.

Bessen, J. "Riding the Marketing Information Wave." *Harvard Business Review*, September–October 1993.

Betts, M. "Manage My Inventory or Else!" *Computerworld*, January 31, 1994.

———. "As Easy as ABC?" *Computerworld*, May 23, 1994.

Blattberg, R. C., and J. Deighton. "Interactive Marketing: Exploiting the Age of Addressability." *Business Edge*, May 1992.

Bloxill, M. F., and T. M. Hout. "The Fallacy of the Overhead Quick Fix." *Harvard Business Review*, July–August 1991.

Booker, E. "Fighting Your Battles in a World of the Future." *Computerworld*, March 18, 1991.

Bowles, J., and J. Hammond. *Beyond Quality, How 50 Winning Companies Use Continuous Improvement*. New York: G. P. Putnam's Sons, 1990.

Bozer, K. M., D. N. Hester, and R. C. Maloney. "Planning for a Computerized Accounting System." *Journal of Accountancy*, June 1992.

Broderick, R., and J. W. Boudreau. "Human Resource Management, Information Technology, and the Competitive Edge.'' *Academy of Management Executive*, May 1992.

Brown, J. S. "Research That Reinvents the Corporation." *Harvard Business Review*, January–February 1991.

Bryson, S., and C. Levit. "The Virtual Wind Tunnel." *IEEE Computer Graphics and Applications*, July 1992.

Bunnell, D. "Virtual Accounting." *NewMedia Magazine*, October 1993.

Buta, P. "Mining for Financial Knowledge with CBR." *AI Expert*, February 1994.

Buzzell, R. D., and B. T. Gale. *The PIMS Principles, Linking Strategy to Performance.* New York: Free Press, 1988.

Bylinsky, G. "The Marvels of 'Virtual Reality.' " *Fortune*, June 3, 1991.

———. "The Payoff from 3-D Computing." *Fortune, Special Report*, Autumn 1993.

Cafasso, R. "Rethinking Re-Engineering." *Computerworld*, March 13, 1993.

Canton, M. "AutoCAD Data Extensions Offer Query Power." *PC Week*, November 22, 1993.

Caroni, J. "Business Reports Get Graphic." *Datamation*, June 1, 1991.

Chaudhry, A. "From Art to Part." *Computerworld*, November 9, 1992.

Cheatham, C. "Updating Standard Cost System." *Journal of Accountancy*, December 1990.

Chepetsky, S. "MRP II Software Moves to Embrace Client/Server Computing." *Digital News & Review*, December 7, 1992.

Churbuck, D. C. "Applied Reality." *Forbes*, September 14, 1992.

Cole, R. E. "The Quality Revolution." *Production and Operations Management*, Winter 1992.

Converse, C. "Accounting Software's Client/Server Architecture Adds Up to Savings." *Digital News & Review*, March 1, 1993.

———. "CAD Packages Broaden Their Reach." *PC Week*, June 14, 1993.

Cooper, R., and R. S. Kaplan. "Profit Priorities From Activity-Based Costing." *Harvard Business Review*, May–June 1991.

Damarin, S. K. "Schooling and Situated Knowledge: Travel or Tourism?" *Educational Technology*, March 1993.

De Jager, P. "Oceanic Views and a Visit to the Holodeck." *Computing Canada*, February, 1993.

De Jong, J. "Smart Marketing." *Computerworld*, February 7, 1994.

Delaney, B. "Where Virtual Rubber Meets the Road." *Virtual Reality Special Report*, published by *AI Expert*. San Francisco: Miller Freeman, 1993.

———. "Virtual Reality Lands the Job." *NewMedia Magazine*, August 1994.

Dertouzos, M. L., R. K. Lester, and R. M. Solow. *Made in America: Regaining the Productive Edge.* Boston: MIT Press, 1989.

Desmond, J. "Windows to MIS: Graphics Focuses Business Picture." *Software News*, April 1987.

Dickinson, J. "A New Generation of Intelligent Objects Will Enhance Our Daily Lives." *PC Computing*, March 1992.

Drucker, P. F. "The Emerging Theory of Manufacturing." *Harvard Business Review*, May–June 1990.

Dumaine, B. "Closing the Innovation Gap." *Fortune*, December 2, 1991.

Dysort, J. "Wall Street Meets VR: Animated Investment Tracking." *Virtual Reality World*, September–October 1994.

Earls, A. R. "Agile Manufacturing Finds Firmer Ground." *Computerworld*, February 24, 1994.

Ehrenfeld, T., P. Hise, R. H. Mamis, and A. Murphy. "Where Great Ideas for New Businesses Come From." *Inc.*, September 1993.

Endoso, J. "DOD Hopes 3-D Systems Find Home in Civilian Sector." *Government Computer News*, August 17, 1992.

Fierman, J. "The Contingency Work Force." *Fortune*, January 24, 1994.

Francett, B. "Downsized Financial Apps Challenge DBMS." *Software Magazine*, December 1993.

Francis, B. "A New Vision of Quality Control." *Datamation*, April 1, 1990.

———. "MRP II Rides the PC Bandwagon." *Datamation*, August 15, 1990.

Freedman, D. H. "Quick Change Artists." *CIO*, September 15, 1993.

Freichs, D. "Bringing Real Applications to the Virtual Environment." *Virtual Reality World*, July–August 1994.

Fritz, M. "The World of Virtual Reality." *Training*, February 1991.

Frost, N. "Outsourcing: The Right Move for Today's Virtual Organization." *The Office*, May 1993.

Fuller, J. B., J. O'Conor, and R. Rawlinson. "Tailored Logistics: The Next Advantage." *Harvard Business Review*, May–June 1993.

Garcia, B. J. "Training the American Team." *EDGE*, July–August 1990.

Gargan, E. A. "Virtual Companies Leave the Manufacturing to Others." *New York Times*, July 17, 1994.

Garvin, D. A. "Building a Learning Organization." *Harvard Business Review*, July–August 1993.

Gellerman, S. W. "The Tests of a Good Salesperson." *Harvard Business Review*, May–June 1990.

Gembicki, M., and D. Rousseau. "Naval Applications of Virtual Reality." *Virtual Reality Special Report*, published by *AI Expert*. San Francisco: Miller Freeman, 1993.

Goldstein, D. "Modeling and Manufacturing: Preparation for CIM." *DEC Professional*, August 1991.

Good, M., and L. Tan. "VR in Architecture: Today's Use and Tomorrow's Promise." *Virtual Reality World*, November–December 1994.

Goodrich, B. E. "Creating a 'Virtual' Magnet School." *T.H.E. Journal*, May 1994.

Gouillart, F. J., and F. D. Sturdivant. "Spend a Day in the Life of Your Customers." *Harvard Business Review*, January–February 1994.

Greco, A. J., and J. T. Hogue. "Developing Marketing Decision Support Systems." *The Journal of Business & Industrial Marketing*, Summer–Fall 1990.

Greene, A. "MRP II: Out with the Old . . ." *Computerworld*, June 8, 1992.

Hamel, G., and C. K. Prahalad. "The Core Competence of the Corporation." *Harvard Business Review,* May–June 1990.

———. "Corporate Imagination and Expeditionary Marketing." *Harvard Business Review*, July–August 1991.

———. "Competing for the Future." *Harvard Business Review*, July–August 1994.

———. "Seeing the Future First." *Fortune*, September 5, 1994.

Hamilton, J. O'C., E. T. Smith, G. McWilliams, E. I. Schwartz, and J Carey. "Virtual Reality: How a Computer-Generated World Could Change the Real World." *Business Week*, October 5, 1992.

Hammer, M., and J. Champy. "In Depth: Explosive Thinking." *Computerworld*, May 3, 1993.

———. "The Promise of Reengineering." *Fortune*, May 3, 1993.

———. *Reengineering the Corporation: A Manifesto For Business Revolution.* New York: Harper Collins, 1993.

Harding, E. W. "Cost-Justifying Robots Gets Easier." *Software Magazine*, June 1991.

Hauser, J. R., and D. Clausing. "The House of Quality." *Harvard Business Review*, May–June 1988.

Hayes, R. H., and G. P. Pisano. "Beyond World-Class: The New Manufacturing Strategy." *Harvard Business Review*. January–Febraury 1994.

Henkoff, R. "Cost Cutting: How to Do It Right." *Fortune*, April 9, 1990.

———. "Companies That Train Best." *Fortune*, March 22, 1993.

Hildebrand, C., and C. Wilder. "Never Fear—'Re-engineering' Is Here!" *Computerworld*, December 23, 1991–January 2, 1992.

———. "Financial Affairs." *CIO*, March 15, 1994.

Hill, G. C. "Electronic 'Agents' Bring Virtual Shopping a Bit Closer to Reality." *Wall Street Journal*, September 24, 1994.

Hinterhuber, H. H., and W. Popp. "Are You a Strategist or Just a Manager?" *Harvard Business Review*, January–February 1992.

Hitt, M. A., R. E. Haskisson, and J. S. Harrison. "Strategic Competitiveness in the 1990s: Challenges and Opportunities for U.S. Executives." *Academy of Management Executive*, May 1991.

Holbrook, D. "Stereo Viewing: Looking 'into' Manufacturing." *Manufacturing Systems*, January 1991.

House, G. "Going to the Shopping Mall Via VR." *Virtual Reality World*, November–December 1994.

Ives, B., and R. O. Mason. "Can Information Technology Revitalize Your Customer Service?" *Academy of Management Executive*, November 1990.

Jacob, R. "How to Gain to Regain the Productive Edge." *Fortune*, May 22, 1989.

———. "The Search for the Organization of Tomorrow." *Fortune*, May 18, 1992.

Jacobson, L. "Virtual Reality: A Status Report." *AI Expert*, August 1991.

———. "Reading, 'Riting, 'Rithmetic, and Reality." *Virtual Reality Special Report*, published by *AI Expert*. San Francisco: Miller Freeman, 1993.

Jacobson, R. "Virtual Worlds: A New Type of Design Environment." *Virtual Reality World*, May–June 1994.

———. "Applying the Virtual Worlds Paradigm to Mapping and Surveying Data." *Virtual Reality World*, September–October 1994.

Johnston, S. J. "Virtual Reality Takes Architectural Leap." *Computerworld*, June 20, 1994.

Jones, J. P. "Ad Spending: Maintaining Market Share." *Harvard Business Review*, January–February 1990.

Kanter, J., S. Schiffman, and J. F. Horn. "Let the Customer Do It." *Computerworld*, August 27, 1990.

Kanter, R. M. "Collaborative Advantage: The Art of Alliances." *Harvard Business Review*, July–August 1994.

Kaplan, R. S. "The Four Stage Model of Cost Systems Design." *Management Accounting*, February 1990.

Kellar, D. "Virtual Reality, Real Money." *Computerworld*, November 15, 1993.

Kiechel, W., III. "How We Will Work in the Year 2000." *Fortune*, May 17, 1993.

Kiely, T. "The Creative Process." *CIO*, September 1, 1993.

Kimura, E. H. "Integrating HR Systems for Daily Valuations." *Payroll Exchange*, October 1992.

King, P. "Financial Apps Open Client-Server Door." *Open Systems Today*, July 4, 1994.

Knight, R. "New Architecture Aligning Manufacturing and RDBMs." *Software Magazine*, March 1994.

Korzeniowski, P. "Accounting Platform Slow in Shaping Up." *Software Magazine*, August 1993.

Kuhn, S. E. "The New Perilous Stock Market." *Fortune*, December 27, 1993.

Kumada, M. "Customers Enter Virtual Reality to Design Own World." *Japan Times Weekly International Edition*, Volume 32, Issue 14.

Labich, K. "The Innovators." *Fortune*, June 6, 1988.

LaPlante, A. "Virtual Capitalists." *CIO*, June 15, 1992.

Larson-Mogal, J. S. "An Immersive Paradigm for Product Design and Ergonomic Analysis." *Virtual Reality World*, July–August 1994.

Levine, J. Z. "Reality Testing." *Planning*, May 1991.

Liker, J. K., M. Fleischer, M. Nagamachi, and M. S. Zonnevylle. "Designers and Their Machines: CAD Use and Support in the US and Japan." *Communications of the ACM*, February 1992.

Lindholm, C. "CAD on the Desktop." *Datamation*, January 1, 1992.

Lowe, R. "Three UK Case Studies in Virtual Reality." *Virtual Reality World*, March–April 1994.

Mahnke, J. "Manufacturers Gain by Uniting Plant Flow Systems with MIS." *MIS Week*, January 6, 1990.

Main, J. "At Last, Software CEOs Can Use." *Fortune*, March 13, 1989.

———. "Manufacturing the Right Way." *Fortune*, May 21, 1990.

March, J., and J. Bernhards. "Software for Training Administration." *Training & Development Journal*, June 1989.

Mayer, D., and D. M. Greenberg, "What Makes a Good Salesperson." *Harvard Business Review*, January–February 1992.

McKenna, R. "Marketing Is Everything." *Harvard Business Review*, January–February 1991.

Merril, J. R., "VR for Medical Training and Trade Show 'Fly-Paper.' " *Virtual Reality World*, May–June 1994.

Moad, J. "Tools to Automate Quality Production." *Datamation*, April 15, 1991.

Morgan, C. "Federal Projects Taken to New Directions with Virtual Reality." *Government Computer News*, August 3, 1992.

Morris, C. R., and C. H. Ferguson. "How Architecture Wins Technology Wars." *Harvard Business Review*, March–April 1993.

Moshell, J. M., and C. E. Hughes. "Shared Virtual Worlds for Education." *Virtual Reality World*, January–February 1994.

Myhre, B. L. "Human Resource Environment: Ensuring a Quality Workforce by Handling HR Over." *EDGE*, July–August 1990.

Nadel, R. D., "Just How Good Is Low-Cost Accounting Software?" *Computers in Accounting*, April–May 1992.

Nash, J. "Our Man in Cyberspace Checks Out Virtual Reality." *Computerworld*, October 15, 1990.

Needle, S. "Microcomputer-Based Manufacturing Software." *Journal of Accountancy*, June 1990.

Newquist, H. P. "Virtual Reality's Commercial Reality." *Computerworld*, March 30, 1992.

Normann, R., and R. Ramirez. "From Value Chain to Value Constellation: Designing Interactive Strategy." *Harvard Business Review*, July–August 1993.

O'Boyle, T. F. "Last In, Right Out: Firms' Newfound Skill in Managing Inventory May Soften Downturn." *Wall Street Journal*, November 19, 1990.

O'Connell, B. "Bean Counters at the Crossroads." *DEC Professional*, August 1993.

Pantelidis, V. S. "Virtual Reality in the Classroom." *Educational Technology*, April 1993.

Paré, T. P. "A New Tool for Managing Costs." *Fortune*, June 14, 1993.

Pastore, R. "A Virtual Visionary." *CIO*, July 1993.

Patch, K. "Virtual Reality Becoming More Real." *PC Week*, October 4, 1993.

Peavey, D., and J. DePalma. "Do You Know the Cost of Your Products?" *Coopers & Lybrand Executive Briefing*, May 1990.

Phillips, M. E., and C. E. Brown. "Need an Expert?, Ask a Computer." *Journal of Accountancy*, November 1991.

Pierson, J. "Virtual Reality Offers a View with a Room." *Wall Street Journal*, December 3, 1993.

Pimentel, K., and K. Teixeira. *Virtual Reality: Through the New Looking Glass.* New York: McGraw-Hill, 1993.

Pine, B. J., Jr., B. Victor, and A. C. Boynton. "Making Mass Customization Work." *Harvard Business Review*, September–October 1993.

Port, O., and J. Carey. "Questing for the Best: In Itself, the Search for Quality Is Creating a Revolution." *Business Edge*, May 1992.

Portante, T. "Cyberspace: Reality Is No Longer Enough." *Patricia Seybold's Office Computing Report*, October 1990.

Products. "Colt Virtual Reality Ltd. Using VR to Make Buildings Safer." *Virtual Reality World*, July–August 1994.

———. "Volvo Demonstration Uses VR." *Virtual Reality World*, July–August 1994.

Purcell, J. D. "Designing New Learning Environments." *Autodesk*, A Supplement to *T.H.E. Journal*, October 1993.

Puttre. M. "Virtual Reality Comes Into Focus." *Mechanical Engineering*, April 1991.

Rappaport, A. "CFO's and Strategists: Forging a Common Framework." *Harvard Business Review*, May–June 1992.

Rheingold, H. *Virtual Reality.* New York: Touchstone, 1991.

Roehm, H. A., M. A. Critchfield, and J. F. Castellano. "Yes, ABC Works with Purchasing Too." *Journal of Accountancy*, November 1992.

Romei, L. K. "Quality Becomes Integral to American Business." *Modern Office Technology*, July 1991.

Rose, F. "Now Quality Means Service Too." *Fortune*, April 22, 1991.

Roth, H.P., and A. F. Borthick. "Getting Closer to Real Product Costs." *Management Accounting*, May 1989.

Ryan, A. J. "Sales Force Automation." *Computerworld*, April 8, 1991.

Saffo, P. "Virtual Reality Is More Than Goggles, Gloves, and Fantasies." *InfoWorld*, September 16, 1991.

Sarkissian, R. V. "Retailing Trends in the 1990s." *Journal of Accountancy*, December 1989.

Schell, E. H. "How to Make Millions with Database Marketing." *Datamation*, August 1, 1992.

Schlack, M. "IS Has a New Job in Manufacturing." *Datamation*, January 15, 1992.

Schmitz, B. "Virtual Reality: On the Brink of Greatness." *Computer-Aided Engineering*, April 1993.

Schonberger, R. *Building a Chain of Customers: Linking Business Functions to Create a World Class Company.* New York: The Free Press, 1990.

Seidman, L. W. "What Is the Future of Banking?" *Harvard Business Review*, July–August 1991.

Seiter, C. "Forecasting the Future." *MacWorld*, September 1993.

Sellers, P. "What Customers Really Want." *Fortune*, June 4, 1990.

———. "Winning Over the New Consumer." *Fortune*, July 29, 1991.

———. "How to Remake Your Sales Force." *Fortune*, May 4, 1992.

Semich, J. W. "Information Replaces Inventory at the Virtual Corporation." *Datamation*, July 15, 1994.

Shapiro, B. P., V. K. Rangan, and J. J. Sviokla. "Staple Yourself to an Order." *Harvard Business Review*, July–August 1992.

Shaw, J. "Getting a Virtual Education." *AI Expert*, August 1993.

Sherman, S. "Will the Information Superhighway Be the Death of Retailing?" *Fortune*, April 18, 1994.

Simpson, D. "Alpha Makes Its Way Onto the Production Floor." *Digital News & Review*, November 22, 1993.

Slywotzky, A. J., and B. P. Shapiro. "Leveraging to Beat the Odds: The New Marketing Mind-Set." *Harvard Business Review*, September–October 1993.

Smith, J. M. "Space Center's Rising Star Says His Job Is a Real Blast." *Government Computer News*, October 26, 1992.

Smith, P. "Unique Tools for Marketers: PIMS." *Management Review*, January 1977.

Snell, N. "How Hard Is Our Advertising Working?" *EDGE*, January–February 1990.

———. "Software to Tame the Sales Force." *Datamation*, June 1, 1991.

Spiers, J. "Upper-Middle-Class Woes." *Fortune*, December 27, 1993.

Stalk, G., Jr., and A. M. Webber. "Japan's Dark Side of Time." *Harvard Business Review*, July–August 1993.

St. Antoine, A. "The World's Greatest Toy." *Car and Driver*, June 1993.

Stark, J. *Competitive Manufacturing Through Information Technology: The Executive Challenge.* New York: Van Nostrand Reinhold, 1990.

Stefanae, S. "Interactive Advertising." *NewMedia Magazine*, April 1994.

Stewart, T. A. "Why Budgets Are Bad for Business." *Fortune*, June 4, 1990.

———. "The Search for the Organization of Tomorrow." *Fortune*, May 18, 1992.

———. "Reengineering: The Hot New Managing Tool." *Fortune*, August 23, 1993.

Stone, B., and A. Connell. "The UK's Virtual Reality and Simulation Initiative: A Year Later." *Virtual Reality World*, October 1994.

Stone, R. J. "Towards Telepresence Imaging's Answer to Virtual Reality." *Advanced Imaging* (Special Issue), August 1992.

———. "Virtual Reality and Telepresence." *Robotics*, October 1992.

———. "A Year in the Life of British Virtual Reality: Will the UK's Answer to Al Gore Please Stand Up!!!" *Virtual Reality World*, January–February 1994.

Taguchi, G., and D. Clausing. "Robust Quality." *Harvard Business Review*, January–February 1990.

Tait, A. "Authoring Virtual Worlds on the Desktop." *Virtual Reality Special Report*, published by *AI Expert*. San Francisco: Miller Freeman, 1993.

Taylor, A., III. "The New Golden Age of Autos." *Fortune*, April 4, 1994.

Teresko, J. "Robots Poised for New Arms Race." *Industry Week*, December 7, 1992.

Thierauf, R. J. *Group Decision Support Systems for Effective Decision Making: A Guide for MIS Practitioners and End Users.* Westport, Conn.: Quorum Books, 1989.

———. *Electronic Data Interchange in Finance and Accounting.* Westport, Conn.: Quorum Books, 1990.

———. *Executive Information Systems: A Guide for Senior Management and MIS Professionals.* Westport, Conn.: Quorum Books, 1991.

———. *Image Processing Systems in Business: A Guide for MIS Professionals and End Users.* Westport, Conn.: Quorum Books, 1992.

———. *Creative Computer Software for Strategic Thinking and Decision Making: A Guide for Senior Management and MIS Professionals.* Westport, Conn.: Quorum Books, 1993.

Ulrich, K., D. Sartorius, S. Peason, and M. Jakiela. "Including the Value of Time in Design-for-Manufacturing Decision Making." *Management Science*, April 1993.

Ulusory, G., and R. Uzsoy. "Computer-Aided Process Planning and Material Requirements Planning: First Steps Toward Computer-Integrated Manufacturing." *Interfaces*, March–April 1992.

Van Name, M. L., and B. Catchings. "Virtual Reality Represents New Level of Communications." *PC Week*, October 15, 1990.

Varney, S. E. "Manufacturing Requirements Move Beyond MRP II." *Digital Review*, November 4, 1991.

Vaughn, R. *Quality Assurance.* Ames: Iowa State University Press, 1990.

Veit, S. "What Ever Happened to . . . Personal Robots?" *Computer Shopper*, November 1992.

Vesey, J. T. "The New Competitor: They Think in Terms of 'Speed to Market.' " *Academy of Management Executive*, May 1991.

Wallace, P. "Virtual Classes Teach a Real Sense of Community." *InfoWorld*, September 26, 1994.

Warivick, K., J. Gray, and D. Roberts, eds. *Virtual Reality in Engineering.* London, England: The Institution of Electrical Engineers, 1993.

Webster, J. "An Engine of Change." *Computer Graphics World*, October 1992.

Welco, T. V. "HR Computer Study: Who Buys? What? How? and Why?" *Personnel*, February 1990.

Welles, E. O. "Virtual Realities." *Inc.*, August 1993.

Wexler, J. W. "Ties That Bind." *Computerworld*, June 28, 1993.

Wiggenhorn, W. "Motorola U: When Training Becomes an Education." *Harvard Business Review*, July–August 1990.

Wilder, C. "Virtual Reality Seeks Practicality: Firm's Drive Toward Real-World Applications Shows Promise of Potentially Big Market." *Computerworld*, April 27, 1992.

Williamson, M. "Some Simulating Experiences." *CIO*, November 1, 1993.

Wilson, L. "The Online Economy." *Information Week*, July 4, 1994.

Worthington, P. "Multimedia Is Taking on Training." *InfoWorld*, September 3, 1990.

Worthy, F. S. "Japan's Smart Secret Weapon." *Fortune*, August 12, 1991.

Zachmann, W. F. "Simulation: The Ultimate Virtual Reality." *PC Magazine*, March 31, 1992.

Zarowin, S. "How CPAs Count on Computers." *Journal of Accountancy*, April 1993.

Zipkin, P. H. "Does Manufacturing Need a JIT Revolution?" *Harvard Business Review*, January–February 1991.

Zurier, S., and J. Liebowitz. "Multimedia: Government Embraces Technology Poised on Brink of Revolution." *Government Computer News*, August 3, 1992.

Index

About the Author

ROBERT J. THIERAUF is Professor of Information Systems at Xavier University, Cincinnati. Formerly a staff accountant (CPA) and consultant at Coopers & Lybrand, Thierauf writes extensively on all facets of information systems, particularly decision support systems, expert systems, and information system management. This is his eleventh Quorum book.